MOTIVATING AND PREPARING BLACK YOUTH TO WORK

by Jawanza Kunjufu

AFRICAN AMERICAN IMAGES
Chicago, Illinois

Cover photo by William Hall

Cover design by Eugene Winslow

First Edition

Seventh Printing

DEDICATION

To the youth studying in the library, working on a
science project, singing in the church choir, watching
television, listening to the radio, and playing basketball; no generation can choose the age or circumstances in which it is born, but through faith and
work you must develop your talents and "use yourself up." Because, it is unfortunately true that to be
Black in White America requires more than a score
of 100 percent, it means scoring 110 percent.

SPECIAL THANKS

Special thanks is given to my wife Rita, for her
understanding and editorial assistance. A special
thanks is given to Larry Hawkins for the introduction and Eugene Winslow for his editing. Deep respect and appreciation are given to Sanyika Anwisye
for the scholarship lended to the book.

TABLE OF CONTENTS

PREFACE

I had more difficulty in writing *Motivating and Preparing Black Youth to Work*, than either *Countering The Conspiracy to Destroy Black Boys*, or *Developing Positive Self-Images and Discipline in Black Children*. Part of the problem was deciding for whom the book was to be written. My ultimate desire was to reach the reader between thirteen and twenty-one years of age. I saw vast numbers of young people filled with talents, but with very little motivation or adult guidance. I read studies that postulate large percentages of Black youth may never work. The predicament is that few thirteen to twenty-one year olds may read this book because most read only required school materials.

I also contemplated writing for the primary grade student with hopes of stemming the decline in motivation with each passing year. My reservations lie in the realization that this would place on this age group the difficult task of developing their own motivational techniques. I have resolved the dilemma by appealing to teachers, parents, counselors, administrators, librarians, Upward Bound and Manpower staff, and all concerned adults who interact with youth, to pass this book along to them. I further request that they share my ideas with the primary grade group, so that we can begin being proactive with preventive measures, rather than reactive with crisis intervention and band-aid programs.

I am an advocate of moving from theory to practice. I believe that the majority of people have a good assessment of what the problems are, but few have furnished solutions. All of my books are action oriented; their titles use key words such as *countering*, *developing* and, this book chooses *motivating* and *preparing*. When I tell people the title of this book, their first response, is "How do we motivate Black youth?" I gather they want me to reduce all my research and pages of the book down to the ABC's of motivating and preparing Black youth to work. I strongly encourage reading all six chapters which include: (1) "The Politics of Work", (2) "Values as the Foundation for Motivation," (3) "Motivation to Work," (4) "The Development of Talents into a Career," (5) "Jobs: The Present and Beyond," and (6) "How to Become Economically Self-Sufficient." Those who either don't have the time or the interest in absorbing the details of the book can motivate and prepare Black youth to work by: (a) changing their values from consumption to self-improvement,

(b) maintaining their enthusiasm to learn with continued encouragement or questions, (c) making a dedicated effort to identify and develop their talents, and (d) teaching our youth to consider becoming future employers.

There are numerous books on the market concerning the work ethic, employment, and business ventures. Fewer titles are available on values, motivation, and talents. I have found no books that, from a Black youth perspective, combine the above mentioned areas with the sense of direction needed for them to reach their fullest potential.

I realize that my objective for writing this book is much more ambitious than can be achieved by a book alone. I would like for the book to rejuvenate Black youth and reduce the preposterously high Black unemployment rate. But books don't do that; people with vision and ideas do. However, with your help, we can make a positive difference in the Black youth of today and the future of all African-Americans.

Jawanza Kunjufu
August 1986

INTRODUCTION

The many problems that plague our youth have no single cure. Jawanza advocates the need to instill motivation, many experts feel the lack of, has created our high dropout rate. There is a growing need to revitalize the educational system across the board. At the same time, there is a sharper need for parents and the Black community to undergo dramatic restructuring of the resources available and attitudes controlling its schools.

The author's point of the anti-intellectual environment of the Black community is indeed a prime target in this proposed restructuring. The ideas and societal perceptions that our students are unable to perform academically must be refuted. As we demand more from students they will achieve academically; our students are as capable as any other students. They must be convinced of that.

Paralleled to the concept of anti-intellectualism is the view that schools are solely responsible for educating students. This leads to the fallacy that only schools can and do teach, and further, to the dangerous assumption that parents need only send their children to school.

Education is the specific responsibility of the *parents*. They are the source, and all other agencies, school, churches and community, are secondary resources that parents and students should make use of. Parents must view this as their responsibility until their child is of age to assume the task of learning.

What exactly should parents be doing for their children? Through a series of deliberately planned activities, parents should give students a sense of self-worth, providing the basis for a value system that equips the child to function in American society. Within this value system the parent helps to shape the concept of service. The concept of community service should not be allowed to disappear when the youth moves away to gain higher education or to work for others. During the "moving away" process, a young person should apply their knowledge and become a producer who in turn provides opportunities for others. This positive, mature outlook by the young person is dependent upon him being encouraged by his parents *early on* to develop that fundamental value of self-worth.

Beyond instilling these strong values, parents must play a key role in monitoring the student's school, the student himself, and the student's environment in order to assure values taught at home have the proper context in which to mature. Parents should insist that schools teach and that students study and learn. Mastery of the tools of learning is crucial. Therefore, the parent must insist that the student is disciplined as a learner. Without discipline and respect, little will be achieved.

Community agencies can be a potent force in the student's educational process. Social agencies, clubs, and sports groups should be viewed as vital to the student and, consequently, to the student's education. Again, the road leads home. It is the parents that must understand and coordinate these talent centers to ensure they support and complement the child's education.

Summers should also be planned to complement the child's learning process. Summers should be considered a prime time for learning, not for working. The work of youth is to learn. Learning about work is, of course, part of the process, but should not be all of it. The confidence necessary to secure a job comes from secure knowledge and a positive self-image. This is acquired over time through education. If students are to be creative and to create, they must spend time learning about the people who build organizations. Students must study the experiences of others to develop their own sense of the importance of learning and the necessity of hard work to achieve. In this way, when they do approach the working world, it will be with the values, attitudes, and premises of achievement.

This point of view will of necessity come from a community perspective. We must find local neighborhood constituencies that, along with parents, motivate Black youth to work. The goal for all of us involved with youth should be to prepare an individual capable of competing internationally, who is socially concerned, and community-based in outlook. We seem to have a diminishing number of agencies and people in our communities to instill collective values, motivation, and talent development. The task for all of us is to remember where we came from, remain informed of where we are, and to reach back and help someone.

Larry Hawkins
Director of Special Programs
    and The Institute for Athletics And Education
University of Chicago

Chapter 1
The Politics of Work

It's 8:30 Monday morning. Willie is lying in the bed watching television and dozing off between commercials. He is twenty years old, six feet tall and weighs 170 pounds. His day has been divided between the television and the street corner since age sixteen. Willie was a good student in the primary grades where his natural ability was sufficient, but in the upper grades where discipline and study habits are expected, Willie adhered more to the culture and rigors of the street and its highly influential peer group. Willie does not know in retrospect, whether he dropped out or was pushed out at the first "legal" age of sixteen. Willie knows that both he and school had been together since day care at the ripe age of three, and that thirteen years of being still and listening to ideas unrelated to his world were enough.

His mother has been working at the phone company all of his life; his older brother works at the post office, and his younger sister presently is in college. Willie has never known his father. From time to time, Willie drops into a community center that offers GED training. He has taken several courses but not the test.

There are large numbers of teenagers and young adults who parallel Willie — male, female, younger and older, from two parent affluent homes as well as single parent welfare dwellings.

What actually happened to Willie? When did it happen? What prevented Willie from maintaining his development like his brother and sister? What will happen to Willie's talents while he watches television? Did someone fail Willie? If so, who? Was it the family, school, economy, church, or government? In succeeding chapters we will ask: What does Willie value? How can Willie be motivated? What are Willie's talents? What is the present employment picture for him? How can he become economically self-sufficient?

Let's return to the first question, What happened to Willie and when? I believe the first step toward self-actualization is the de-

1

velopment of self-esteem. This becomes extremely significant for Black people because we live in a world controlled by an insecure minority. Eighty percent of the world's population is Black, brown, red or yellow; the remaining twenty percent is White. The White minority have developed the theory of racism, by claiming that their differences make them better. Secure people are comfortable with differences and have no need to demonstrate or prove their superiority. Unfortunately, many Blacks assume the inferior role of the victim and defensively respond to the myths and stereotypes. Our problem commences when we believe the myths and stereotypes are true. Please remember, it was Africans who built the pyramids and the Grand Lodge of Wa'set, now in the city renamed Luxor.

As a result, Willie, his peers, parents, and the larger society often believe that Black people are lazy, prefer welfare, and lack qualifications. I advocate that many things are political, i.e.,determined by *interest*. For example, many White historians say that Columbus discovered America, while many Black historians state that Columbus was lost and native Americans, in fact, discovered him. The criteria used to determine which view will be included in the curriculum will probably not be decided on empirical research, but by political interests. If Black children have not read Walter Rodney's, *How Europe Underdeveloped Africa* or Manning Marable's, *How Capitalism Underdeveloped Black America* they may not know that the people who are being classified as lazy provided the labor to make Europe and America rich. Marable states,

> Where would the original accumulation of capital used in Western industry have come from if not from the extraction of wealth from colonies, piracy, and the slave trade. The constant expropriation of surplus created by Black labor is the heart and soul of underdevelopment. Underdevelopment is not the absence of development; it is the inevitable product of an oppressed population's integration into the world market economy and political system. Once "freed," Black Americans were not compensated for their 246 years of free labor to this country's slave oligarchy. The current economic amnesia of the West is therefore no accident, because it reveals the true roots of massive exploitation and human degradation upon which the current world order rests.[1]

Why bring a lazy people to America? Why spend six to nine months on a slave ship incurring expenses for transporting a worthless people? Why not use indentured servants or native

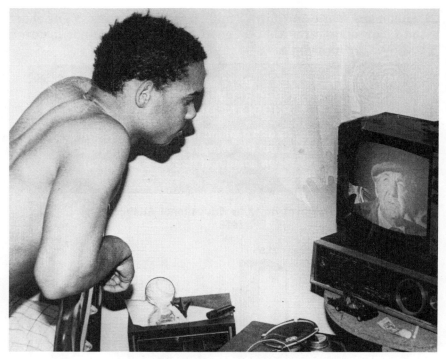

Beyond the streets, radio and television, where can Willie channel his energy and intellect?

Americans? Do you think European slave traders would take slaves without observing their work ethic before the journey? Why accuse a people of being dirty and lacking family cohesiveness and then, during and after slavery, employ Blacks as maids and nannies? Why allow your house and children to be cared for by people lacking competence? Why declare that Blacks don't want to work, when television news shows massive crowds of people, including Blacks, gathered to apply for a few positions that may not even be available. Why should Blacks, who were here "unofficially" in 1619, be compared to illegal aliens who came right off the boat yesterday? America often ignores the fact that its treatment of Blacks has been that of second-class citizens for over 300 years. Why spread the stereotype that welfare is predominantly Black when governmental reports note that of the 35 million who receive financial assistance,

23 million are White and only 12 million are "minorities."[2] The chart listed below illustrates that a "good education" may not insure a "good job" for all people.

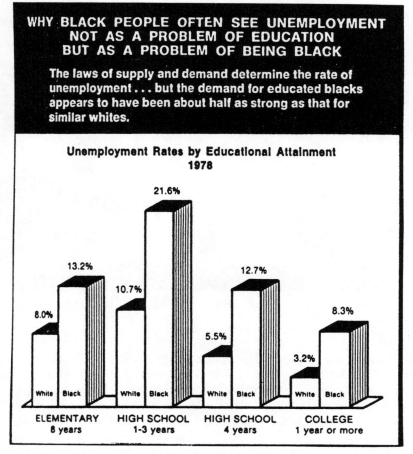

From *Black Power Imperative* by Theodore Cross. Copyright 1984 by Faulkner. Reprinted by permission of the publisher.

Willie's lack of motivation and preparation to work begins with overt and institutional racism, but becomes compounded with low self-esteem, and indifferent adults who perpetuate the self-fulfilling prophecy. These are the "offensive" responses needed to counter the practice of blaming the victim. They become essential because although Willie is not others such as, the "talented tenth," Willie's brother and sister are progressing. The widening gap between the "haves" and the "have nots" has reached epidemic proportions. Simultaneously, in the Black community are "buppies" (Black urban professionals) and Blacks who have not worked and may never work. One segment of the talented tenth has no desire to help the Black masses and will quickly articulate how the "bootstrap theory" worked for them, and will place failure squarely at the feet of the individual. Large numbers of the talented tenth are not even seen by the masses. They do not live, shop, recreate, fellowship, or educate their children near the masses. Another segment of the talented tenth has good intentions and/or an African worldview, but is having difficulty reaching the masses and providing positive role models.

Youth unemployment over the past two decades has been between 16 and 25 percent. Black youth statistics indicate a rate twice the national average.[3] Major reasons often cited are racial discrimination, teenage pregnancy, distance, and lack of work readiness skills. In the year 2,000, if you're a young man and black, brown or tan, the odds are about two to one that you won't have a job. The largest obstacle facing females of color is teenage pregnancy and inadequate child care. Labor participation rates of young Black women are expected to increase from 55 percent in 1983 to 70 percent by the year 2000.[4] The semi-skilled jobs that appeal to young men have moved to the White suburbs, away from the inner city, while clerical jobs, rapidly increasing and 80 percent female, are growing in downtown areas that are more accessible, both physically and psychologically, to inner-city residents. A major reason for the decline in male participation in the family is due to the change in the economy.

Many job counselors tell me that before we find these teenagers a job, we need to locate one for their parents. This book will continue to look at *motivating and preparing Black youth to work*, but I am not oblivious to the plight of Black adults. The major question is, what are half the Black teenagers who are unable to find employment going to do? Beyond the streets, radio and television, where can Willie channel his energy and intellect?

Thousands of unemployed teenagers are on the streets trying to find ways to survive. What's open to them is not always legal, much less approved by society. In a *Chicago Tribune* article, young men talked about life on the street corner.

The People:

Willie Cintron is twenty.
Pedro Perez is seventeen.
Robert Caldero, a friend of Orlando and Pedro, is a project director for the American Friends Service Committee.

WILLIE: I've been unemployed for a year and a half. I worked at Playskool. I was laid off. I get money. I got my ways.

PEDRO: I've been out of work about a year. I've done some work for my cousin off and on by rehabilitating old buildings. But there ain't much of that work.

WILLIE: Other guys I know are pushing drugs. They stand on the corners and throw it (deal in drugs). If a person's got good stuff, the customers'll come from everywhere. That's why people try to get the best.

PEDRO: Or you can make it stealing. Stripping cars or just taking what's around, jewelry, that kind of thing. Also, dealers have money and they make good fences for stolen goods.

PEDRO: On summer days you can get pretty good business. Some guys make $500 or $600 a week. It depends on the drugs. And it depends on the area. A lot of it's marijuana. But, it's also cocaine and pills. The customers drive up in cars. They ride bikes. They walk up.

WILLIE: Everybody is out there doing it. You see maybe fifty guys in my community on the corner throwing it.

PEDRO: Where I grew up there were a lot of factories around there. If you quit one, you could have always gone to another and get a job. But nobody leaves a job anymore, no matter how bad it is.

WILLIE: All my friends are stealing or dealing. They look for jobs but they can't find them. It's better to work, because of the chance you're going to get caught if you deal or steal, but the only jobs you can get are the slave jobs. That's what they call them in the neighborhood. A slave job is one in which you do heavy labor for the minimum wage. The people say, "The guy's a fool. He could be dealing."

PEDRO: Also, guns are a very heavy industry. If you have a good connection for guns, you can really make money.

6

WILLIE: When gangs are building up, it's the number of weapons that count.

ROBERT: It's just like the arms race between countries.

PEDRO: I am out trying to find a job. I have a diploma. Willie doesn't. It makes no difference. They want experience and they want training.

WILLIE: Dealing drugs is like a job. The guys are not all hoggish. They take turns throwing. They watch each other's back when the other guy is throwing. Mostly all my friends are in jail for dealing.

PEDRO: There are people who don't ever get caught. I'd say it's fifty-fifty. I know a guy who has been caught twelve times. He spends three nights of the week in jail and the other four he is out dealing. Another dude never had to spend a night in jail. He goes through channels and he has connections.

ROBERT: What's out there is worse than I've ever seen it. There's more people on the street corners and they are there all day. They have nothing to do. They are divorced from the rest of the economy and from the rest of society. The biggest factor is unemployment. It's strange to see that world out there with guys getting up at 10 a.m. and drinking beer and staying out there all day and dealing or stealing or doing nothing.

PEDRO: We got to get something. That's why people turn to stealing and drugs.

ROBERT: The worse part is you see guys really go out there and try. You see guys at 7 and 7:30 a.m. hop on a bus maybe four days a week to go to the suburbs to try to find a job. On the average, I'd say it takes a year or a year and a half doing that to find a job. That long is not considered unusual at all.

WILLIE: People sleep in the Humboldt Park just to be first in line to get day labor work from an office there. It's worse than slave labor. The guy who owns the place gets $45 a day each for them. He pays them $25 a day and charges them each $2 for bus fare. How can you support a family on $23 a day? That's for the dogs.

ROBERT: People do make money selling drugs, but only a few of

7

them. I now have gotten a house and car out of it. It's small time. Say, the ordinary street corner dealer really keeps at it and does not get busted, he makes maybe $12,000 a year. He has to live with the fear of being arrested or his supply drying up. Only a few guys make real bucks.[5]

I believe when a problem is incurred by a few it may be an individual concern, but when the problem affects larger numbers the issues may rest within the society. Sidney Wilhelm, in the classic, *Who Needs the Negro* states,

the Negro is caught in the jaws of a technological vise operating in accord with economic and racist motives of white America. The technological trend implemented in terms of economic incentives and racism points to what seems to be an inevitable dispensability for the Black race. Under preindustrial technology whites exploited the Negro as an economic commodity to be bought, sold, and traded in an agricultural economy; under industrial technology the Negro transformed into an economic serf complementing the economic incentives of Northern capitalists. In the past, it was incumbent upon white America to balance racial values against economic incentives. But with the introduction of automation, the necessity virtually disappears. White America hopes the Negro will accept its design and passively accept the fate of total isolation within the ghetto. The ghetto is the equivalent of the Indian reservation. Just as the people of one reservation were debauched with whiskey sold by white men, so the people of the other are ravaged by drugs.[6]

It is not my desire to be so depressing in a book designed to motivate Black youth, but I do believe that to solve the problems facing Black youth requires a better understanding of the relationships between racism and economics. The melting pot theory is applicable to immigrants who voluntarily left Europe with the sole objective of improving their station in life. African-Americans were forced to relocate to America, and it was understood it was not for a better life, but servitude. The economic reason for the journey was to work; racism "justified" why Blacks were chosen. Alvin Toffler's, *Third Wave*, explains the waves as agriculture, industrialism, and post-industrialism or automation. With each passing wave, white America had less economic need for Black labor, consequently racism is expressed more with disdain, and best described in Wilhelm's book titled, *Who Needs the Negro?*

I also believe the change in the economy has affected our motivation. Who determines our value? Who determines if we're needed?

Should Willie stay in bed because plantations and factories are closed and robots don't need him? Self-definition and self-esteem are the first step toward self-control and self-actualization.

Let's take a look at the typical parental view of the present generation's work ethic. I recently was taking a taxi from the airport to a convention site for a presentation and entered into a conversation with the Black driver. He told me he was sixty-one years old, had been working on various jobs for the past fifty-one years, and planned retirement within the next four years. He said both he and his wife are hard workers, but his youngest son of fifteen is downright lazy. "I don't know what's wrong with these children today. They got more opportunities than I ever had, and all I wanted to do was *make it easier for them than it was for me.*" How many times have you heard that classic statement? Adults really do not know why children do not possess their drive and work ethic. Youth add to this communication problem with phrases such as, "Whatever," "You know," "Straight up." Young people actually believe they have communicated with such jargon, and to their peer group they have succeeded. The future of the Black race may be dependent on bridging this communication gap.

I don't believe adults or youths exclusively can be faulted for their views. I like to consider myself an advocate for youth. I try to see the world from their perspective which requires listening, eye contact, and observing their mannerisms. Somewhere in "whatever, you know, straight up" are significant clues. I think youth are growing up too fast. The combination of diet, television, and the economy has caused havoc during the period labeled childhood.

The American diet has changed over the years for complex reasons including profit, urbanization, and convenience. Since 1930, little girls have started their menstrual cycle six months earlier for every decade. Young girls are now starting their menstrual cycle as early as eight years of age.[7] The major reason is the increased protein in the diet. Every mother in the animal kingdom has the appropriate milk for her offspring. Dogs feed their puppies, cats feed their kittens, cows feed their calves but humans, the most sophisticated animal, send their babies to another animal for milk. Cow's milk develops the body; breast milk develops the brain. The move away from breast milk and the continued rise in the consumption of red meat coupled with the dietary decline in green vegetables has accelerated the developmental growth in youth.

Television has also increased the maturation rate of children with the overexposure of sophisticated information at earlier ages. Neil Postman in the *Disappearance of Childhood* remarks:

> Children have command over speech at the age of seven. The printing press created a new definition of adulthood, based on reading competence. In an oral world where information is disseminated more through television than the printed word, first literacy disappears. The second is that education disappears. The third is that shame disappears. And the fourth, as a consequence of the other three, is that childhood disappears.[8]

You now can see parents and children wearing the same clothes and going to the same entertainment places. Parents are often called by their first names and want to be their children's buddies. Many parents no longer know how a eight-year-old girl should wear her hair, and when a twelve-year-old boy should be inside the house. The economic incentive for the disappearance of childhood lies in the fact that consumers spend the most money between twenty and thirty years of age. Advertisers have created a buying teenage market.

Conversely, the complex economy has delayed the entrance of youth into the work force. Young people historically have been able to work on a farm or enter a factory between thirteen and seventeen years of age. Witness that in 1910, only 10 percent of the American populus received a high school diploma, in contrast to 1980 when 85 percent of European-Americans, 75 percent of all African-Americans, and 55 percent of all Hispanic-Americans graduated from high school.[9] Now, however, the economy has moved into the third wave, automation, and therefore fewer unskilled positions are available. As a result, children are now staying in school longer than ever before, not because they like school more, but because it is required.

It is ironic that the diet and television have accelerated their physical growth and maturation, the economy has delayed their entrance into the world of work, and schools are being used primarily as a holding station. I do not believe the problem lies exclusively with our youth. More fundamentally, I feel we do not know *what* to do with young people and rather than address this issue we give children a speech on how hard we worked delivering morning papers, walking miles to schools, stocking and clerking after school and being a provider before our eighteenth birthday. I challenge adults to ask themselves, if they were sixteen living in this present day,

Most children do not lack money, clothes or diversion, but they do lack the emotional security of stable, loving parents.

could they weave their way through dietary changes, television, automation along with the larger societal problems of drugs, moral decadence, low teacher expectations, and family instability?

I hope now both adults and youths are more open-minded about the complex circumstances affecting motivation and work, and will not blame one another. What has happened to the work ethic? Remember the classic parental statement, "They got more opportunities than I ever had, and all I wanted to do was make it *easier* for them than it was for me." The key word was *easier*; humans, unlike other parents of the animal world, often make children more dependent. I stated in *Countering the Conspiracy to Destroy Black Boys*, some mothers *raise* their daughters and *love* their sons. We have too many sons over twenty dependent on their parents in the animal kingdom. Nature documentaries illustrate how other parents in the animal kingdom push their offspring out to learn survival and developmental skills. We suffer from a two-edged sword: poverty and affluence — poverty of the things in life that give life substance and meaning; affluence in the material rewards and diversions that increasingly demand our time, planning and constant vigilance to acquire and maintain.

Children suffer from a new kind of neglect. They do not lack money to spend, clothes to wear (for the most part), or diversions to occupy them, but they do lack terribly in having within them the kind of emotional security only stable and loving parents can provide. According to some researchers, work values are generally transferred from parent to child, and are well developed by the fifth grade.[10]

What effects does it have on children's potential work ethic when their parents work away from home? What is different between lacking knowledge about what your parents do and not having a working parent, one who receives welfare? What effect does it have on the work ethic when parents are unable to find work or are not paid enough to afford child care? What effect does acknowledging the fact that drug pushers and garbage men make more than teachers? Studs Terkel, in his book *Working*, interviewed hundreds of workers in every conceivable occupation, and heard these comments regarding the work ethic:

> What a lot of young people rebel against is having to go into corporations where they have to spend thirty years of their lives and come out a wornout human being on a pension. The depression in the thirties was a unique period. People were willing to work and there wasn't work around. I think the mentality of the thirties and the mentality today is different. Then people really wanted to work. Now the thing is to want something *meaningful*: I didn't start out as president. It was necessary for me to scrub toilets. Not that I liked doing it. But I didn't feel debased by it. It was better than doing nothing. Any work is better than no work. Work makes a person noble. Another worker responds: Jobs are not big enough for people. It's not just the assembly line worker whose job is too small for his spirit. A job like mine, if you really put your spirit into it you would sabotage it immediately. You don't dare. So you absent your spirit from it. My mind has been so divorced from my job except as a source of income.[11]

A review of all major studies on work satisfaction concluded that there has been a significant decline in overall job satisfaction. The trend includes a shorter workday and week, flextime, more frequent vacations, early and better financed retirement, and greater interest in leisure. One of eight consumable dollars goes to recreation, and the industry nears 300 billion dollars annually.[12] Alvin Toffler in the *Third Wave* describes it very succinctly.

We must recognize three basic requirements of any individual: The needs for community, structure, and meaning. The complex changes in our society creating diversity caused feelings of loneliness. In the past economy, the structure resulted from the trio of home, school, and corporation, but with each year they have declined in their influence on youth. Ultimately, people are looking for a sense of purpose or meaning in their lives. The rising influence of "dogmatic" organizations or cults propose having the sole truth about life. The cult, however sells community, structure and meaning at an extremely high price. The mindless surrender of self. For many of course this price is too high, but the search for community, structure, and meaning continues.[13]

The first chapter in *Motivating and Preparing Black Youth to Work* has looked at "the politics of work". Willie represents many Black youth not operating at their full potential. The reasons are numerous, and include racism, low self-esteem, lack of concerned positive role models, and the changing economy from labor to capital-intensive. This change has made a large part of the population, and specifically Black youth, expendable. Large numbers of unmotivated Black youth turn to welfare and crime for survival. Segments of the Black talented tenth, many adults, and White media propagandists blame the victim for his plight without considering all pertinent factors. The issues may be that White America does not know what to do with Black people, and Black parents don't know what to do with their youth.

The work ethic has changed from 1619 and 1930 to the present. In order to motivate Black youth, we must go beyond understanding the economic, political, and social arena; and determine in the next chapter the role values play in motivation.

Deluged with new products, bombarded by advertising, and armed with credit cards, for many the motivation in life has become consumption.

Chapter 2

Values as the Foundation for Motivation

My two sons, thirteen and eight, are riding in the back seat of our four-year-old Volkswagen Rabbit. They are involved in one of their favorite games: "That's my car." The objective of the game is to be the first to point at the most desirable car; the favorites include sport cars and large automobiles, preferably limousines. In our home, I have taught them to play concentration, scrabble, boggle, checkers, cards and ball games, but neither I nor their mother taught them "that's my car." They did not formally or consciously learn this game from electronic or print media. Where did they learn it? Who taught them these values?

I recently spoke at an annual Black Men's conference. The analysis of the preceding year had determined that the number one problem facing Black men was unemployment. The solution appeared simple: provide employment for Black men and the major problem has been resolved. A change in government personnel could eradicate the problem, and, conversely, a subsequent change could restore the problem. I pondered if the plight of Black men and their masculinity rested on economic policies and governmental shifts. I wondered how a job determined if a Black man would stay with his children and help with their homework, moral and cultural lessons, and domestic responsibilities. I contemplated how Black women feel about their man when he receives a pink slip.

The headline in a major Chicago newspaper reads, "East Meets West — and Finds Decadence." Shown below it are two female Japanese teenagers, one wearing blue jeans and a Boy George tee-shirt, and the other wearing an above the knee length dress. Two months ago, at the peak of its popularity, the hit song "One Night in Bangkok," was banned by the Japanese government. Over the past two years, the average Japanese has increased in weight by fifteen pounds with the emergence of McDonald's, Kentucky Fried Chicken, and Shakey's Pizza.[1]

Values are the "invisible institution" says Richard Simmons in the *Crucial Element in The Development of Black Children,*[2] and they are so deep and interwoven that my sons, Black men, Asians and most of us never had a chance to determine our own values. The Purchasing Council reports 60 percent of all supermarket purchases were not predetermined by the consumer, but were bought because of suggestive advertising. It becomes almost suicidal to enter a store without a list and a made-up mind to stick to it. Similarly, our values may also be largely determined by external pressures.

What make this subject and chapter so difficult is because values are often intangible. Most of us don't know why we do what we do or like what we like, but are convinced that whatever the reason, its ours and original. When I hear my sons enthusiastically claim their cars, I think of my possible responses. I could tell them to stop playing the game, but that would not eliminate the desire, change the values, nor prevent them from playing the game in my absence. I could make the game intellectual and raise technical questions concerning gas mileage, maintenance, durability, and costs. I could be emotionally disappointed that they don't value our car, or I could say nothing and think about what Eastern utilitarian value I could offer to compete against a Trans Am or a Mercedes. I don't have to leave my car to better understand the tremendous impact Western values have on youth. I actually believe I'm competing for the minds of my children and I'm pleased that I see it as competition rather than collaboration.

The challenge of providing alternative values is a very difficult task. Johari Amini comments:

> A value base is the foundation of every society. And as a consequence, desired changes in institutions or systems can take place only on a superficial level at best unless changes have first occurred in the value base of the society. Therefore, changing an imperialist exploitative peoples economic system from capitalism to socialism or communism will not retard or change their imperio-exploitative behavior; if the values of a society dictate that the people believe in competition, exploitation of others, and imperialism, those people will continue behaving in those ways, regardless of their economic system, until their society's value base itself is changed.[3]

I believe that Black men have something very valuable to offer their children regardless of their present employment status. When man got separated from the land and self-sufficiency and sold his labor into the marketplace, values, self-esteem, and sufficiency were predicated on money. Masculinity, marriage, and parenting for almost all men hinges on income. As Amini pointed out, it is difficult to change individual values beyond a superficial level without a societal change, but it is suicidal for us to allow our children to play "that's my car," for men to leave their family because they can't find work, and for Asian teenagers to forfeit their ancient rich tradition for the recent ideas of Madison and Fifth Avenue. Let's take a historical look at how society became inculcated with its present value system.

Quality	Southern Cradle (African)	Northern Cradle (European)
Descent	Matrilineal	Patrilineal
Gods	One Universal God	Familistia Gods
Social Philosophy	Collective, Xenophilic	Individualistic Xenophobic
Ancestor Worship	Burial	Cremation
Mode of Existence	Agrarian, Settled	Nomadic

Cheikh Anta Diop's two-cradle theory is based on three premises. Firstly, differences had to do with the climate and the specific conditions of life. Secondly, in passing from South to North, all cultural values were overthrown and became opposite as the poles. Ancient Africa was opposed to Europe in its conceptions of domestic life, state craft, philosophy, etc. Thirdly, the requirements of nomadic life and those of settled life provide all the elements of an explanation which makes it possible to clarify the subject. Diop's two-cradle theory links a matrilineal descent system (not matriarchy) to African agrarian life, and a patrilineal descent system (male supremacy) to European nomadic life.[4]

Please remember it was Europeans traveling into Africa not the reverse, and the major reason was the need for life-sustaining natural resources. Climate not only affected personalities historically, but I've noticed many people have a much more relaxed, giving disposition when the weather is warm rather than in arctic conditions. Secondly, paralleling Diop's analysis, secure people are comfortable with differences, they do not see opposite as being in conflict.

European	**African**
God vs. Man	God
Faith vs. intellect	Nature Family
Man vs. woman	Community
Color vs. non-color	

Thirdly, our agrarian lifestyle respected land, glorified home and family, and respected women and children. Our ability to survive the worst oppression ever placed on a people may well be attributed to these values, and in order to survive the present onslaught of value changes we should return to them.

Our objective is "motivating and preparing Black youth to work," but this is predicated on values. What are we motivating Black youth to work for? Money? Fame? Individualism? Do I motivate my sons with a Trans Am or a Mercedes? If not, how do I motivate them? When are they affected by society's present values? How did my sons begin to receive messages from the "invisible institution?"

Johari Amini provides the following model.

Values   Frame of Reference   Motivation   Behavior

"There is no contradiction or inconsistency between what one's true beliefs or values are, and what one actually does. There are no contradictions, errors, or mistakes in behavior. We *act out what is in us*, nothing more, nothing less."[5]

I firmly believe that values and images don't lie. What a person says may be false, but what a person does and wears is consistent. How men treat their wives, mothers and sister tell me more about how they feel toward Black women than what they say. What a person puts in his/her hair, on his/her face, and walls at home says more than words can describe.

The model provides four key stages: values, frame of reference, motivation and behavior. My objective is to motivate and prepare Black youth to work. If this is the desired result, a better understanding of values is necessary because of their impact on the latter three stages. I appeal to the reader to make this invisible institution of values as concrete as possible, either by reflecting on your own examples or that of my sons playing "that's my car."

Diop and Amini provided a historical/psychological analysis of values. Christopher Lasch in *Culture of Narcissism* offers a contemporary view.

To live for the moment is the prevailing passion — to live for yourself, not for your predecessor or posterity. We are quickly losing the sense of historical continuity, the sense of belonging to a succession of generations originating in the past and stretching into the future. A society that fears it has no future is not likely to give much attention to the needs of its children. Until recently, the Protestant work ethic stood as one of the most important underpinnings of American culture. According to the myth, thrift and industry held the key to material success and spiritual fulfillment. In an age of diminishing expectations these virtues no longer excite enthusiasm, in a simpler time advertising called attention to the product, now it manufactures a product of its own: The consumer perpetually unsatisfied, restless, anxious and bored. Advertising serves not so much to advertise products as to promote consumption as a way of life. The tired worker, instead of attempting to change the conditions of his work, seeks renewal in brightening his immediate surroundings with new goods and services.[6]

It is very difficult for a consumer, bombarded by a 70 billion dollar advertising industry and banks that conveniently offer credit cards, to resist purchasing. For many living in a self-centered society, bored with work or school, deluged with new products or old products with different shapes and colors, their motivation in life has become consumption. You need not be denied whatever your heart or their ad persuade you to purchase. I'm sure many of us have read about credit card abuse, but it should be obvious by the growth in installment purchases and bankruptcy, that it continues. I also am concerned with tempering the use of credit cards *before* insolvency has transpired. Credit cards are ideal as a substitute for cash or in lieu of a check in those institutions that do not accept them, but it should not be used to live above our means.

One day I was glancing through magazines and began critically looking at the advertisements. Black magazines are filled with alcohol, cigarette, and cosmetics ads. (Blacks are 13 percent of the population, earn only 6 percent of the income, but spend 39, 38 and 30 percent respectively in these areas.) I began cutting the ads out to show that what we purchase may be the result of sophisticated promotion. The first test case was my family. Right after dinner we had "Show and Tell." I showed the ads, but covered up the product name and asked then what was advertised. One ad was for cigarettes, but no one was smoking! There were two Black men and one woman having fun on a skateboard; the message was, smoking is as invigorating as exercising outdoors. Another ad was for liquor. A

Black couple are walking into a ballroom dressed in after-five attire. My children thought they were advertising clothes! The ad, not implicitly but explicitly, showed that drinking whiskey will make you look like a model. The last ad they never figured out. A very well-dressed, handsome, Black man is standing in the doorway. In front of him are two legs of a Black woman, the legs are spread apart forming a triangle effect, with the floor as the base. The three-dimensional effect has the man's head at the top of the triangle or in between the legs! What do you think was being advertised? A product? What type? The man's hair care? His clothes? Her stocking or shoes? Wrong. They were advertising cologne. In reality, they were advertising sex and values through "Night Musk."

I asked the boys, "How do television actors get paid? Do you put coins in the set in order to turn it on?" It took some time for them to appreciate the relationship between commercials and income for television owners and actors. Advertisers are confident enough in their ability to persuade, to spend up to a half a million dollars on a thirty-second ad during the Super Bowl game, and expect a sizeable rate of return.

In this chapter on values, I'm looking at their relationship to motivating Black youth to work. What is it that we value? What do adults value? What do children value? Are the values of the adults different from youths? What is the purpose in life? I have learned through conducting workshops and teaching that people tend to provide what they think will be the right answer regardless of whether it's their answer. If I asked most people, "What is your purpose?" They would probably answer by saying, "To help somebody, to make the world better, to get closer to God." But if I asked them, "What do you spend most of your working hours doing, or what would you like to do with these hours?" I believe the responses would be, "Making money, shopping, feeling and looking good."

I asked young people if they had only one choice between money, house, car, clothes, land, and time, which would they choose? Many brothers choose cars. Many sisters choose clothes. Adults often prefer houses. Large numbers select money. But when I inquire, "What would you do with the money?" They respond with, "Buy a house, car, and clothes." Very few choose land. Yet it is the only commodity that can't be made in a factory, and it's the source of our food, clothing, and shelter. Even fewer choose time, and many chose it because they felt it's the "right answer," not because they value it. Returning to Amini the model, our behavior doesn't indicate that we value time more than money, cars, clothes and houses. Many of us give our time to soap operas, gossiping, and street life, but will fight and kill over the mistreatment of our money, cars, clothes and houses.

There are many adults who do not like their work, but love money and what it will buy. The term "TGIF" (Thank God it's Friday) illustrates that large numbers of people are dissatisfied with how they spend the largest part of their week and life, consequently use the shortest part to pacify a dying spirit. The average adult spends eight hours working a job he doesn't like. They spend two hours for transportation, three hours for breakfast, lunch, dinner and their preparation. This total of thirteen hours, plus eight hours sleeping leaves three hours for recreation. Many adults dislike Monday through Friday, but enjoy weekends. Some adults do not like what they do from ages twenty-one to sixty-five, and look forward to enjoying life upon retirement. I believe a strong motivation would be finding enjoyment during the longest period of your life.

I have been accused of being too critical and over-simplifying the above scenario. But if you tell me you value time more than anything else, as Amini's model points out, "then the truth ain't in it." I would admit, though, that if you're thirty-five years or older, have a spouse and children, and are over-committed in debt and living from paycheck to paycheck it is difficult to quit a job you don't like, return to school or start the business you've often thought about. Going back to school or starting your business doesn't pay the salary in the first year your present lifestyle requires.

My father made sure I didn't work with him in the post office. He told me he saw talented youth work there while in school and enjoyed making a good income, often one that would surpass many "degreed" professions. Many of them dropped out of school, continued to work for money rather than personal satisfaction, and started their merry journey to "over-extended city and bankruptcy USA."

I believe people value time, but a synonym for values is priorities. A value or priority is more significant when placed within the context of choices. Behavior, not words, is the best indication of values. For many of us when forced to choose, prioritize between money and time, value money. The University of Michigan conducted a survey in 1950 and repeated it in 1980 to determine the major influences on children. Listed below are its findings.

1950		**1980**	
1)	home	1)	home
2)	school	2)	peers
3)	church	3)	television
4)	peers	4)	school
5)	television	5)	church[7]

If we accept the position that values determine behavior and values are a result of exposure to information, then suffice to say whoever controls print and electronic media will have a lot to say about values. What institutions teach youth to value time? What institutions or advertisements teach youth the difference between needs and wants? Who will teach youth the value of savings? I believe this is the responsibility of parents and educators — and it starts by example. It is very difficult to teach children when our behavior is in direct contradiction to our professed values. I encourage us to manage our time better than we do our check books. I recommend that we develop a time chart for the day and allocate the appropriate time for each task. I've often pondered that many of our talented people made their invention, record or contribution to society while the rest of the populace was watching television, talking on the telephone or hanging on the streets. These "gifted" stars may be ordinary people, but they use their time like a gift.

I also suggest that we equip children with an "advertising defense" to the avalanche of promotion directed at them. Youth should be taught the difference between needs and wants. When children are watching commercials, parents should quiz them on which is which. For example, designer jeans are a want, while regular jeans may be a need if your wardrobe warrants it. This game can also be played in the grocery store. They can put needs in the basket, but not wants. As mentioned earlier with magazine ads, we should ask what is being advertised? A product? Exercise? Good looks? Sex?

We should also teach our children the significance of savings. Many view savings as anything leftover after we've gone shopping. As a result, very little if anything ever ends up in savings. To insure that savings receives its share, I recommend savings be allocated *before* not *after* consumption. My wife and I give our children an allowance of which a certain percentage is for savings, and if they allow it to grow throughout the year, then at the end we will provide a "matching grant." We have found this not only encourages savings, but teaches them how savings can become an investment. (More will be said about investment in the concluding chapter.)

As Johari Amini pointed out, values of the individual are difficult to change if the values of the society remain the same.

African	Euro-American
We	I
Cooperation	Competition
Internal	External

Maulana Karenga in *The Theory of Kawaida* offers the Nguzo Saba.

UMOJA (Unity)
To strive for and maintain unity in the family, community, nation and race.

KUJICHAGULIA (Self-determination)
To define ourselves, name ourselves, create for ourselves and speak for ourselves instead of being defined, named, created for and spoken for by others.

UJIMA (Collective Work and Responsibility)
To build and maintain our community together and make our sister's and brother's problems our problems, and to solve them together.

UJAMAA (Cooperative Economics)
To build and maintain our own stores, shops and other business, and to profit from them together.

NIA (Purpose)
To make our collective vocation the building and developing of our community in order to restore our people to their traditional greatness.

KUUMBA (Creativity)
To do always as much as we can, in the way we can, in order to leave our community more beautiful and beneficial than we inherited it.

IMANI (Faith)
To believe with all our heart in our people, our parents, our teachers, our leaders and the righteousness and victory of our struggle.[8]

Val Jordan offers *The Black Value System*.

Commitment to God
Commitment to the Black community
Commitment to the Black family
Dedication to the pursuit of education

Dedication to the pursuit of excellence
Adherence to the Black work ethic
Commitment to self-discipline and self-respect
Disavowal of the pursuit of middle classness[9]

Karenga's and Jordan's value systems are positive contributions in our quest to reorder our society. Many homes, schools, churches, and other institutions teach their youth and members these values. Unfortunately, many times these positive values have been memorized and regurgitated in rote fashion. The first step is for these values to be given to youth, but the next step is their internalization. We need youths and adults who will depict in their behavior a commitment to God, the Black community, family, education, excellence, work ethic, and self-discipline.

In a society obsessed with self-preservation and "what's in it for me" there are few advertisements promoting unity, self-determination, collective work and responsibility, cooperative economics, purpose, creativity and faith.

We have to select books for children that encourage sharing and being your brother's keeper. Family rituals ranging from having dinner together, cleaning together, and being considerate when there is only one glass of juice left and two people want it. This reminded me of a church retreat I went on where we talked all day about sharing with one another. At dinner, shrimp was served and "sharing Christians" became selfish animals fighting over an inadequate amount of shrimp for the group. In contrast, at the same retreat a little girl was told to pass out candy to the group. She was one piece short and an adult still needed candy. She pondered her options, gave the lady her candy and smiled.

I acknowledge Amini's respect for the values of the dominant society, but if she did not think they could be changed, she never would have written her article, Karenga and Jordan would not have created their value system, and I would not be thinking of strategies to counter "that's my car." And I would not appeal to youth to value time over money. *I do not believe we can motivate Black youth to work if the highest value in life is to make money.* I believe our youth have found other ways to make money besides working hard and receiving a "good education." I strongly suggest a change of our values from money to time, from materialism to the Nguzo Saba and the Black Value System. The next two chapters on motivation and talent, begin to offer alternatives to our present value system.

Chapter 3

Motivation to Work

Rick and Anthony's two young brothers are too excited to fall asleep. For the past hour their parents have told them that if they don't get any rest they will be sleeping in school. Rick and Anthony are so eager to go to school they can't sleep. This will be Anthony's first year, and he's heard from his brother, who is a "one year veteran," how great it is to be in school. Rick says, "There are more children in school than in the whole wide world. We sing songs, color, listen to stories, play at recess, and eat lunch. They even give you papers to do at home. I like to do mine as soon as I eat my snack. I really like school."

Leon and Kathy, two high school students, are sitting in the park "shooting the breeze," during their seventh-period class. They've been friends since sixth grade which was four years ago. They checked into their "home room" between third and fourth period to be officially in attendance. Unofficially, they've been talking, eating, smoking reefer, and drinking beer for the last three periods in the park. Leon's says, "School is a drag and all I want is some paper to enlist in the Army." Kathy knows the three classes she missed base their grades on a mid-term and a final exam. She has friends with copies of the exams, so there is no need to attend or study.

What happened between kindergarten and tenth grade to the eagerness and enthusiasm to learn? Were Leon and Kathy always that way? Did they ever feel like Rick and Anthony? Will Rick and Anthony feel like Leon and Kathy when they become teenagers? In one of my earlier books, *Countering the Conspiracy to Destroy Black Boys*, one chapter is called "The Fourth Grade Failure Syndrome." Research showed a decline in academic achievement with age, which probably paralleled their enthusiasm.[1]

Our children are bored; adolescence isn't a training ground for adulthood, it is a holding pattern for aging youth.

Harry Morgan says: "When Blacks enter first grade, the stories they create express positive feelings about themselves in the schooling situation, but by the second grade their stories express negative imagery of the teacher and school environment and by the fifth grade, the overall feeling expressed by students is that of criticism. In other words, upon entering school in primary grades, Black children possess enthusiasm and eager interest, however, by fifth grade, the liveliness and interest are gone, replaced by passivity and apathy. Primary grades presented a more nurturing enn-vironment than intermediate or upper grades. In early childhood education, much of the activity is child-teacher centered and a great deal of interaction between children. The classroom environment in the upper grades is transformed from a socially interactive style to a competitive individualistic and minimally socially interactive style of learning."[2]

The drop-out rate has reached epidemic levels ranging from 23 percent nationally to 49 and 55 percent respectively in the Black and Brown communities.[3] A table of Chicago Public High Schools illustrates the plight.

Percentage of freshmen tested who read
at or above the national average:

Lane	88	Westinghouse	17
Young	83	Fenger	15
Lindblom	74	Harlan	14
Von Steuben	66	Bowen	14
Kenwood	63	Clemente	14
Lincoln Park	49	Gage Park	14
Mather	49	Hirsch	14
Taft	45	Corliss	14
Morgan Park	43	Richards	13
Prosser	41	Carver	13
Curie	40	Near North	13
Metro	39	Kelvyn Park	13
Washington	37	Wells	13
Bogan	37	South Shore	13
Hyde Park	33	Crane	9
Steinmetz	33	Farragut	9
Kennedy	30	King	9
Amundsen	28	Tilden	7
Roosevelt	26	Robeson	7
Dunbar	27	Marshall	7
Hubbard	24	Manley	7
Julian	24	Collins	6
Juarez	24	Austin	6
C.V.S.	23	DuSable	6
Schurz	22	Calumet	5
Foreman	22	Flower	5
Simeon	22	Harper	5
Senn	21	Cregier	5
Kelly	20	Phillips	5
Sullivan	17	Orr	4[4]

Chicago schools are not the exception, but the norm. Each year schools receive students like Rick and Anthony, and we must prevent them from becoming like Leon and Kathy. High school teachers cite the lack of motivation as their number-one problem. Students drop out for this reason, as well as poor grades, student-teacher incompatibility, economics, and pregnancy.[5] A decade ago the adults and the college crowd were the principal users of marijuana. Then it became the high school crowd, until it started experimenting with speed pills and cocaine. More recently, the big growth in marijuana use has been among the junior-high crowd. A common reason given for the upsurge in drug use by youngsters is boredom.[6]

Our children are bored, and this is expressed in their slang when they say, "whatever," "you know," and "straight up." In an earlier chapter, I mentioned the terrible trick that has been played on them. The combination of accelerated physical maturation coupled with overexposure to electronic media has produced youth unable to accept their invisible role in the "Third Wave Economy" of automation.

I believe youths have a story to tell if adults will listen. When I ask youth, "What do your parents and teacher tell you about school?" The youth respond with, "Get a good education and work hard." When I ask them how they feel about those comments, they answer, "Get a good education for *what*? Work hard for *who*?" The youth also want to know the relevancy, need or reason why for each lesson.

Youth observe adults with their "good education" and they wonder what adults end up with. A j-o-b which they don't like, consequently, they end up living for "TGIF" (Thank God It's Friday). Youths quickly conclude that life is about money, not a good education or a job. They also wonder, "If working hard is the solution, why aren't Black people more advanced since Blacks were brought here to work?" I believe adults have not been honest with youth. Have you ever thought about the inverse relationship between age and asking questions, or the direct relationship between age and cheating? Rick and Anthony entered school assuming the learning experience would be shared between students and teachers, so they asked all kinds of questions. Why is it that Leon and Kathy don't ask as many questions as they did in the primary grades? Do you think Rick and Anthony would cheat on a test given the first day of school? When would they begin to cheat? Why? Do you think Leon and Kathy cheat? When did they start?

I believe our youth stopped asking questions and began cheating when they found out the most important objective in school was not learning, but receiving good *grades*. I further postulate our youth have determined that securing employment is based more on *who* you know than *what* you know. I do not believe you can motivate and prepare Black youth with a lie.

If the objective in life is to make money, our youths see numerous ways to achieve this without a "good education or working hard." If we encourage a good education and working hard, the motive will have to be something other than money. How can adults — specifically educators — promote learning without simultaneously insisting on more questions? Many adults view education (degrees) as a plateau rather than a process. The first and probably greatest university, The Grand Lodge of Wa'set in Egypt, admitted students at the age of seven, and studies were not completed until forty years later! Many contemporary educators become masters and doctors much earlier and stop learning.

I agree our youth do need to work hard and receive a good education, but do the same parents who advocate this know the distinction between being educated and being trained? The latter is a very passive experience and an exercise in information regurgitation while the former is active, challenging, relevant, and encourages youth to be inquisitive.

Working hard has always been an admirable goal, slaves did not slow down because they were lazy, but because they were not the beneficiaries of their labor. Employers opt to work longer far more often than employees who require overtime compensation in contrast to owners who do it for long-term growth. Parents have always found dirt in the house that their children didn't see, one reason being pride in ownership was more instilled in the parents. Parents reinforce this view by saying, "You don't do that in *my* house!" The desire to work hard has to be connected to benefits and goals. Students work harder when they see the relationship between theory and practice, a more hands-on experience. Black youth, and specifically Black male youth, literally demand to see the connection between the classroom and the streets.

Black adults may know that schools value grades more than learning, and employers reply more to referrals than credentials, but they do not know anything else to tell Black youth other than to work hard and get a good education. Very few Black adults equip Black youth with a sense of cultural and racial pride, so that when they see racism, they don't view *themselves* as inferior, but view the *discriminator* as having an insecurity problem. Even fewer Black adults encourage their youth to start their own business. The combination of mass public school education geared toward manufacturing employees, and parents not instilling pride to be the boss creates frustration for Black youth. Almost half the Black youth drop out, and the other half who believed a good education would make them the chief executive officer of a "Fortune 500" corporation, now bitterly accept the reality they can only go so far in someone else's corporation.

Our objective is to motivate Black youth to work. Parents, peers and media may motivate them to consume, but that doesn't always create a burning desire to work hard and receive a good education. Our youth today often desire a $200,000 lifestyle but possess only five-dollar skills. Youth tell me they're going to *be* a doctor, lawyer, or engineer, but when I ask about their progress in math, reading, and science they give lackadaisical responses. Youths say, "I'm going to *be* Magic Johnson or Whitney Houston" without an appreciation of what it requires to *become* anything.

Youth are motivated to *be* great, but not motivated to *become* great which requires discipline, time management, vision, patience, and, above all else, work. This misconception of the rigors involved are best attributed to youth watching "instant success" stories on television, and not observing how their parents earn a living. When I ask youth what kind of lifestyle they want, their answer includes a large house, a two-car garage with, of course, two luxury cars, fine clothes and appliances, and the money to travel. I then ask what kind of career will pay for it and what are its requirements? The answers are not forthcoming. Somehow youth feel they can skate from kindergarten to twelfth grade then accelerate, bloom and blossom in college.

I again do not fault our youth. I believe they are the product of their experiences. Earlier, I mentioned the terrible trick that has been played on youth via the diet, media, and the economy. I believe adults do not know what to do with youth. Today, school is what young people do for a living. While a high school diploma or a college degree no longer guarantees a job, there are more jobs you can't even apply for without them. So the payoff is less certain, but the pressure is even greater to go to school longer and longer, to extend the state of semi-autonomy further and further.

The irony is that society worries more when the young try to grasp at adult "privileges" than when they remain in the passive fraternity-house state of mind. We worry about teenage drinking and driving and pregnancy — all perhaps misguided attempts at "grown-up behavior." School just isn't enough. It demands only certain skills, tests only for certain concepts. Adolescence isn't a training ground for adulthood now, it is a holding pattern for aging youth.

Many adults respond to this dilemma with advice from the "good old days" — days filled with two parents, of which only one worked; little to no television; music void of "Sexual Healing" and "In Between The Sheets"; a reverence for teachers, an extended-family neighborhood where every child could be disciplined by an adult, and a church-going community. I respect and encourage adults who want to maintain a more "traditional" lifestyle, but I have concerns when adults give "traditional" advice without providing a "traditional" home, school, and church environment which monitors the peer group and television. Adults need to give advice which includes the *present* reality youths find themselves.

I often challenge adults by asking, "If you were a teenager could you weave your way through what they have to endure?" I want to focus briefly on the peer group; presently it has the second greatest influence nationally on youth, after the home and before television. Why? The peer group has more time. The declining hours from the home have been divided between peer group and television — and the peer group reinforces much of what is seen on television.

Many parents have become very liberal and passive in rearing their children. While the problems of inadequate time and not listening to their children should be obvious, the subtle mistake is not sharing their perspective on contemporary issues. What was our analysis when our youths saw "Purple Rain" or any television show, movie, video, or commercial? What was our opinion when educational and developmental programs solicited their attendance? How are youths going to understand our position on anynynything if they do not work with us, and we do not communicate with them when we arrive home? In the movie "Purple Rain," there was a scene where Prince drove Appolonia (the leading actress) to the lake, and talked her into undressing. What was your position with your son and/or daughter?

I am involved with several youth programs. The major reason for their creation was to provide viable options to our youth, but I learned to realize that the problem often is not the lack of community programs but their sparse attendance due to parents allowing teenagers to decide if they should attend Bible study, piano lessons, academic tutoring and cultural awareness sessions or staying home on Saturday morning watching videos or playing basketball. Adults need to push their values, if for no other reason than that the peer group and media will push theirs.

We offer few alternatives, few meaningful opportunities for

adulthood training. We have virtually allowed sex, drinking, and driving to become rites of passage. Without enough alternatives, schools are left to produce adults, but schools are where the young are kept, not where they grow up.

Listed below are some alternatives for young people:

1) Volunteer in a blue-collar field to learn skills such as carpentry, electricity, and plumbing.
2) Manage the family budget and do the grocery shopping.
3) Volunteer to work for a firm to learn about word processing and computers.
4) Join the school newspaper and learn writing, editing, and graphic design.
5) Learn maintenance of the family car.
6) Volunteer for work with an investment firm to learn the stock market.
7) Join a science club.
8) Learn to play a musical instrument.
9) Improve your personality, communication skills, and income by selling a product.
10) Visit the sick in hospitals.

I have read numerous articles describing the plight of youth and the ambivalance of adolescence. Many writers advocate the need for such alternatives as the above. The assumption is based on the notion that our youth are bored and feel unproductive, therefore, by providing these alternatives and more, we can motivate them. Wrong! When I gave youth an option to choose the above or eat pizza and watch videos, they chose the latter in every case. These options can only be useful if we encourage and/or demand their participation.

In conclusion, our children did not come to us bored, but teacher pedagogy, parental dishonesty or ambiguity about how to "make it" in America, have left youth asking fewer questions, cheating on tests, and dropping out of school. I believe we are not going to motivate youth without being honest, sensitive to the present reality, and assertive in our views. I strongly encourage the use of the alternatives provided to make adolescents more productive, but it might require adults mandating their participation.

I also believe that an appreciation of African-American history can motivate youth. I did not say Negro history which is taught only in February, memorizing names and dates, or allocating one week each to Africa and the middle passage, and the remaining weeks of the course to America. Many youths are ashamed of Africa and slavery. A historian or a teacher decides *before* they write or teach where they want the reader or student to be upon completion. When we teach African-American history do we want to make the students docile and ashamed or assertive and proud? Our youths have a right to know how a people so great went from pyramid to projects. I strongly feel that a committed teacher or parent can motivate our youths with the African-American experience. We were a great people and we withstood the greatest oppression ever placed on a people. In whatever industry or occupation we've been "permitted" to enter we have excelled. We must teach our youth their history and potential. We must use racial pride to motivate them to become the best they can be.

Lastly, I believe the best way to motivate Black youth is not with money, but through the development of their God-given talents. The next chapter will look at how these talents can be identified, developed, and used for motivation.

Children have innate ability, potential and intellect, the full development of which is dependent on opportunities and encouragement.

Chapter 4

The Development of Talents into a Career

From the book of Matthew:

And unto one he gave five talents, to another two, and to another, one to every man according to his ability. Then he that had received the five talents went and traded with the same, and made them five other talents. And likewise he that had received two, he also gained another two. But he that had received one went and digged in the earth, and hid his Lord's talent. After a long time the Lord of those servants cometh, and reckoneth with them. And so he that had received five talents came and brought other five talents, saying Lord, thou deliveredst unto me five talents: behold I have gained beside them five talents more. His Lord said unto him, well done, thou good and faithful servant: thou hast been faithful over a few things, I will make thee ruler over many things: enter thou into the joy of the Lord. He also that had received two talents came and said, Lord, thou deliveredst unto me two talents: behold, I have gained two other talents beside them. His Lord said unto him, well done, good and faithful servant. Then he which had received the one talent came and said Lord I was afraid, and went and hid thy talent in the earth. The Lord said take therefore the talent from him and give it unto him which hath ten talents. For to whom much is given, much is required.[1]

God has given all of us talents, but as the Scripture explains, if you don't *use* them, you will *lose* them. Recognizing your talents should provoke humility and responsibility. When you acknowledge that your gifts come from God, it should make you humble, but it should also encourage you to develop them. Let me offer three brief profiles for illumination: Paul Robeson, Smokey Robinson, and Jeremiah Wright.

Paul Robeson was a star football, baseball and basketball player; a Phi Beta Kappa student who delivered the senior commencement address at Rutgers; a prolific singer of over 300 recorded songs; and a brilliant actor performing on stages internationally, all coupled with a law degree from Columbia University.

William "Smokey" Robinson has survived thirty years in a musical industry based more on fads than stability. Smokey has been either involved as a singer, writer, or producer in over 250 hit records. He has founded and developed some of the most popular artists. He has starred in several films, and has learned the business end of the field, becoming vice-president of Motown. He has blended all of this with an appreciation of African culture, natural diet, and putting God and family first in his life.

Dr. Jeremiah Wright is pastor of Trinity United Church of Christ, one of the fastest growing congregations in America. His degrees range from the social sciences to theology, he speaks four different languages, he writes music, sings, and plays four different instruments, and serves on numerous boards of distinction. He was a cardio-pulmonary technician in the Navy and is actively involved in Trans-Africa and other African liberation movements. A friend of mine, Eugene Winslow, brilliant in his own right, has coined the phrase "use yourself up." Many people go all of their lives unfulfilled and continuously searching for happiness and contentment. Advertisements steer them to cars, clothes, houses, sex, drugs, and exotic resorts, but the pursuit continues. Our youth will take that same journey unless we have adults who will encourage them to look within, to "use themselves up." In the previous chapter on motivation, I declared money may not be adequate to inspire all youth to work hard and get a good education. I propose that in order to motivate youth to study and work requires them to "use yourself up." The major purpose in life should be the exploration and development of all your talents. Robeson, Robinson, and Wright are three fine examples of people who were given certain talents, but have added and multiplied them into many more.

I believe God has given *all* children talents and this chapter will explore how they can be developed and used for motivation. Unfortunately, when most people think of talents, what comes to mind are persons with extraordinary gifts and abilities. Even worse are Blacks who think of talents primarily in sports and music. Most would accept that Dr. J. (Julius Erving) and Michael Jackson are talented, but do not conceive all children as being talented.

Benjamin Bloom comments in *Developing Talent in Young People*,

> After forty years of intensive research, my major conclusion is: What any person in the world can learn, 95% can also if provided with the appropriate conditions. (The remaining 5% is divided among the 2-3% with impairments and the 1-2% with exceptional learning skills.) By talent we mean an unusually high level of demonstrated ability, achievement, or skill in some special field of study or interest. This is in contrast with earlier definitions, which equate talent with natural gifts or aptitudes. This study has provided strong evidence that no matter what the initial characteristics (or gifts) of the individuals, unless there is a long and intensive process of encouragement, nurturance, education, and training, the individuals will not attain extreme levels of capability in these particular fields.[2]

I support Bloom's premise that children have innate ability, potential, aptitude, and talent; and its development is dependent on its nurturance. Bloom cites parental involvement, teachers, and the surrounding environment as key factors in talent development. The research examined the backgrounds of world-class performers in concert piano, sculpture, swimming, tennis and mathematical and neurological research. Parents were instrumental in their children's development by providing them time, money, the work ethic, and commitment. It was also noticed that children selected areas in which their parents had previously demonstrated interest and/or skill. Children did not necessarily choose the exact instrument or sport, but if their parents were musically or athletically inclined it was a catalyst for their child's decision. Income was needed for special tutors, teachers, and programs for talent enhancement. Teacher selection was critical because each stage of talent development requires a certain type of mentor. Lastly, the home, siblings, peers, and the larger community sanctioned and supported the endeavor.

From a Black perspective there is much extrapolation necessary to fully appreciate the study. The full development of talents is dependent on the extent to which there are opportunities and encouragement for individuals to find meaning and enjoyment. Blacks are talented in music and sports because of innate ability coupled with a society that encourages this form of expression. Jackie Robinson was "our first accepted," Henry Aaron hit the most homers, and Ricky Henderson stole the most bases, but don't you believe they had the most baseball talent in the history of our race. Blacks in Africa and America before the 1950's simply were denied the opportunity to express baseball talent. It does not mean they didn't have talents, but the environment was not conducive.

If a major incentive for being a concert pianist, sculptor, swimmer, tennis player, or researcher is dependent on parental interest and accomplishment, it could explain the limited scope to which many Blacks confine their talents. Blacks may be more talented in basketball, football, baseball, boxing and track than in swimming, tennis, bowling, golf and hockey because the former require less money and are supported by their peers. The large number of men who spend their evenings as baseball and basketball coaches, and churches who will teach singing in the choirs may help explain our excellence; and the lack of men and women who provide coaching in math, science, and debate programs may explain our detriment in these areas.

Jeff Howard and Ray Hammond from the Efficacy Committee commented in an article titled "Black America and the Psychology of Performance:"

> Important as the reality of racism may be in understanding the origins of our present problems, we believe our tendency to avoid intellectual engagement and competition limits our potential for development and progress. We contend that avoidance is rooted in reactions of fear and self-doubt engendered by strong negative stereotypes. Competition spurs development. The willingness to engage in competitive activity with commitment to high standards and success stimulates the discipline and effort that underlie intellectual development.[3]

The NAACP has done a fine job with the Academic Olympics, but we need far more. Where are the schools that will give more glory to their scholars than their athletes? That will give pep rallies, medals and trophies to the winners of debate, math, spelling, and science competitions. Young people see schools give more glory and employers give more money to ballplayers than to academicians. Our youth are motivated to make money, play ball, and sing, but we have not provided the support system for the development of other talents.

God has given "talents" to the entire human body. Many educators are familiar with the "split-brain theory." The brain is divided into two apparently symmetrical parts. The left side of the brain is analytical, divides things into sections and specializes in the functions of math and science. The right hemisphere is more holistic, relational, and appreciates the areas of music, art, dance, and sports. It has been rumored that men are better on the left and women better on the right. It has also been felt that people with greater levels of melanin are better on the right, and people with lower levels are better on the left. Are these theories accurate? Did God go to sleep with men on the right and wake up on the left? Did God wake up for Blacks on the right and fall back asleep on the left?

Is the above phenomenon nature (physical) or nurture (environment)? What can explain the tremendous rhythm of Black people and 86 percent of the starting players on NBA teams being Black, yet comprising only 1 percent of the engineers? Consider the following: If you practice dancing and playing basketball six hours daily after school, and spend little time in the library or laboratory, chances are you'll be a better dancer than dentist. If Black parents and teachers emphasize one style of learning over another or are afraid of math and science, this will have implications on the child's development. For example, teachers may offer 100 points for extra reading, 75 points for writing a research paper, but only 10 points for an original drawing. The large number of "degreed" people who can only draw on a primary level is appalling.

Talents are like hidden gifts dispersed throughout the body. It takes time and nurturance to identify and develop them all. Listed below is a miniature diagram.

Body	Characteristic	Possible careers
Right-brain	intuitive, holistic, visual	music/art/writing
Left- brain	logical, analytical	doctor/engineer accountant
mouth	good communication skill, extrovert	sales/media/ singer
hands	good dexterity	sewing/mechanics carpentry
larger body muscles	eye-hand coordination, graceful, strength, speed	athlete/dancer
heart	good listener, compassionate	minister/social worker/teacher
ego	leader	manager/ administrator

My major objective in this chapter is to change the concept that talents are held only held by a few, and that Blacks only have talents for playing ball and musical entertainment. I would like to see parents, schools, and churches look at all children very early and provide them with numerous opportunities to develop their talents. One of the popular manuals used by guidance counselors is the *Self Directed Search*. First, it assumes that people can be loosely classified into six different groups: realistic, investigative, artistic, social, enterprising, and conventional. Some of the major characteristics of each group are as follows:

Realistic	Persistent, mechanical
Investigative	Critical, curious, independent, precise, good memory
Artistic	Original, imaginative
Social	Communicative, convincing, friendly
Enterprising	Adventurous, ambitious, domineering, efficient, orderly
Conventional	Efficient, orderly

I believe a major parental responsibility is to identify and develop children's talents. I also encourage adults who still do not know their children's talents to explore their possibilities. Reviewing the last two diagrams, the following characteristics were provided:

intuitive	holistic	visual
logical	analytical	communicative
extroverted	dexterous	graceful
speed	strength	eye-hand coordination
listening	leadership	persistent
mechanical	critical	curious
independent	good memory	precise
original	imaginative	compassionate
convincing	friendly	adventurous
ambitious	domineering	efficient
orderly		

I'm recommending that parents look at their children for all these characteristics (talents) and provide them with opportunities for major further enrichment. Bloom's study showed that parents were the major catalyst. One of the major obstacles for Black parents is the cost involved in talent development. The magazine, *Black Enterprise* featured an article, "Everything You'd Like to Give Your Kids But Weren't Sure You Could Afford." The article was a cursory look at the cost nationwide for various lessons in piano, drama, computers, and tennis. The average cost was *ten dollars per half-hour*, and, of course, to maximize instruction, each instructor encouraged the purchase of the equipment to practice at home.[5] Many Black parents don't have the advantages included in the demographics of the *Black Enterprise* subscriber — income, education, assets, etc. — consequently would have difficulty paying those fees. This further explains the perception that violin and tennis lessons are for the more well-to-do, and the excellence demonstrated by Blacks in basketball and singing is due to the combination of natural talent and free access to the means of developing these talents. The article, as an afterthought, mentioned the use of the Y. I further suggest the park district, day and evening schools.

My major recommendation in this area would be the Black church. The church has often been criticized for being open only on Sundays, and closed the rest of the week. The church should solicit from members talented instructors in math, science, writing, carpentry, electronics, sewing, speech, music, and sports, etc. These instructors could provide lessons to youth for much less than the cost cited in the article of ten dollars per half-hour.

The four factors preventing our youth from developing their talents are lack of adult identification, institutions, cost, and time. I have already addressed the first three; let's take a closer look at the obstacles of time. Much of the hyperactivity demonstrated by children can be attributed to diet and television. Today's generation of children are uncomfortable with "free time." They are either outside playing or watching television. If parents monitored television and often told them to turn it off, many children would say, "There is nothing to do and I'm bored." What they mean is "There is nothing to watch on television, and I don't know *how* to do anything." Boredom does not come from the *outside* in but the *inside* out. The African term is *inner*attainment, where there is no separation between performer and audience, when the drummer plays, the people dance. The European term is *enter*tainment, best illustrated at the opera where there is not only a distinct separation, but the audience only claps at designated intervals.

How could children filled with talents all over the body and abundant amounts of energy be bored? Besides the obvious fact that watching television takes vital time away from talent development, most children and adults do not have *hobbies*. Webster's Dictionary defines hobbies as "a favorite occupation or something pursued for amusement." I make a distinction between job and career. Jobs are something we have to do for income. Careers are like hobbies, they are a favorite occupation, something pursued for amusement. Can you imagine being paid for something you enjoy so much that you would do it for free, but because you do it so well, you get paid?

The merging of hobbies and talents should be a parental goal in children's development. I don't believe Paul Robeson, Smokey Robinson, and Jeremiah Wright are exceptional or geniuses; I believe they just made the best use of their time to develop their talents.

I believe many of the great contributions of our day could have been made by a number of people if they had reduced their television viewing and other time wasters. This book is being written while some of my peers watch television, gossip on the telephone, and hang out on the streets. Children need hobbies for their free time. Listed below is a partial list of hobbies.

animals: care, hunting, fishing
baking: cooking
carpentry
collections: cards, coins, stamps
dance
drawing: painting, design
electronics
games: chess, checkers, Scrabble, etc.
gardening
musical instrument
photography
reading
sculpture
sewing
singing
sports
travel: geography
writing

Please note I did not mention watching television and listening to music. These are passive (entertainment) experiences. You develop very few little talents watching and listening to electronic media.

This may explain why our youth participate in Michael Jackson and Prince look-alike contests rather than being original. It is very difficult to be bored if you participate in several hobbies.

There is a thin line between achievers and underachievers. A popular statement teachers make to parents at conferences is, "He has the ability, but he's not using it." This statement lets most teachers and parents off the hook and places the weight on the youth for not maximizing his potential. The parents would have been upset with the teacher if he/she had said "their child" is lacking ability. The burden of motivation is erroneously placed squarely on the child. Sally Todd, in *You and the Gifted Child*, provides the following characteristics of the underachiever:

1. They have a low self-concept demonstrated by distrust, lack of concern, and even hostility toward others.
2. They often feel rejected by their family; and feel that their parents are dissatisfied with them.
3. They take little responsibility for their actions.
4. They often do not like school or their teacher, and choose companions who have the same attitude.
5. They lack motivation for academic achievement.
6. They may not have hobbies that could occupy their spare time.
7. They tend to state their goals very late, have much lower aspirations than achievers, and often choose goals that are not in line with their major interest or abilities.[6]

I spoke at a youth camp recently, and attended one of the workshops on concentration and brain control. The workshop conductor had the group form a circle, and then placed an object in the center. He then wanted all of us to see how long we could concentrate on the object without allowing distractions to enter our mind. Everyone acknowledged how difficult it was to do even for two to three minutes. He commented that the brain is a little baby and needs to be disciplined. He mimmicked how children act restless in class, crossing their legs, playing with their hands, mouth, hair, etc. I thought about free-throw shooting in basketball, where the range of accuracy is from 45 to 92 percent. What explains the differential? The ball and the distance are the same, but some shooters can control their brains and concentrate better than others.

Upon completion of that workshop, I felt that very early in school, children should be given exercises in concentration. I realized that whatever you want to achieve in life will require the ability to discipline the brain. Some people can focus talents and energy on one objective for longer periods of time than others. This ability to discipline the brain and maximize concentration may be essential in talent development. Frequently, in our home, our family plays concentration with a deck of cards turned over. Observing my sons affords me an opportunity to measure this vital ability. This talent may be essential to the release of all other talents throughout the body.

I believe the key factor in motivating Black youth to work is to "use yourself up." The search to identify and develop your talents is a lifelong process, as demonstrated by Paul Robeson, Smokey Robinson, and Jeremiah Wright. Students may cheat for a grade, but when you go all of your life not knowing what your talents are — consequently not developing them — you cheat yourself. Money may not be enough to motivate all youth to work hard and get a good education. I suggest one major purpose in life is to *identify* and *develop* your *talents*.

The next chapter takes a look at the present and future employment picture. We now must begin to merge the politics of work, values, motivation, and talents into the present economy and beyond.

Chapter 5

Jobs: The Present and Beyond

Where did the jobs go? Made in Hong Kong, Korea, Taiwan, or Mexico. America has always had international interests, starting from importing slaves and natural resources from Africa to exporting over-priced or finished products back to the "Third World." The international link became more complex with OPEC oil negotiations and the rising cost of U.S. labor. Heavy industrial areas such as steel, cars, and electronics have joined with toys and clothes to be produced overseas. Simultaneously, domestic firms display "Buy American" bumper stickers. U.S. companies want their workers and consumers to be patriotic and loyal while they prostitute and imperialize the rest of the world.

This country would have very little difficulty achieving full employment if they simply created a national employment policy that would reverse the jobs lost overseas. The mistake that many well-intentioned advocates make is assuming owners have the same values as workers and consumers. Capitalists never said their objective was full employment; their first and major obsession is to make a profit, *wherever* it's possible. The contradictions of capitalism are better explained in the Marxist literature, but suffice to say, if capitalism is always looking for new frontiers and people to exploit profitably, the supply will eventually be exhausted. When owners suppress wages, they reduce available consumable dollars, consequently products are either bought with governmental subsidies to corporations and families or exported overseas.

My major reason for providing this brief overview in economic theory is to encourage workers to begin operating from their own interests. When workers enter the marketplace looking for work, we need to be clear where the values of both parties lie. Workers enter the labor force to sell their skills for the top dollar. If the owner did not value their skills or could find any other way to produce his product without it, he would. For example, I don't have any problem with athletes securing large salaries from their owners. First, if the owner can pay that kind of salary to a player, what does he pay himself. Secondly, if the owner doesn't think the player is worth it, he is not forced to sign him, *but* the player should have the opportunity to see what he is worth on the open market. Thirdly, players like Vida Blue, Reggie Jackson, Patrick Ewing, and others have documented that when they play, attendance figures increase, which is the best index to justify additional compensation. Lastly, many non-athletes are simply jealous that their chosen field does not command the same compensation; but I wonder how many critics, given the same opportunity in their occupation would pass it up, especially in sports where the average career lasts only five years.

My major suggestion to workers is to always develop your talents and skills to increase your marketability. The negotiations between owners and workers are based on different interests. Joe McDonald, twenty-year veteran at U.S. Steel in Gary has been laid off the past six years. He is forty years old with a wife, three children, and a mortgage. Joe had moved up the ranks and had become a welder making $18.00 an hour plus benefits. Joe felt very secure on his job, expressed by his large accumulation of debt, and his not developing other skills "just in case." He never thought U.S. Steel would close or, more precisely, relocate to Korea. Joe waited for two years to be recalled while receiving unemployment benefits and union support. The last four years he's found there are few $18.00 per hour jobs in the "third wave" economy. Wages once paid in the second wave of industrialism are not being offered in the third wave of automation and the service sector. In 1960, manufacturing accounted for one out of every four jobs. By 1980 it was responsible for one out of five, and by 1990 will be only one out of six. After hitting a high-water mark of about 45 percent in the 1950s, unions now claim only 22 percent of the nation's workers.[1] Illustrated on the next page are some of the reasons why automation and the anticipated 17,000 robots per year, will decrease Black employment.

Jobs: The Present and Beyond

Occupation	Number of Black Workers 1980	Percentage of Total Jobs Held by Blacks — 1980	Reason for Projected Decline in Employment by 1990
Cleaners and Servants	262,194	53.4%	Mechanized Commercial Cleaning Services
Clothing Ironers	46,056	40.4%	Synthetic Fibers and Automatic Pressers
Farm Laborers	151,255	16.9%	Robot Planters, Sorters and Harvesters
Packers and Wrappers	115,200	19.2%	Mechanical Sorting and Packaging
Sewers and Stitchers	156,812	19.9%	Automatic Fusing Machines
Postal Service Workers	68,970	24.2%	Electronic Mail and Optical Mail Scanners
Transit Workers	114,920	22.1%	Automatic Transportation Systems
Textile Workers	72,998	22.6%	Computer-Controlled Looms and Knitters
Typists	158,565	15.5%	Electronic Voice Transcribers
Steel Workers	63,802	14.6%	Computerized Production
Automobile Washers	33,970	21.5%	Self-Service Car Washes
Loggers	19,008	19.9%	Automatic Tree Harvesters
Bakers	13,965	10.5%	Continuous Mix Systems
Metal Molders	14,025	25.5%	Automatic Sand Slingers
Assembly Line Workers	175,864	15.2%	Industrial Robots
Paper Mill Workers	58,860	16.4%	Automatic Continuous Pulp Digestors
Boiler Tenders	9,996	14.7%	Thermostat Control Systems
Library Attendants	20,064	13.2%	Home Computer Access to Library Files
Telephone Operators	49,928	15.8%	Automatic Switching Devices
Stock Clerks	66,092	12.4%	Computerized Storage and Retrieval Systems

Welders (Joe McDonald)	78,888	11.4%	Robotic Arc Welding
Cashiers	167,832	10.8%	Universal Product Code Scanners
File Clerks	69,984	21.6%	Electronic File Retrieval
Tailors and Dressmakers	21,017	15.8%	Computer-Controlled Stitching
Messengers	15,974	16.3%	Telecommunications and Electronic Mail
Fabric Cutters	42,987	16.1%	Computer-Guided Laser Scissors
Gardeners	97,963	16.3%	Robot Lawn Mowers and Sprinklers
Key Punch Oper.	57,988	21.8%	Optical Scanners and Readers
Stenographers	9,984	15.6%	Automatic Dictation Machines
Private Mail Carriers	37,950	23.0%	Electronic Mail

Jobs Vulnerable to Robots

Farm laborers	Meat cutters
Mail carriers	Gas station attendants
Messengers	Railroad workers
Stock clerks	Ticket collectors
Food counter workers	Mass transit workers
Steel workers	Utility meter readers
Dishwashers	Bottlers and canners
Key punch operators	Fork lift operators
Bank tellers	Payroll clerks
Checkout clerks	File clerks
Telephone operators	Textile workers
Assembly line workers	Shipping clerks
Parking lot attendants	Elevator operators
Garbage collectors	Freight handlers
Automobile workers	Clothing ironers
Welders	Stenographers
Gardeners[2]	

Joe McDonald's major question is, where are the jobs for the future? This is a question not only asked by workers, but by employment counselors and forecasters. The advancement in technology supposedly will create new jobs to replace extinct positions. High-tech should provide more leisure time, and accelerate the growth in recreation, services, and specialty shops. Listed below is a table showing those areas with the fastest growth rate followed by a table showing those occupations with the greatest aggregate increase projected in 1990.

Projected Employment

Occupation	Growth 1978-1990
Computer programmers	73.6%
Systems analysts	107.8
Electronic technicians	45.4
Vocational trainers	26.5
Laboratory technicians	43.9
Crane operators	40.4
Appliance repairers	24.1
Health care technicians	45.0
Auto body repairers	27.0
Physical therapists	57.5
X-Ray technicians	47.4
Bulldozer operators	57.0
Travel agents	55.6
Paralegals	132.4
Plumbers	20.0
Nurses	50.3
Accountants	32.7
Law clerks	44.0
Firemen	22.7
Lithographers	45.8
Electricians	24.6
Tax preparers	64.5
Mechanics	29.7
Policemen	23.23

Forty Occupations with
Largest Projected Growth: 1982-1995

Occupation	Change in total employment (in thousands)	Percent of total job growth	Percent change
Building custodians	779	3.0	27.5
Cashiers	744	2.9	47.4
Secretaries	719	2.8	29.5
General clerks, office	696	2.7	29.6
Salesclerks	685	2.7	23.5
Nurses, registered	642	2.5	48.9
Waiters and waitresses	562	2.2	33.8
Teachers, kindergarten and elementary	511	2.0	37.4
Truck drivers	425	1.7	26.5
Nursing aides and orderlies	423	1.7	4.8
Sales representatives, technical	386	1.5	29.3
Accountants and auditors	344	1.3	40.2
Automotive mechanics	324	1.3	38.3
Supervisors of blue collar workers	319	1.2	26.6
Kitchen helpers	305	1.2	35.9
Guards and doorkeepers	300	1.2	47.3
Food preparation and service workers, fast food restaurants	297	1.2	36.7
Managers store	292	1.1	30.1
Carpenters	247	1.0	28.6
Electrical and electronic technicians	222	.9	60.7
Licensed practical nurses	220	.9	37.1
Computer systems analysts	217	.8	85.3
Electrical engineers	209	.8	65.3
Computer programmers	205	.8	76.9
Maintenance repairers, general utility	193	.8	27.8
Helpers trades	190	.7	31.2
Receptionist	189	.7	48.8
Electricians	173	.7	31.8
Physicians	163	.7	34.0
Clerical supervisors	162	.6	34.6
Computer operators	160	.6	75.8
Sales representatives nontechnical	160	.6	27.4
Lawyers	159	.6	34.3

Stock clerks, stockroom and warehouse	156	.6	18.8
Typists	155	.6	15.7
Delivery and route workers	153	.6	19.2
Bookkeepers, hand	152	.6	15.9
Cooks, restaurants	149	.6	42.3
Bank tellers	142	.6	30.0
Cooks, short order, specialty and fast food	141	.6	32.2[4]

It is not my desire to disappoint or confuse Black youth in a book designed to motivate, but as I have said in previous chapters, I do not believe you can motivate Black youth with a lie. Those areas with the fastest rate are primarily high-tech which require a math and science background. I encourage Black youth to be prepared in these subjects. The complexity lies in the fact that high-tech will probably represent only seven percent of the labor force; of the top ten occupations in *total* numbers, only nursing and teaching require a college degree, and the leading occupations are custodians, cashiers, and secretaries.

How do we motivate Joe McDonald and Black youth with the above analysis? There will be increased competition for the "elite" jobs of the future. A college degree will remain a valued commodity, but its stock will increase if its concentration is in engineering, computers, accounting, education, medicine, or marketing. Specialists in word processing, paralegals, auto and appliance repairers, plumbers, electricians and carpenters will be lucrative occupations. There will be a widening gap between the haves and have-nots, with a small number needed in the growth fields and a larger number needed in low-skilled areas. The major advice any counselor should give to youth would be for them to familiarize themselves with the above charts, remain flexible, continue to learn new skills, and understand that the marketplace between owner and worker is based on negotiated interests and values.

One of the frequent comments heard from "the political right" and some Blacks who blame the victims is the numerous pages of want ads. The sentiment expressed is that the problem is not unemployment, but workers lacking "third wave" skills. I encourage everyone to play "the want ad exercise." The *Sunday Chicago Tribune* may have 20 pages of employment advertisements; if you called every position you may find half of them have been filled through their internal apparatus. (Often times personnel departments publicly show a position to protect themselves from charges of discriminatory practices, while all along they knew the position was to be filled from within.) Secondly, for many inner-city residents the jobs are either not accessible by public transportation or are so far by car or bus that an inordinate amount of salary is spent on transportation. I see numerous fast-food chains advertising in the suburbs for part-time help. But can we blame Black youth for not being able to reach it? Or adults for not feeling minimum-wage salaries warrant four hours each day of commuting? There is no excuse though for idleness, and the need to learn new skills and volunteer time in the Black community.

After eliminating jobs that no longer exist and/or are inaccessible, we come to those engineering, computer, accounting, medical, marketing, word processing, and paralegal positions that some of us are qualified for, but which require one to five years experience. Where and when are Joe McDonald and Black youth going to be able to learn the skill and gain experience simultaneously? Black youth, both qualified and unqualified, then call the few remaining positions not affected by the above.

On a more optimistic note are the many job training and manpower programs nationwide providing an excellent service to our community. I have had the fortunate opportunity to observe and interview numerous directors about their full range of services. While there is no question that a greater commitment of time and money are needed from the government, these directors also said that their programs are often *under-utilized* by their constituency. Many of these programs provide GED certificates, training in high-tech areas, self-esteem, grooming and interviewing techniques, and job placement.

The Neighborhood Institute, based in Chicago, provides an eight-week course that concentrates on appearance, communication, and thinking skills. Employers have targeted these areas along with technical skills as their major concerns. The Institute helps clients in goal clarification, resume preparation, and interviewing strategies. Here are some of their "Stress Interview Questions" and the major reasons why people lose their jobs.

STRESS INTERVIEW QUESTIONS

What are your short-range objectives?

What are your long-range objectives?

What can you do for us that someone else cannot do?

Why should we hire you?

Can you work under pressure, deadlines, etc.?

What is your philosophy of management?

Do you prefer staff or line work? Why?

What kind of salary are you worth?

What are your five biggest accomplishments in: Your present or last job? Your career so far?

Why didn't you do better in college? What is your biggest strength/ weakness?

How long would it take you to make a contribution to our firm?

How long would you stay with us?

How do you feel about people from minority groups?

If you could start again, what would you do differently?

What new goals or objectives have you established recently?

How have you changed the nature of your job?

What position do you expect to have in five years?

What do you think of your boss?

Why haven't you obtained a job so far?

What features of your previous jobs have you disliked?

Would you describe a few situations in which your work was criticized?

Would you object to working for a woman?

Some of your experience isn't related to the position. How can you compensate for that?

How would you evaluate your present job?

Do you generally speak to people before they speak to you?

How would you describe the essence of success?

What was the last book you read? Movie you saw? Sporting event you attended?

In your present position, what problems have you identified that had previously been overlooked?

What interests you most about the position we have? The least?

Don't you feel you might be better off in a different size company? Different type company?

Why aren't you earning more at your job?

Will you be out to take your boss's job?
Are you creative? Give an example.
Are you analytical? Give an example.
Are you a leader? Give an example.
How would you describe your own performance?
Have you helped increase sales? How?
Have you helped reduce costs? How?
What do your subordinates think of you?
Have you fired people before?
Have you hired people before? What do you look for?
Why do you want to work for us?
If you had your choice of jobs and companies, where would you go?
What other types of jobs are you considering? What companies?
Why do you feel you have top management potential?
Tell us about yourself. Are you conceptual? Give an example.
If you had only one question that you could ask of me, what would it be?

Why People Lose Their Jobs:

1. Coming to work late or leaving early
2. Taking too many breaks or staying too long on them
3. Being dishonest or stealing from the boss
4. Missing too many days from work
5. Not following company rules
6. Not getting along well with others
7. Being lazy and not doing a fair work share
8. Not willing to train for the job
9. Doing messy or incomplete work
10. Being too slow or not trying to improve[5]

In looking at the chapter on jobs, we should not only be concerned about the kinds of positions, but where they are located. We all have heard about industry's move south and west toward the Sun Belt. Listed are the high and low growth rate states.

High-Growth States Through 1993

	Annual Percentage Growth	Total Growth
Arizona	2.94	351,560
Nevada	2.8	7,135,680
Florida	2.67	1,167,130
New Mexico	2.55	137,790
Colorado	2.49	371,700
Georgia	2.4	5,614,610
Texas	2.4	11,658,140
California	2.39	2,626,310
New Hampshire	2.30	100,060
Virginia	2.29	547,490

Low-Growth States

	Percentage Growth	Total Growth
Delaware	1.65	46,370
New Jersey	1.63	544,650
Ohio	1.61	711,790
Maine	1.59	70,320
Illinois	1.57	762,000
West Virginia	1.55	97,900
Dist. of Columbia	1.40	88,870
Pennsylvania	1.31	618,300
New York	1.25	957,050
North Dakota	1.22	32,590[6]

The high-growth states have a much smaller percentage of Blacks than the industrial Northeast and Midwest. Statistical tables can also be confusing. For example, let's compare Arizona with New York. The rate of growth for Arizona is twice the rate of New York, but New York will produce almost three times as many jobs over the decade; but the greater population in New York will increase competition. Joe McDonald lives in Gary, and, like so many other cities that were dependent on one industry, it has become a virtual ghost town. (Richard Hatcher needs to be commended for the additional resources brought into Gary.) It is often said Black people are landlocked, living primarily in the largest thirty cities regardless of their economic conditions.

The decision to relocate is complex. Blacks obviously proved they were not landlocked in the 1920s with the large migrations northward. Recently there have been traces of a return migration southward and to California. The Black population in the South still represents 53 percent of its total. One of the major strengths of the Black community is the extended family. Blacks are less inclined than other groups to move cross-country and leave behind relatives for a few more dollars. I am reminded of the White affluent suburb of Dallas, and the rising teenage suicides. A high school counselor said she had not seen a grandparent out of 3,000 students, and one of the teenage suicide victims, who hung himself to a tree, left a note saying, "This was the only thing that had *roots*." Relocation is a middle-class phenomenon that assumes you have skills and/or a position on the other end. A person is less likely to relocate to Arizona with no skills.

Lastly, I'd like to look at the military, specifically, the U.S. Army and its impact on our youth. Their favorite slogan is "Be all that you can be," and for a youth struggling to graduate from high school with an economy as complex as previously described, it *seems* like the best thing to do. I have seen students drop out of school, return for a GED, with the sole purpose being enlistment. I have even seen cases where our youth have been registered without GED or diploma! There are mothers who, after eighteen years of "loving" (unconditional love creating irresponsibility) their sons versus "raising" (unconditional love creating responsiblity and self-actualization) them, *give* them to the Army in hopes they will make him a responsible man. The enlistment meetings remind me of the EMR (Educable Mentally Retarded) meetings that took place when Black boys were nine years old. Unfortunately, at this meeting, nine years later, many parents don't even attend. Parents who have participated in these military meetings, have told me their presence may very well have determined whether their son was placed on the front line or in electronics. If the parent and the larger Black community had been more involved, challenged the school, curriculum, and the teacher about the disproportionate number of Black boys placed in EMR, this subsequent army meeting might have been unnecessary. For every isolated "success" story in the Army, I can provide nine that were failures. Blacks are 12 percent of the population, but are 33 percent of the Army, were 41 percent of the deaths in Vietnam, and only 7 percent of the officers.[7]

In conclusion, I did not want you to understand the politics of work, change your values, become motivated to learn, identify and develop your talents, for you to *look* for a job. If you must do that, I hope this chapter has been of some assistance. Many counselors confine their advice to seeking employment. I view this as a temporary phase with the ultimate destination being developing a career, starting your own business, and making the Black community strong and viable. I believe the best way to motivate and prepare Black youth to work is to identify and develop their talents.

A good education should make you economically independent and self-sufficient by teaching you the skills to make a product or provide a service.

Chapter 6

How to Become Economically Self-Sufficient

I travel on airplanes about two or three days a week, and have noticed that the "world runners" — White men — make up 90 percent of the occupancy, with the remaining 10 percent divided among White and Black women and Black men. It hurts me sometimes to see all these financially successful White men and so few Black men when I can so vividly remember the night before college graduation, White men were still having panty raids and beer fights, but because of their white privileges, have risen high up in the corporate ranks. I will never forget one particular trip where two White men were talking about their professions. (I wish more Blacks, especially those in college, would talk about career options and possible business ventures.) One of the men was a personnel recruiter for a firm that produces nails. When most of us see nails, that is probably all we see.

Let me share from the above experience what I see. I envision one to three men who decided years ago that they wanted to work for themselves, and they sat down and created Nails, Inc. Years later, this company not only sends its staff on expensive recruiting trips, but has an engineering department charged with combining raw materials to achieve product quality and safety specifications. It also has a purchasing department responsible for securing all needed materials, and which is very much aware that one part missing could cause costly delays. Nails, Inc. has an accounting department assigned to oversee the budget and operate the disbursements, receivables, income and balance sheet statements, and plan investment strategies. The company also has a marketing division which handles its print advertisement, administers the sales force, and provides the company with a good image. I see a million square foot plant which also has a maintenance staff. When I see a nail, I recognize a company behind it that employs over 500 people with a $5 million dollar payroll, which multiplies itself four times by contributing additional jobs to the city of Nailville. It is called Nailville because it is the largest employer in town, pays thousands of dollars in taxes, has three officers on various municipal boards, and its former CEO (Chief Executive Officer) and founder is the present mayor. What do you see when you see a nail? I see the above that started with one to three men who had a vision.

What keeps so many Blacks away from starting their own businesses? George Subira, in *Black Folks' Guide to Making Big Money in America*, says a "good job." He further states:

> to be Black and have a "good job" usually means you went to college, competed against other blacks and whites for the job and won, you have responsibility, proud of your social image, and lastly and most dangerously have been promised advancement and security. Now for this company man to risk all of this to operate his own business for many is inconceivable. A Black with a "good job" for more than ten years is very much like a convict who has been in prison for ten years. Neither one of them can make it on "the outside" regardless of how much strength and character they demonstrate "inside."[1]

I believe we need a new generation of youth, motivated, talented, with a budget based on needs, who will have the confidence to start their own businesses. Employers have more faith in us than we have in ourselves. Why would they hire us, if they did not believe our contribution to the company would pay not only our salary but operating expenses, and help bring substantial profits. Many of us talk a good "black game", but would rather someone else have the responsibility of Friday payroll. It is amazing that Carter G. Woodson's writings from fifty years ago are still so applicable.

> In the schools of business administration Negroes are trained exclusive in the psychology and economics of Wall Street and are, therefore, made to despise the opportunities to run ice wagons, push banana carts, and sell peanuts among their own people. Foreigners, who have not studied economics, but have studied Negroes, take up this business and grow rich.[2]

The accuracy of this historical quote is astonishing. Our talented tenth prefer to work downtown, and the few Black businesses we have are often operated by those lacking in economic principles. How nice it would be if our talented tenth had the vision to "do for self" instead of Arabs and Koreans in the Black community, and leaving the business opportunities to the Jews, Arabs, and Asians who now operate in the Black community.

Many of us believe that business is comprised solely of capital, labor, and a physical plant. While these are essential resources, what precedes all of this is attitude or "social capital." Glen Loury coined the phrase, to refer to:

> those institutions within a community, that generate economic dividends, by shaping the values and attitudes of individuals. There is ample evidence that the home and church can yield significant economic benefits. We discovered that young men who had been taught to aspire to relatively high-status occupations, later in life worked nearly 25 percent more weeks per year than otherwise similar youths who had no such aspirations. It was revealed that those who reported religion is important in their lives worked about 15 percent more weeks per year than comparable youths who lacked a religious background.[3]

There are numerous books promoting positive mental attitude (PMA). Some of the most important attitudes to possess are: good self-esteem, think big, take risks, avoid use of the word "can't," accept responsibility for your actions, work hard, become knowledgeable, monitor your time, keep healthy and energetic, be decisive, interact with positive peers.

What should a motivated youth do when he/she is out of work? First, I believe all of us should learn how to make a product and provide a service. When you can't do either, you have to ask someone for a job. If you can make a product or provide a service, you will reduce the chance of being unemployed. A good education should make you independent and self-sufficient by teaching these skills. I would recommend that our youth learn both a blue-collar and white-collar skill. We need to quit choosing between the philosophy of DuBois and Booker T. Washington and accept both. Many white-collar professionals look down at blue-collar workers until they have to pay $30.00 plus per hour to plumbers, carpenters, and electricians. The latter have so much contempt for the scholars, they seldom master the business side of their professions, which would enable them to secure large governmental contracts requiring an extensive amount of paperwork. Secondly, I would encourage our youth to understand the field of selling. I have found many people are afraid of sales and public speaking. I believe one reason is they did not believe in what they were selling or speaking. I am against students first encountering public speaking with a topic they do not believe, and I am not in favor of youths and adults selling any product indiscriminately. You must first ask yourself, what do I like? Secondly, can I make any money selling it? And lastly, how many other people can I convince to buy what I like?

For example, most people think I am a writer, public speaker, and salesman, but I don't write, speak, or sell everything. My next book will be titled *Marketing Black Consciousness*; my doctoral dissertation was "The Marketability of Black Literature." I write and speak about the liberation of Black people, and sell books and related items committed to that position. I am not as effective writing, talking, or selling a product or concept I do not believe in.

I encourage Black youth to understand sales. This field is the basic way goods and services are distributed, consequently it employs large numbers and offers unlimited income. But please remember, only sell what you enjoy, then it won't feel like work, but an extension of yourself. We have too many people working and selling things they do not enjoy. As mentioned earlier, a major hinderance to starting your own business is a "good job"; a major obstacle to sales is the desire for a guaranteed salary. Many people who lack confidence in their abilities would prefer a guaranteed salary, versus working on commissions with unlimited income. George Subira recommends that those conservative-minded individuals try sales part-time, so that their bills are placed on the "good job," while they try sales. I also encourage you to take advantage of the creative and innovative marketing plans companies have designed, where you not only sell products, but have other people selling them for you.

The first step in starting your own business is to have a positive attitude, followed by identifying something you enjoy selling. Then we must understand the value of money, real estate, and taxes. Black youths often go to school from pre-kindergarten through twelfth grade, plus undergraduate and above, and are not knowledgeable of the fundamentals of this economy. Most Blacks work harder for their money than their money works for them. Many of us value cars more than real estate, and we pay more taxes while earning less income. I find no better way to motivate Black youth than to encourage them to use their talents for themselves by

Selling is the way goods and services are distributed; it employs large numbers and offers unlimited income.

understanding money, real estate, and taxes.

The greatest hinderance to investment is again the desire for a guarantee. Blacks, more than most people, would prefer a "guaranteed" 5 percent interest from a bank or savings and loan, or 8 to 10 percent interest from a certificate of deposit with strict time limitations, than investing in money market, mutual funds, common stocks, leasing, or real estate. I wonder if we ever ask if banks and savings and loans institutions pay us 5 to 10 percent interest, where do they make their 15 to 50 percent interest? Just as employers do with our labor, banks have more confidence with our money in "unguaranteed" places than we do. The formula for investment is time-rate-capital, the combination of investing young with a good rate of return with as little capital as fifty dollars per month can provide a college education or the capital needed to start Nails, Inc.

In a book titled *Motivating and Preparing Black Youth to Work*, I do not want to provide an in-depth analysis of business theory, but I do encourage you to read *The Power of Money Dynamics* by Venita Van Caspel, *Black Folks' Guide to Making Big Money in America* by

George Subira, *101 Businesses You Can Start and Run with Less than $1,000* by H.S. Kahm, and *How to Become a Successful Consultant in Your Own Field* by Hubert Bermont.

Finally, on the idea of starting your own business, you must ask yourself, "Am I starting the business to serve the customer or to provide myself a means of employment where I am the boss and do whatever, whenever, and wherever I feel?" Many Blacks think that having your own business makes you the boss with no accountability; while in contrast, many Whites understand that the customer is the most important asset of the business, and that a harmonious, cohesive staff is necessary to provide customer satisfaction.

I remember two "negotiations" I was in with Black businesses. The first was a pizza shop advertising free pop with a family-size pizza. I ordered the largest size available in deep dish, which exceeded the dollar value of a family-size thin crust. I calmly explained that the ad did not specify thin crust, that I had ordered the largest deep dish and it had a greater dollar value, and, in addition, I was a frequent customer. The second example was a owner of a facility our school wanted to rent for classroom purposes. We knew the owner was having financial problems; the space was not being used, and we offered a fair price for rental. In both cases the owners took a attitude of a HNIC (Head Negro in Charge) with them holding the trump card. They didn't realize how valuable I was to their operation, and treated me as an enemy rather than the person who puts bread on their table. It takes a lot of my political commitment to continue to support these kinds of businesses. These same owners will be the first to condemn the Black community for lack of support, without ever looking at themselves.

Listed below are a few good reasons to start your own business:
1) An opportunity to work longer hours and to give more of your love, creativity and talent to a task than what is provided by most job situations;

2) An opportunity to receive a fair return (money and other benefits) for such additional work output in ways that are not tied to "wage guidelines" or other artificial, limiting, subjective or arbitrary decisions by others;

3) An opportunity to build something of lasting value that can be sold or passed on to heirs; (A job's benefits obviously last only as long as the job lasts, and cannot be passed on to anyone.)

4) An opportunity to gain additional tax advantages and build a

substantial net worth;

5) An opportunity to employ others;
6) An opportunity to give some kind of community service;
7) An opportunity to attract other business opportunities or financial investors;
8) An opportunity for a degree of independence, "freedom," and a greater sense of security than jobs can usually provide;
9) An opportunity for a significant identity so that your fellow man can know you exist, and appreciate you and work with you.

My desire has been motivating and preparing Black youth to work. We are not a lazy people, but a proud people who would like to be compensated fairly. We have excelled in every industry where we've been allowed to participate; we have the capacity to be good ballplayers or scholars if given the opportunity. A large part of the problem has been an erosion of our values. The larger society, and Black youth specifically, often want to "feel good and look good" at any cost. Values such as hard work, savings and the liberation of Black people can only be taught by concerned adults who are willing to compete against the onslaught of media bombardment.

Many Black youths have lost the desire to learn because they have not been encouraged to ask questions and to develop critical thinking skills. Many youths have determined that the motive for schools is to get good grades by whatever means; securing employment is based more on who you know than what you know. We are not going to motivate and prepare Black youth without being honest about the complexity of school, diet, media, and economy. The problem may not be with Black youths, but with adults who don't know how to develop teenagers.

Unfortunately, many Black youths spend their entire lives neither finding nor developing their God-given talents. I believe the best way to motivate and prepare Black youth is to encourage them to "use themselves up." Many adults have already discovered the void in their lives thinking cars, clothes, appliances, drugs, and sex could make up for working a job. I have attempted pragmatically to show how Black youth with limited resources can discover and develop their talents. This same pragmatism was used in exploring employment opportunities. This last chapter was an attempt to show our youth who are motivated, talented, and operating on a "needs" value system, how they can start their own business and contribute to the vitality of the Black community.

EPILOGUE

I often think about what I would like to do for the future. Two project ideas have been generated by this book. Just as with *Countering the Conspiracy to Destroy Black Boys*, which helped promote the continuance of Simba program (activities designed by men to take boys through the rites of passage) and are now operating in over fifteen cities across the country, I'd like to share these two projects, either for your assistance to me, and/or your development in your respective city.

Kuumba (Creativity) House

This is a talent center located in the Black community. It provides one general location to learn and develop hobbies and talents. The few places in our community that provide talent development concentrate primarily on basketball, football, baseball, track, singing, dancing, and sometimes piano. Kuumba House may consider these but, with limited dollars and space will concentrate on science, mathematics, debate, writing, spelling, art, mechanics, gymnastics, marital arts, drama, and musical instruments.

There is a fear in many Black youths of competing academically. This is reflected in a lack of competitive academic activities and an over-abundance of athletic events. The Kuumba House will not only offer all these "talent centers" but will provide "healthy competition" to stimulate its growth.

The School of Kujichagulia (Self-Determination)

This school is designed for the aggressive learner who wants a hands-on approach to learning. Many Black students who ask questions or demand relevancy, are labeled EMR (Educable Mentally Retarded) or BD (Behavioral Disorder) and end up in prisons. I believe some of our best minds are incarcerated. The requirements to enter would be a high school diploma or its equivalent. While we would like to attract the talented tenth, most of them have the ability to make it in college. Our focus would be attracting those youths that normally might not succeed in "traditional" institutions.

67

The objective of the school would be to teach how to produce a good or provide a service that can be developed into a business. Upon completion of all course work, the students, with the assistance of faculty members, will design a business plan that will be presented to banks. The school will not only provide the curriculum to achieve this goal, but will align itself with the financial community to secure financing. The school will co-sign all loans. Board members and alumni from the school will provide an excellent pool of networking which will enhance contract procurement and continued business expertise.

FOOTNOTES

Chapter 1

1) Marable, Manning. *How Capitalism Underdeveloped Black America.* Boston: South End Press, 1983, pp 3,7.

2) U. S. Dept. of Commerce Bureau of Census, America's Black Population 1984, p4.

3) U.S. Dept. of Labor, Bureau of Labor Statistics, Special Labor Force Report 225.

4) Thomas, Veronica. "Black Youth Unemployment." Issues, Concerns and Strategies For Change. *Urban Research Review*, Vol. 9, No. 3, 1984 pp 1-4.
Curwood, Steve. "Minorities Face Grim Employment Future," Chicago Sun Times, November 9, 1983, p74.

5) Chicago Tribune, "For Some Jobless, Survival Means They Steal and Deal," July 16, Section 2, pp3.

6) Wilhelm, Sidney. *Who Needs the Negro.* New York: Doubleday 1971, pp XIII, 222,223.

7) Colt, Allan. "Orthornolecular Approach to the Treatment of Children with Behavior Disorder and Learning Disabilities." *Journal of Applied Nutrition*, 1973, Vol. 25, Nos. 1 & 2, Winter, pp. 25-36.

8) Postman, Neil. *The Disappearance of Childhood.* New York: Delacorte Press, 1982, pp 10,13,14,18.

9) Goodlad, John. *A Place Called School.* New York: McGraw Hill, 1984, p.12.

10) Thomas. O.P. Cit, p3.

11) Terkel, Studs. *Working.* New York: Pantheon Books 1972, pp 449,521.

12) McDaniels, Carl. "The Work/Leisure Connection." Vocational Guidance Quarterly, Vol 33, No. I, pp 35-42.

13) Toffler, Alvin. *The Third Wave.* New York: William Morrow, 1980, pp. 367-376.

Chapter 2

1) Yates, Ronald. "East meet West — and Find Decadence." *Chicago Tribune*, August 4, 1984, Section I, p. 5.

2) Simmons, Richard. *The Crucial Element.* Chicago: Richard Simmons, 1985, pix.

3) Amini, Johari. "Behavior and Its Value Base." *Black Books Bulletin*, Volume 4, No. 3, 1976, p.43.

4) Wobogo, Vulinedela. "Two Cradle Theory and the Origin of White Racism." *Black Books Bulletin*, Volume 4, No. 4, 1976, p.23.

5) Amini Op. Cit pp. 40-41.
6) Lasch, Christopher. *The Culture of Narcissism.* New York: W.W. Norton, 1979, pp 30-31, 101, 106-107, 137.
7) Black Child Care Conference, Columbus, Ohio, September 1981.
8) Karenga, Maulana. *Kwanzaa, Origin, Concepts, Practice.* Los Angeles: Kawaida Publication, p.1.
9) Jordan Val. *The Black Value System.* (Chicago: Trinity Church, 1981).

Chapter 3

1) Kunjufu, Jawanza. *Countering The Conspiracy to Destroy Black Boys.* Chicago: African American Images, 1983, p. 7.
2) Morgan, Harry. "How Schools Fail Black Children." *Social Policy*, Jan-Feb, 1980, pp. 49-54.
3) U. S. Department of Labor, Bureau of Labor Statistics Press Release pp. 79-90.
4) *Chicago Tribune.* "A Reading on School's Freshman Class." April 28, 1985, Tempo Section.
5) Minority College Report Manual. "The High Cost of Dropping Out," Education Section.
6) Packard, Vance. *Our Endangered Children.* Boston: Little, Brown and Co., 1983 p. 16.

Chapter 4

1) *Holy Bible*, King James Version, Matthew 25:15. 29
2) Bloom, Benjamin. *Developing Talent In Young People.* New York: Ballantine, 1985, pp. 3-5.
3) Howard, Jeff and Hammond, Ray. "The Intellectual Inferiority Game." Boston: The Efficacy Committee, 1985, pp. 2, 4, and 8.
4) Holland, John. *The Self Directed Search.* Palo Alto: Consulting Psychologists Press, 1977, p. 2-3.
5) Black Enterprise. "Everything You'd Like to Give Your Kids But Weren't Sure You Could Afford." October, 1985, pp. 48-50.
6) Todd, Sally. *You and the Gifted Child.* Springfield: Charles Thomas Publishers, 1983 p. 111.

Chapter 5

1) Quinlan, Tim. "The new high-tech employment market will offer many jobs at mini-wages." *Chicago Sun-Times*, May 23, 1983, p. 29
2) Cross, Theodore. *The Black Power Imperative.* New York: Faulkner, 1984, pp. 448-449, 622.

FOOTNOTES

3) ibid. p. 623

4) *Monthly Labor Review*, "Occupational Employment Projections to 1995," p. 45

5) The Neighborhood Institute Career Education and Employment Cennter, "Try-out Employment Placement Program." Participant's Manual, Chicago

6) Saunders, Dick. "Sun Belt big winner in jobs survey." *Chicago Sun-Times*, August 26, 1984, p. 55

7) Staples, Robert. *Black Masculinity.* San Francisco: Black Scholar Press, 1982, p. 24.

8) U.S. Department of Commerce Bureau of Census "America's Black Population," 1983, pp 23-24.

Chapter 6

1) Subira, George. *Black Folks' Guide to Making Big Money in America.* Newark: Very Serious Business Enterprises, p. 62.

2) Woodson, Carter G. *Miseducation of the Negro.* Washington: Associated Publishers, 1933, p. 5.

3) Loury, Glenn. "New Dividends Through Social Capital." *Black Enterprise*, July 1985, p. 36.

4) Subira, p. 156.

INDEX

FAITH AND WILL

By Julia Cameron

BOOKS IN THE ARTIST'S WAY SERIES

The Artist's Way

Walking in This World

Finding Water

The Complete Artist's Way

The Artist's Way Workbook

The Artist's Way Every Day

The Artist's Way at Work *(with Mark Bryan and Catherine Allen)*

Inspirations: Meditations from *The Artist's Way*

The Artist's Way Morning Pages Journal

The Artist's Date Book, *illustrated by Elizabeth Cameron*

OTHER BOOKS ON CREATIVITY

The Writing Diet

The Right to Write

The Sound of Paper

The Vein of Gold

How to Avoid Making Art (or Anything Else You Enjoy),
illustrated by Elizabeth Cameron

Supplies: A Troubleshooting Guide for Creative Difficulties,
illustrated by Elizabeth Cameron

The Writer's Life: Insights from *The Right to Write*

Money Drunk, Money Sober: 90 Days to Financial Freedom
(with Mark Bryan)

FAITH AND WILL

Weathering the Storms in Our Spiritual Lives

JULIA CAMERON

JEREMY P. TARCHER/PENGUIN

A MEMBER OF PENGUIN GROUP (USA) INC.

New York

JEREMY P. TARCHER/PENGUIN
Published by the Penguin Group
Penguin Group (USA) Inc., 375 Hudson Street, New York, New York 10014, USA •
Penguin Group (Canada), 90 Eglinton Avenue East, Suite 700, Toronto, Ontario M4P 2Y3,
Canada (a division of Pearson Penguin Canada Inc.) • Penguin Books Ltd, 80 Strand, London
WC2R 0RL, England • Penguin Ireland, 25 St Stephen's Green, Dublin 2, Ireland
(a division of Penguin Books Ltd) • Penguin Group (Australia), 250 Camberwell Road,
Camberwell, Victoria 3124, Australia (a division of Pearson Australia Group Pty Ltd) •
Penguin Books India Pvt Ltd, 11 Community Centre, Panchsheel Park, New Delhi–110 017,
India • Penguin Group (NZ), 67 Apollo Drive, Rosedale, North Shore 0632, New Zealand
(a division of Pearson New Zealand Ltd) • Penguin Books (South Africa) (Pty) Ltd,
24 Sturdee Avenue, Rosebank, Johannesburg 2196, South Africa

Penguin Books Ltd, Registered Offices: 80 Strand, London WC2R 0RL, England

First trade paperback edition 2010

Most Tarcher/Penguin books are available at special quantity discounts for bulk purchase for sales
promotions, premiums, fund-raising, and educational needs. Special books or book excerpts also can
be created to fit specific needs. For details, write Penguin Group (USA) Inc. Special Markets, 375
Hudson Street, New York, NY 10014.

The Library of Congress catalogued the hardcover edition as follows:

Cameron, Julia.
Faith and will : weathering the storms in our spiritual lives / Julia Cameron.
p.   cm.
ISBN 978-1-58542-714-7
1. Spirituality.   2. Faith.   I. Title.
BL624.C3318   2009   2009002379
204'.4—dc22

ISBN 978-1-58542-801-4 (paperback edition)

Printed in the United States of America
1 3 5 7 9 10 8 6 4 2

Book design by Marysarah Quinn

Some names and identifying characteristics have been changed to protect the privacy of the individuals
involved.

While the author has made every effort to provide accurate telephone numbers and Internet addresses
at the time of publication, neither the publisher nor the author assumes any responsibility for errors,
or for changes that occur after publication. Further, the publisher does not have any control over and
does not assume any responsibility for author or third-party websites or their content.

To my creative elders

FAITH AND WILL

I WOULD LIKE TO BEGIN at the beginning, but I do not
know what the beginning is anymore. I am a person at
midlife. I am a believer who is trying one more time to
believe. That is to say I am caught off guard by life and by
feelings of emptiness.

I want there to be more reassurance than I currently feel
that we are on the right path. By "we" I mean God and me. I
have been trying consciously to work with God for twenty-
five years now, and a great deal has been made of my life that
I think has a lot of value—but I am one more time asking
for something to be made of me and it that I myself can hold
on to. Me. Personally. Not as some abstract but as a genuine
comfort.

I am a writer and a teacher—"worthy" things, but I am
not feeling my worth in them right now. I must again come
to some relationship to God that will enable me to pursue

my career as an outward manifestation of inwardly held values. In other words, what needs mending here is probably not the outward form—I suspect that after a great deal of soul-searching I would still come back to being a writer and a teacher—but the inward connection. I must feel I am doing what God would have me do.

To be comforted, I must feel connected to God and that I am acting out of some inner sense of guidance. Guidance is what is missing right now. I feel that I have come so far and suddenly, *pfft*, God is missing. I know that the phrase for the period I am in is "dark night of the soul," but that seems very dramatic for what is essentially a broad daylight problem. It is three o'clock on a dreary, gray early autumn day and I do not know where God is.

It seems to me it takes faith to say "God is right here. Right now. Right where we are." To do that is to assume that no mistakes have been made. But maybe no mistakes have been made or, if mistakes have been made, they must be able to be unmade. God, merciful God, must be able to incline himself to the exact point, here, where we are crying in the wilderness.

And so, because there is no point in positing God as misplaced, let us assume God is right where God is supposed to be, right where we are. Here. Now. In the midst. If God is right here, then what is my problem?

My problem then comes back to faith. God is here, but I do not believe God is here. I do not believe, but that does not mean I am right. I may very well be blind to God right now. God may be everywhere, all around me, completely involved and infusing all of my affairs and I still might just miss his presence if what is going on is somehow counter to my sense of God or godliness. If I cannot see how and why God is using me as he does, then I stubbornly find myself thinking that there must again be some mistake and I must have lost God somehow. I turned left and God turned right. I went north while God went south.

Ah, but I have not.

God is our milieu, every compass point, our entire universe. God cannot be misplaced. Then it follows that everything is in divine order and that I am exactly where I am supposed to be, feeling exactly what it is I am supposed to be feeling—which is lost. Why, God, must I feel lost?

There must be some purpose to my feeling lost. If it is God's will for me to be wandering without a compass, there must be some point to such meanderings. God, where are you? I ask, and in the question there must be some worth because God's will is not purposeless. God has intentions for us and the one intention that I can see in my current dilemma is that God must want me to grow and to grow toward God. Well, I am trying. I am sending stalks out blindly, like a plant seeking the light and groping upward.

"God, where are you, God?"

"I am right here," I can imagine God answering me, so real I must report it. "I am in the very air you breathe. I sit with you at your desk. I look outward with you to regard your vista. I am not lost. I am not missing."

If God is not missing, then why is my sense of God missing? It may be something as simple as "absence makes the heart grow fonder" and God is growing me a fonder heart. For my own good. I could use a fonder heart. I could enjoy having a heart more fondly open to God and more open to seeing God in all I encounter. Surely, living in New York as I do and encountering great crowds of people as I do, it would be comforting to see the eyes of God looking outward from each face.

"Now you are onto something," I can hear God saying—almost.

If I let myself, I can imagine how God might talk with me, gently, as though trying not to startle a child. "Here I am," I can hear God saying to me, "not lost at all, just misplaced by you. Why do you need to have such a sense of emergency?"

When I have a sense of God, there is no sense of emergency. There is a sense of wonder and calm unfolding. Then I can watch my life as time-lapse photography and see the great good being brought to bear simply because I am practicing enough patience and faith to let God have his way with me. I am cooperating. That is, co-operating.

When I have a sense of God, there is a sense of synchronicity. All things work toward the good, and I am able to see that good when I look with the eyes of faith. But the eyes of faith are blinded right now. I grope in the darkness. Again, I can hear God saying to me, "What darkness? I am right beside you. See things in my light."

The light of God is the light of optimism, the light of hope. The light of God sees all things as potential good. The light of God sees things being made right, and again, more right. The light of God sees all creation as ever coming more perfectly into form—and that includes myself. "I am on the right track," the eyes of faith tell me. They see visible progress and they report to me what they see. "You are well and carefully led."

The light of God is a beacon and we need not be blind to it. I can use it like a flashlight to examine my life and to ask that I be pointed toward the good. There is always some corner of my life that is still dark, some area that is still being run by self-will that can yet be surrendered to God. Take money. In my time I have made a great deal of money. I would like to keep on making money, a great deal of money. This is an area where I do not want to let God run my life for me. I am afraid lest his will for me be less abundant. And so I say, "Sure, God, you can run the seasons and the planets and this green earth, but you cannot run my financial affairs." You see where my faith has holes in it.

And yet a faith with holes in it is better than no faith at all and that is the terrifying point that I have come to lately. I have misplaced my faith. I search for it with both hands but cannot lay hold of it. I have faith, surely I have faith in something, but faith in what? God must be the great reality and we must somehow live our life relative to that. We must on some level be able to grasp God. God must on some level be real as bread.

Two months a year I go to New Mexico. God is real in New Mexico. Clearly visible as the Sacred Mountain or as the clouds that wreathe it. God is in the vast horizons and the far peaks. God is in the snowy crags, the cascading mountain streams, the hawks that ride the thermals. God is everywhere and God is glorious. The Great Creator shows forth in his creation. In New Mexico it is easy to believe.

But ten months a year I live in New York City. God must be just as real in New York. God doesn't choose to live only in scenic beauty. God is everywhere. God is on the crowded street. God is visible in the faces of strangers. God is in place and active in all human affairs. God is in the skyscraper. God is on the brownstone stoop. At the deli. At the newsstand. On the subway platform.

In order to find God, we must look for God and we must begin that looking in our own heart. "God? Are you there?"

"Of course I am here," I can hear God answering, but is that answer just my comfortable imagination?

How can we know when God is real and answering? Must we be content with "It seems to me"? Is conscious contact one-sided?

Every morning I seek to find God. I do it by writing three pages of long-hand writing, a position statement. "Here is where I am, God. Can you find me?" Every morning I find enough of God to go forward. I state where I am and I believe that somewhere the Great Something is listening and responds back. There are other ways to pray. Some people start their days with small books, daily reminders of God. Other people start with sitting meditation. Some people start with both. We are all looking for God, looking for a connection that will feel real enough to get us through the day. What we are seeking is a sense of companionship and connection.

God as daily. God as guidance.

How do we know if we are being guided by God? How

do we know if we are moving in the right direction? There is an inner sense of rightness, a feeling that all may yet be puzzling yet all is well. When we are being guided by God, we may not know what step to take months from now, but we will know, usually, the next right step and, taking that step, we again know the next right step that follows. Rarely are we given great bolts of knowledge. God's will comes to us in daily increments, "Do this next."

There are ways that we can romance knowledge of God's will for us. We can take walks, asking God to companion us. On these walks we may feel a strong sense of connection and direction. Walking is simple. Walking is doable. We all do it and we can all do more of it, talking with God.

We can also take ourselves to the page. Writing yields clarity. There is something in moving our hand across the page that can also help to make God's will visible to us. "I don't know what to do," we write. "It seems to me I should try X." Then, a little later, "I could also try Y." In seeing our alternatives, we can sometimes see the face of God. We are not powerless. We are not choiceless. We are not trapped. We do have dignity. All of this can be revealed by time at the page.

There is a way to live each day that feels in accord with God's will for us. We may act differently at the office. We may be kind to a stranger boarding a bus. Riding crosstown, we might view the leafy green canopy of Central Park and resolve that next time we will walk. All of these choices are points where our life touches God's. God touches our lives everywhere and at all times.

The great question is not "Where is God?" but "Where

am I?" Am I pretending that God cannot see me or hear me? Am I pretending to be living a life without God? Most of us do that most of the time. Take me. I am writing and I am wondering what to write next.

Am I asking?

If God is with us every moment, then we can ask for direction at all times. There will never be a moment in which our prayer is unheard, although we may hurry onward, not taking time for the answer. To know God takes a beat. We must reach out and allow the time to feel that what we have reached out to has reached out back to us. Most of us are too hurried to know God. And yet we act as if God is too hurried to know us.

Most of the time we have it inside out. We complain that God has abandoned us when it is we who have abandoned God. God is waiting for us at all times, at all moments. God is always there ready for us to make contact and willing, when we make contact, to make contact back.

"God, are you there?"

"Of course I am here."

Let us start with this idea: "Of course, I am here."

If God is always there and always available, then we are the ones who lag behind. Perhaps we do what I do and tag base with God only in the morning, forgetting about God the rest of the day, just going from thing to thing without taking God into account. Is it possible that in light of this, God gets lonely? Is it possible that God misses us? I think it is possible. I think that God is always glad to hear from us.

"Of course I am glad to hear from you."

Was that thought God or just wishful thinking?

I began this writing by saying that I was estranged from God, and yet I notice how quickly that sense of estrangement passes as I try, however feebly, to be honest and to reach toward God. Perhaps God does not make difficult terms for us. Perhaps we are the ones who make difficult terms for God. Perhaps we are the ones who are so afraid to believe that we believe in our disbelief. Why are we afraid of being gullible? Why are we afraid of being naïve? Why are we afraid of being believers? Is it too much for us—the degree of comfort we can take—if we believe we are on the right track and trying to find God?

Perhaps it is.

It is easy to be addicted to anxiety. It is easy to make worry our home vibration. The world, after all, is tuned to anxiety and worry. We need only switch on CNN to be aware that anxiety is what we are being tutored in. We need only glance at a headline to realize that the "news," as we are trained to perceive it, is all bad news. But what if this news is only half the news? What if good news is as real as bad?

What if God really is the good news?

What if God is real and our attempts to reach God are enough? What if there is no hard test to be passed, no high quotient of misery we are required to undergo? What if there really is a benevolent God, one that will try to work with us as we labor to work with him? What if the harmony that we see in the natural world is possible also in the world of human affairs? What if we can move toward this harmony by simply trying to move toward God? What if the trying is enough?

What if God does not play hide and seek with us but stands ready and available for all who seek contact?

What if God really is the Great Comforter?

What if all that stands between us and God is us?

We are back to the same bottom line. If I am uncomfortable, and I am, then what can be done about it? If I have trouble believing, how can I believe? What we are talking about here is "conscious contact," a reliable, *felt* sense that we are in touch with God and God is in touch with us.

Probably the first portal to God comes with slowing down, taking the time in the morning to link up with God, to place our day in God's hands, however we can conceptualize our doing that. For me, writing the three Morning Pages is the way I "turn things over." For others, it may be a more formal prayer: "God, I offer myself to Thee to build with me and do with me what Thou wilt." For still others, it may be more Zen, a quiet period of sitting meditation in which nothing is articulated but everything is somehow addressed and eased. It matters less how you try to link up with God than that you try to link up with God. It doesn't matter that you didn't do it yesterday and that you may forget again to do it tomorrow. What matters is today, the one day that we have got with any certainty. Just for today, I am going to reach out toward God. Just for today, I am going to act as if I am a believer.

The key words *conscious contact* give us many clues. First of all, we must bring God to our consciousness. We must be aware of God. God must become a variable in our life, Something or Somebody to be dealt with. Next, we must make contact. That is we must reach out and touch God. The very phrase implies that it is possible. Having made contact, we must then seek to hold that contact in our consciousness. God must be given a place in our day and in our thoughts. God must become a part of our mental furniture, as real as the chair we are sitting in.

How do we make God real? How do we convince ourselves that there is a God that gives meaning to life? It is so easy to see life as meaningless, random, capricious.

It is so easy to move point to point in life without ever being able to see a larger, overarching whole, a framework that makes it all have context. What we need is a sense of God as grid. God is real and I am real and the way we interact is real. This is probably why Paul Tillich spoke of God as "the ground of being." This sense of God as the very ground is the sense that we are all looking for. If God is the bedrock, then I can build something of meaning. If God is the bedrock, then life has a sustainable meaning.

So often, we have it backward. We want a faith in God, but we are unwilling to take the actions that make that faith possible. We want faith to predate any action on our part. We want faith to not take faith. We want the luxury of faith without having made the decision of faith. For faith is a decision. We decide to believe in God, and having decided that, we then reach out for conscious contact.

I don't know about you, but I don't want faith in God to cost me anything—not really. Not even a decision. I want my faith to be easy and simple. I want to be able to say "I believe" and keep it just that simple, "I believe." Not "I believe sort of." Not "I believe the best I can." Simply, "I believe." In practice, it goes somewhat more bumpily than that. I might say "I believe" but then add to myself, "Why, if I believe, does it still seem so bumpy?"

Notice that I have used the word *bumpy*. That seens to me to be an accurate word. Faith is not all smooth sailing, but it is not all catastrophe either. Faith is bumpy. We don't fall out of the wagon. We just get jostled. Faith is "enough," and enough is not as comfortable as "plenty." I wish I had plenty of faith. I try to have plenty of faith, but what I generally find is that I have "enough." Enough is enough to keep me from throwing in the towel. Enough is enough to keep me in the game. Enough is not enough for me to have deep pockets. I want to be able to dig down into my pockets and keep coming up with handfuls of belief, but the truth is that sometimes I am down to my last two bits and I hold on to that two bits so tightly that no one can get a grip on it but me.

What happens when we clutch our faith tightly? It doesn't work very well. We are barely able to hold on to our faith. When we are able to hold our faith more loosely, "Of course, I believe," then we are able to take in more. "Of course I believe and because I believe I will try X."

They say that faith without works is dead. It is faith that allows us to make our works. It is faith that allows us to take risks. Faith in something greater than ourselves, faith that the bread will somehow land jam side up. Faith is what says, in the face of "bad" news, "I wonder where this is going." Faith knows that life is an evolutionary process and that "all bets are off" is not such a bad position to be in. Faith puts our money on the certain number—"God"—and spins the wheel. It looks risky, but is it?

Faith is no risk at all. It just feels like a risk because we are told faith is risky. We should have more anxiety than we do if we are to believe the odds are not stacked against us. With God on our side, the odds are stacked *for* us. It may not look like that. It may not seem like that, but it is like that, and that is where faith comes in.

"Tell me God is in charge," I phoned a friend to ask this afternoon.

"God *is* in charge," my friend responded, laughing. "What made you doubt it?"

What made me doubt it is that I went to a business lunch where I was told about how smart and aggressive I had to be if I wanted to get anywhere in this world. I was told about a series of actions I had to undertake if I wanted to "make it." Hearing this list of actions, I thought, "Oh, you do it." I thought, "I do not know that my luncheon acquaintance is wrong, but I do know that I cannot race off willy-nilly and try taking these actions helter-skelter. I will have to take them as they come up and as they seem indicated." Then I phoned my friend and asked to be put in the prayer pot.

One of the sanest passages I have ever read belongs to the Big Book of Alcoholics Anonymous. It is the section of that book that is talking about the newcomer's understandable reluctance to turn his worldly affairs over to God. The book states it very simply: God is your new employer.

That is about as complicated as I am able to make it. I need to believe that God does care and will care and that we can strike a bargain with him. "You be the Father. I'll be the child. You be the principle. I'll be the agent." If this sounds naïve, it is also an accurate way to view things. A look at the natural world should be enough to convince any of us that God knows more of what he is doing than we may know of what we are doing. Sea anemones, red cliffs, lilacs, stars—Something made all these things, and it is to this Something that we now turn, asking what part we are to play in the grand scheme of all this. "How do I fit in?" we ask. It is in asking to fit in and not to run the show that we begin to have a sense of God's will for us.

If I let God be the director, then I am more liable to like the part I am cast in. If I try to be the director, there will never be enough for me: enough glory, enough security, enough lime-light. The beauty of having God in charge is that it renders me right-size. And right-size is comfortable.

When there is no overarching viewpoint, God's perspec-tive, it is too easy to panic. It is too easy to take events as they look at the moment and judge them. When God is in charge, all things are fraught with possibility. The most dire circumstance might be revealed to be the most filled with God's good intentions. Out of apparent disaster can come the greatest good.

A friend of mine underwent a harrowing divorce. Her hus-band of fifteen years left her and, in the wake of his leaving, a string of infidelities was revealed. My friend clung to her faith in God. One day at a time she managed to get through her divorce with dignity and grace. She grieved. She ranted and raved and cried, but she did not drink herself to death or run off with someone inappropriate. For years a professional painter, she kept working at her art. She put days and months together, striving always to do what seemed to her to be "the next right thing." Little by little, she edged herself back from what seemed to her to be the brink. Out of the devastating loss, self-worth was born.

The career that she had always pursued but seen as secondary to her husband's career now took on enough muscle and sinew to be her mainstay and support. The many skills she had used to be a good wife now began to be seen in a clearer light: she was good with money, good with managing people, good with juggling the demands of a household and a career. All of this had always been true, but she had never been able to see it as true. When she had the faith to go forward depending upon God to give her a definition of herself, she began to see the lineaments of her own remarkable courage and fortitude. She began to become a woman that she herself could like and respect. And all of this was born out of the apparent catastrophe of "losing" her husband.

In order to have esteem, we must behave in estimable ways. It is easier to behave in estimable ways if we cling to our faith. If we make a daily decision to act as if there is a God and all things just might be working as they are supposed to. If we believe that God is in charge and that all things will work toward the good, then we do not need to act out of desperation. We can take the time to allow a solution to suggest itself. We do not need to act with panicked self-will.

My friend the painter was urged by some of her well-meaning friends to take part-time work, any work, that would bring some cash in. "My God! You've lost your husband! You're a woman alone! You need something safe and steady to fall back on!" She listened, but the advice did not resonate as correct for her, and so she did the next right thing as it suggested itself to her, putting the finishing touches onto a portrait. After all, she had been a portrait artist for many years married, so why not continue now that she was divorced? For all the years of her married life, she had worked as a painter. Should she abandon that life because her husband had left her? Shouldn't she at least finish the portrait commission she was working on at the time he walked out?

That portrait led to a second portrait, and that to a third. A steady flow of work seemed to be gently stabilizing. Her painting skills, honed over twenty-five years, turned out to be more valuable than, say, her working part-time at a florist's. True, she had no regular paycheck, but she did have a slow-and-steady stream of clients who sought her out. Because she was able to resist the temptation to panic, she was able to keep herself from going off on a path that might not have been right for her. Because she asked herself what God's will was rather than just pursuing her own panicky solution, she became able to expand into a larger definition of herself as an artist rather than contract to a smaller definition of herself as an ex-wife. "Then he left her and she had to go to work at a florist's shop. . . ."

Very often when we are in a panic about faith, it is because God is making us larger. We do not see how we are going to be able to make ends meet, and we doubt that God is going to do that for us or through us. We are afraid we are being made smaller, and yet for some of us the temptation to rush back to what once was a right size and is no longer is a very real temptation. "I'll just cut my losses," we decide, and then we set about trying to wedge ourselves back into a former definition of our self that no longer holds true. What happens? It doesn't work very well. We cannot go back, but we do not see how we can go forward either. And the answer is that we cannot go forward of our own steam, left to our own devices. In order to go forward and become larger, we are going to need the grace of God.

It is easy to recognize people who routinely operate out of the grace of God. They are those people who seem able to rise up and meet whatever challenge life throws at them. They are the ones who become larger, not smaller in adversity. They are the ones who are able, with faith, to shoulder their way through. I have such a friend, Elberta.

When her daughter was diagnosed as having a brain tumor, Elberta resolved that they would beat it, *it* being cancer. The odds definitely seemed stacked against them, but for Elberta there was no hearing that. She was determined that her daughter would get better. They would undertake any form of chemotherapy, any form of rehabilitation that seemed indicated, that held the slightest hope.

Cooking special meals, devising special games that helped with memory loss, Elberta went to work to help her daughter get better. As her daughter underwent bout after bout of chemotherapy and long stints living in rehabilitation centers, Elberta made her daughter the focus of her life and attention. We worried that Elberta would burn herself out, but she seemed to draw on a superhuman strength. She acted with confidence that she was doing as God would have her do. She saw her daughter as being restored to health, as being able to resume again her challenging career as a horse trainer. She counted each day as a day toward recovery and made each day's small victory the focus of her consciousness. Her diligence paid off. Her daughter did get better. The cancer went into remission. Memory began to return. The daily chores of horse schooling began to come back into place.

When, after a year with her cancer in remission, the same daughter had a devastating carriage driving accident that left her in a coma, Elberta one more time resolved that they would beat the odds. Her daughter lay hovering between life and death. Elberta saw her as vital and alive and healthy again. No matter what the odds were, she saw that her daughter would walk and talk again. She would have a memory. She would resume a life. She would train horses. And so, one more time, she set about rehabbing her daughter from her new challenge. One more time, her days were spent at the rehab facility. One more time, her own life was put on hold while she focused on her daughter's crisis. Returning to the word games for memory and to card games for concentration, Elberta sat daily by her daughter's side, coaching her gently back up the long mountain down which she had tumbled. One more time, her daughter rallied and got better against all odds.

"You need to take some time to yourself," Elberta was advised by a well-meaning physical therapist. "You cannot spend your whole life with your daughter."

"Oh, but I can. This is my life right now," Elberta replied.

"What's six months out of a whole lifetime, out of eighty years?"

As I write this, Elberta's daughter is walking and talking and beginning to work with her beloved horses again.

In order to work with God, we must assume that God is willing to work with us. To do that, we must assume that God can start right where we are and not at some imaginary place we have to get to in order to meet him. God is not waiting to rendezvous with us once we have earned the right to his attention. God is waiting for us right now, just where we are.

Very often when we think about what we would like to have happen in our lives, we cast ourselves very far forward and out of the day we are in. No wonder everything seems so impossible and so difficult. We cast ourselves far into the future where we stand alone and buffeted, wondering where God is.

God works in the day that we actually have going on. God's miracles are miniature daily miracles. They are miracles of evolution and miracles of progress. They are the small miracles that add up to large miracles. They are tiny right steps that lead us in the right direction. If we want to find God, we need first to find ourselves. That is where God is. Right with us.

Which brings me back to where I am in relationship to God at this time. I began this writing by saying that I felt lost. That God felt lost to me. This is no longer true. By the simple act of moving my hand across the page, I am able one more time to trace the progress of God's hand across my life.

I may not yet feel comfortable, I may not have a cozy feeling of God, but I one more time believe God to be within hailing distance, to be close enough to hear me, to be "right here." I may not know where my life is going, but I have been able to slow down enough to understand that God and I are going there together, that life is proceeding as it always does, one day at a time and that if I am willing to live at that pace, then all will be well with me.

"If I am willing to live at that pace" seems to be an important part of faith. Christ advised us to consider the lilies of the field—who surely live a day at a time. Twelve-step programs advise members to live "one day at a time," and there is hard-won spiritual wisdom in that maxim. So many of our catastrophes never come to pass. We project disaster and we do not allow for the working out of solutions that will happen as the days tick forward. We think that the worst will happen, only to find out, living through it, that what happens actually may be far closer to the best.

What I am talking about here is the silver lining. We may get tired of trying to look for one, but the truth is that one is always there. Inside every adversity lies opportunity. Take the dicey matter of finances. We always think that what we want is more money, when what we may really want is a gut-level assurance that God will provide—and this is something that often comes to us not in periods of abundance but in times of shortfall. It is when we do not know where the rent money is coming from that we notice the "miracle" that puts the cash into our hands. This is not to say that we need to manufacture misery in order for God to rescue us, merely to say that when we are rescued, we have a tendency to know the face of our rescuer and that face is God.

It is during hard times that we come to rely on God and that is a reliance that we can encourage in ourselves at all times. We do not need to be broke to ask God to help us with our money. Consider the flow of the natural world. Supply comes just where it is needed. We can ask God to be for us such a source of supply. We can ask God to make us attuned to our financial seasons, to cue us when we are free to spend and when we should curtail our spending. We can ask God to take away our fear of financial insecurity and to direct us as to where, from what corner, our prosperity might best come from.

We live in an abundant universe. Our share of that abundance comes to us as we rely upon God. Whenever we make our employer into our source—in other words, when we make our employer into God—we enter a period of fear, for our reliance is not squarely where it belongs. We are intended to rely upon God. God intends us good, and we are tutored by God daily in how that good can come to us. God moves in mysterious ways, but his ways become less mysterious as we try to draw closer to him. When we believe that we will be cared for, we fixate less upon exactly how.

I have a good friend who says to me that we tend to think we can second-guess God. We say, "God's will will be A, B, or C—only to have the answer be God's will is H, heliotrope, which never occurred to me."

When we believe in God and put our faith in God, we are asking to be surprised. God is all-powerful and works on our life from all corners. We may think "Now is the time to focus on my career," only to find that God has decided "Now is the time for me to find a fulfilling personal relationship." We may decide "Now is the time for me to find a personal relationship," only to discover that God has decided to stabilize our career. God's version of what is good for us is far more far-seeing than our own. We can seek to cooperate with God, but we do well not to argue too hard with God's sense of timing.

Few things create more misery than a fight with God about the seasons of our life. When we hold out, stubbornly insisting on a certain blessing that we feel God is withholding, we miss the many blessings that God is in the process of bestowing. When we are saying, "I want *this* now," we miss that *that* may be coming to us instead. We may be asking God for a romantic relationship in a period when God is focused on building up our grid of nonromantic friendships. We may be yearning for a special someone to make us feel more special while God is working on giving us that feeling for ourselves, independent of our romantic status. We may be asking God, demanding of God, that we be given someone to make us feel less lonely when God is in the process of teaching us how to be comfortable on our own.

Whenever we get our heart set on a certain agenda, we run the risk of having our self-will separate us from God. I write a novel—as I did this year—and determine that it should sell right away, instantly and with applause for my creative genius. God, meanwhile, does not plan for the novel to sell right away. He plans that I have a year of working on my patience—and on my nonfiction books. A day at a time, I have to let go of the demand that the novel sell *now*. I can hold the hope in my heart. I can tell God that I am dreaming the novel will sell, but I must be openminded with God when the novel does not sell. I cannot afford to get into a fight. I cannot afford to stomp my foot and insist. Insisting gets me nowhere. I only succeed in making myself feel misunderstood and abandoned.

I do better to explore the silver lining of what comes to me when the book does not sell. I find I have more humility, more gratitude for the times that the books have sold. Unable to imperiously insist on my way, I join the majority of us: I am more a worker among workers and a friend among friends. I am not above it all—one of the lucky ones. I am right in the thick of it. I suffer disappointment just like the rest of the human race, and in suffering disappointment, I become more connected to the human condition. I have more compassion. Many people live with disappointments, and I am one among many. I am hoping that my book will sell, and I am saddened as the seasons pass and it does not. I take each "almost" sale to my heart. The disappointments are keen for me. They feel like miscarriages creatively, but that shows me my own drama. This is a disappointment, but does it compare to the years of someone going childless who wants to conceive? My disappointment looms large to me, but it can be drawn to scale. When I look for the silver lining in any disappointment, my grievance with God is always drawn to scale.

It is one of the ironies of the spiritual life that so much can be seen in retrospect as having been designed in our own best interest. When something finally does come to pass, it is often all we can do to manage it. "Why, if this had happened any sooner, I wouldn't have been ready," we catch ourselves thinking. "I needed every instant of preparation for this that I have had." Many times we ask God for help with securing a certain agenda, then rage because God does not cooperate, only to have God's agenda revealed later as far better.

It is in seeking to cooperate with God's agenda for our life that we come to some sense of peace. Is it too much to think that God has an agenda for each of us? I don't think so. Again, a look at the natural world tells us of the exquisite particularity of God's care. The daffodil is given just what it needs to grow and so is the violet. We, too, are given precisely what we need to grow and we are asked only to cooperate. We must be willing to be either the daffodil or the violet, according to God's will for us. We so often do not see the lineaments of our own character as it is being formed. We have an idea of ourselves that may be counter to what God's idea for our self is. I am in the midst of discovering this for myself right now.

I am currently baffled because when I was "home" in New Mexico for the summer, I got very sick. I am prone to nervous breakdowns, and one more time I was at the brink of one of them, with the prospect of the hospital looming. It was suggested to me that I try coming "home" to New York. For some reason, this suggestion had the ring of guidance to it and "home" I came. I have been back in New York nearly a month now and my health is far more stable. I do not know why busy, hectic New York should calm me down. I do not know why, when I had all the beauty in the world to stare at in New Mexico, I should find a more reliable sense of God's safety here in New York. All that I can conclude is that God has business for me in New York.

In New Mexico I do have a beautiful home, and I love it there. I love it there, but I become fragile there, and that is something that I cannot explain and evidently cannot avoid. It is possible that next summer I will not try to go back to New Mexico. I will do what God seems to be unfolding for me here, and that is going to take some faith on my part. That faith comes to me here a day at a time.

In New Mexico I walk on the road to El Salto, a bald-faced cliff. I pass buffalo and llamas. I pass peacocks and large white dogs. It is exotic and very beautiful. In New York I walk in Central Park, where people carefully pilot their baby carriages and the wild flora and fauna have become tame from proximity to people. In New York I cross the Great Lawn and arrive at the Metropolitan Museum, a monument to what man has accomplished over the centuries. If I want something of the same feeling I get in New Mexico, a glimpse of eternity, I go to the Asian Wing of the Metropolitan, where the great unattributed Bodhisattvas feel as timeless as El Salto's rugged face. In New York I feel my wild heart becoming gentled. This must be God's will for me right now.

When we talk about God's will and the possibility that it might be other than what we envision, it is easy to feel frightened. It is easy to say, "So. I knew it would come to this. My will at one end of the table. God's will at another." But that is not really how it works. The daily attempt to find God's will moves us closer together. Often we discover that God's will for us involves more freedom, not less. Our dreams and desires do not come from nowhere. They come from God. God is able to shape both the dreams and desires and our character so that we arrive at a happy medium where our dreams and God's dreams for us can be seen to coincide.

As we become teachable and open to God's will for us, we have many small revelations. "Why, I thought X would make me happy, but it turns out that Y makes me happy instead." All the time we were begging for X, God knew Y would make us happier. This is why, a day at a time, X was denied to us and Y was encouraged. We fight this encouragement. We fight this superior knowledge of our own temperaments. And then, in a fit of willingness, we surrender and we see that God had our best interests at heart all along.

God always has our best interests at heart. If we can believe this, it is easier to have faith. It is easier to believe this if we remember that God has the long view. God knows more of the variables. God knows not only what is best for us but what is best for everyone. God is involved in working out a far more intricate dance than we can know the details of. We work on our corner of the tapestry. We think, "Ah, it is a tapestry about a fox," because the fox is the animal that we can see. What we do not know is that it is a tapestry about a unicorn and that the fox peeking through the shrubbery is way over in a tiny corner at the left. God's eye is on the unicorn and the fox. God's eye brings each one along a stitch at a time.

We must be willing to be brought along. We must slow our willful pace down long enough to begin to get some idea of what it is that God may be up to with us. We must scan our consciousness for the areas where we are insisting that we have our own way. These areas must be gently surrendered to a higher will. "If not this God, something better."

Very often we have a hard time surrendering because we cannot envision something better that God may be up to. We have our ideas of what would make us happy, and we want to pursue them whether they do in fact make us happy or not. I spent my twenties and my thirties pursuing a writing career in film and theater. I was always frustrated not to get further, faster. In my forties, I was given a writing career in nonfiction. This I had not sought out. It gave me a very solid and enjoyable form of success. In my fifties, I began to have the writing career in film and theater that I had wanted twenty years sooner. I found this form of success far harder to handle. Why had I ever imagined I would be able to handle it with grace any sooner?

A lot of coming to terms with God's will for us seems to boil down to acceptance. "Oh, I am really this sort of creature, not that," we may discover. "Oh, I have these needs, not that," we may realize. At bottom there may be a rueful acquiescence, "Oh, God knew best all along."

God knew best all along—if only we could come to accept this as a probability. If only, whenever we seemed to come to loggerheads with God, we could remember this dictum. This may be where friends enter the picture. A friend might remember to tell us that something has actually worked out in our best interests: "It wasn't what you thought you wanted, but it worked out for the best."

I have a woman friend who for years pursued a romantic connection with a man who loved her "but not like that." She fought God on this one. She wanted to be loved as she wanted to be loved. Now, as she is in a period of ill health and her longed-for romantic companion is being revealed to her as the most steadfast of friends, she begins to wonder if she hasn't been given just what is best for her.

Not all stories of God's will boil down to God's will versus our will. Sometimes our yearnings and God's seem to match up. This appears to be particularly true if we strive to make God's will a part of our daily consciousness. In other words, if we work at our conscious contact with God, God seems to gently infiltrate our consciousness with ideas, dreams, and longings that can well be fulfilled. You might want to call this inspiration. But as we work to become closer to God, it is as though God, too, works to become closer to us. We begin to be able to count on an intuitive inner guidance, "Go here. Try that."

So uncanny does this guidance sometimes appear to be that we may be tempted to think of the remote-control guidance system on a toy. God is directing us here and then there. We are cooperating with the guidance. Yes, we have free will, but increasingly our free will is being used in alignment with what we sense may be God's will for us. We get an impulse to call so and so, and we do call so and so, only to find out they had been wanting to talk with us. We begin to gently experience "lucky breaks," being in the right place at the right time. This is what Dr. Carl Jung referred to as synchronicity. It is also sometimes referred to as "being in the flow." In twelve-step programs, where belief in a higher power is often introduced to skeptical newcomers as a desirable thing that seems beyond their emotional reach, it is sometimes taught that a higher power may be found simply in a sense of "Good Orderly Direction." Again, that brings us back to the concept of moving along with the direction that the wave seems to be breaking, *going with the flow.*

This brings us back to the idea of not arguing, trying to see what might be good in the way that life is unfolding. Is there something that we missed that is being brought to bear? I have a friend who says that "God brings us along like fighters." I do not know that I can picture God as being Burgess Meredith to our Rocky, but there is something in this idea that God is working with us, on us. We are asked to be open-minded when God is developing a new muscle group. Say, our patience muscles or our tolerance muscles.

The boss from hell may be an exercise in both patience and tolerance. We may be learning the extent of our capacity to live with an unresolved problem. We may be being given an opportunity to work on our own attitudes, to develop compassion and the ability to put ourselves in the other fellow's shoes. "I have a rotten boss" may be the prelude to "I have a rotten boss and I have learned how to be happy anyhow." We may be being given a black belt opportunity to develop detachment.

The point is that we are not stuck in some emotional cul-de-sac. We are not being taken down a dead-end street into a blind alley. No, we are being taken somewhere, where no matter how "stuck with it" we may appear to be, we can actually make progress. In each day's march, there is always the opportunity for progress. This appears to be spiritual law. In God's world, nothing is wasted and that includes our time. As we seek to make of ourselves what God would have us make of each opportunity, then we are able to prosper and grow.

Sometimes our growth dictates that we make a change in our circumstances. This is best sorted out with the serenity prayer, "God, grant me the serenity to accept the things I cannot change, the courage to change the things I can, and the wisdom to know the difference."

It may be that the rotten boss is a cue not for more patience but for more proactive action on our behalf. We may be being asked not to suffer where we are, working to improve ourselves and our attitudes, but to move on. The regular use of the serenity prayer is a great "sorter outer." The prayer often works in surprising ways. We will think that it will lead us one way only to find that the repeated use of it nudges us toward quite another.

Nowhere is this prayer more useful than in the realm of human relationships. The serenity to accept the things I cannot change means other people, places, and things. The courage to change the things I can means my response to them. When we change our response to people and to events, we alter our relationship to people and to events. We are no longer the helpless victim. Perhaps we learn to speak up for ourselves if we are the quietly resentful and subservient type. Perhaps we learn to hold our tongue if we are the type prone to fly off the handle. One thing is certain: the use of this prayer is a powerful tool and it will alter our lives.

The alterations may be large or small, but they will be

noticeable. Clare began using the prayer on her relationship with Edith. They had been friends for twenty years, but there were things in Edith's personality that drove Clare crazy. They would make a movie date and Edith would habitually arrive late. Clare would wait in the lobby, inevitably missing previews of coming attractions, one of her favorite parts of the show. Using the serenity prayer, Clare found herself not waiting in the lobby any longer. When it was time for coming attractions, she entered the theater and took a seat. Edith, arriving late as usual, did not find Clare as she usually did, pacing and fuming resentfully. In fact, she did not find Clare at all. It was only after the movie ended and she was filing out that she located her friend.

"Did I do something? Are you mad at me?" she asked anxiously.

"You're always late. I decided to go in on time," Clare replied.

"Oh." Edith had no defense because her chronic lateness was indefensible and she well knew it. With a simple single gesture, walking into a theater on time, Clare altered the dynamic between her and Edith. Clare was no longer the hapless victim. Edith was no longer the perpetrator. They were once again equals, two friends who liked to take in a movie. Do I need to say that Edith learned to be on time? At this writing she habitually arrives five minutes early, a change that Clare could not have predicted and which came about only because Clare chose to change her own behavior, "the thing that she could change."

God is the backdrop for our human relationships. God

knows Clare and God knows Edith. God is where all relationships meet. Inviting God to be an active part of our relationships often is the surest way of setting them straight. We learn to see the other person a bit with God's eyes. We develop compassion and empathy. We develop insight: "Ah, that's why he did X." Seeing the other fellow's side of things, it becomes harder to be polarized, harder to have declared enemies. The rotten boss is revealed to have an elderly parent with Alzheimer's. No wonder Monday is so rough for him.

It takes willingness to invite God to be a participant in our affairs. I have a friend who says we are all secret atheists, meaning, we tend to include God out and it is only when the going gets very rough that we remember, "Oh, yes, God," and then we pray. I do not know that I would say we are all secret atheists, but I do think that we tend to posit God at a more comfortable distance. The idea that God is right where we are, intimately involved in every cranny of our life can be uncomfortable. After all, how many of us have lives without mess in them, lives where every corner is presentable? This brings us to another notion, the idea that we must somehow be on our best behavior if we are meeting with God. This is the thinking that keeps our prayers hollow. Instead of saying, "Dear God, I am so fucking angry I could spit," we pray, "Dear God, I seem to be having some trouble with acceptance. . . ."

What we have trouble accepting is the imminence of God. God is right where we are. Right in our faces. There is no scrap of our lives, no detail too small or too sordid for God to have overlooked it. No, God sees everything. God is aware of our shortfalls and we are accepted anyway. This idea of a love so intimate and unconditional can make us very uncomfortable. We can want to freeze into postures that are less vulnerable, "Our Father, Who art in Heaven." Not here. Not now. Not just yet. In heaven. Get it? At a safe remove. But God is right now. God is not pie in the sky. God is not tomorrow. God is the energy infusing all of life, and that means right now when life is necessary to life.

It is difficult to imagine exactly how intimate with us God really is. We can titter and say "God invented sex." God did invent sex. Also bowel movements and menstrual cycles. Not just the far-flung canopy of stars but our tendency to hang-nails. God knows our business. God does not suffer, as we do, from convenient denial. God knows if we are broke or soon to be broke. God knows if we are fighting a drink or contemplating an illicit affair. God is on to us. This is not comfortable.

But who said that God was intended to be comfortable? We have no proof that God ever intended comfortable to be part of the deal. Job was not comfortable. Jacob, wrestling all night with the angel of the Lord, was not comfortable. Mary, in her heartbreak over her son, was not comfortable, and who was more beloved than Mary, the Mother? Comfort may not be a part of God's equation. We may be being brought to something better than comfort. Perhaps to dignity, to grace, to a sense of our own resilience.

With God's help we are resilient, but perhaps part of what we need to be resilient about is also God. We pray for a certain outcome and it is denied us. "Not now," God says and he may mean, "Not ever." We do not know if God's delay is his denial, and so we must work to have resilience. A "no" can be very hard to take, especially if we are hoping against hope for a "yes."

God does not always give us what we want. We can rail against God for this or we can try to understand just what it is that God is giving us. A woman, me, was in love with a man who did not love her back. "Not that way." I prayed for knowledge of God's will and nowhere did God say, "This is the man for you." Instead, I was brought to an independent sense of dignity. I was gently shown exactly how unsuitable the man was for me. I was shown, in the phrase, "More will be revealed," some of the reasons behind the "no" that seemed so unbearable. There was a higher wisdom at hand and, Dear Lord, how I resented it. How I wanted what (and whom) I wanted. But people have free will and so, for that matter, does God. God is no dummy. God is not easily bribed or coerced. God does not fall for our pretty, phony prayers. God is seeking something deeper, and if we cannot muster it, God is stubborn. God holds out for what is in our best interests. God is willing to be unpopular. And there have been many times when God was unpopular with me.

Take now. At this time God seems too distant to me. I try to find him in the streets and he seems to be missing. I walk, looking, and I do not see what I hope to see. Where is the face of God? I want to see him in the faces of all those I encounter. Is it God staring back at me on the subway? Is it God sleeping in a doorway? Is it God laying claim to a park bench? Or are all of these people, just like myself, looking for God, and is God too absent right now to notice?

But God is not absent. God is just selectively elusive. God hides his face and demands that I come looking. I do come looking, but I resent it. I want "faith" to be solved, once and for all. I do not want my faith to ebb and flow. I do not want to be back to being a beginner, begging God for an audience again—and yet, who am I to graduate? I have a woman friend who has spent forty years on a spiritual path. That is a long time. And yet, when I spoke with her recently, she told me God was being elusive again. She was back to reading books about God, seeking to find God in the prayers and lives of others. I wanted to tell God, "Hey, lay off. She's one of yours. Don't you get it? Cut her a break." And yet, it was good for me to hear that she was struggling. It made my own struggles of twenty-five years on a spiritual path seem less dire to me. "Oh, I am in a period when my faith does not come easily to me. That's all. It's a period. It will pass . . ." The "dark night of the soul" does end. It ends in dawn and the coming of the light. If I just make it through the night, an hour at a time, a minute at a time, I will again come to the dawn and I will again see the beloved face of God.

"Why, I was there all the time," God the trickster might tell me then.

I want to write a book about faith. This is the task that I have set for myself to talk me through this rough patch. It is good to remind myself again that there is a God who does come round and that periodic absences are to be expected. I can even see, looking back, that the periods where I have missed God before have been periods that forced me to grow. I can remember after my father died when I was tumbled into a bottomless grief. I walked daily amid the dark sage fields. I cast my eyes toward the Sacred Mountain and I prayed. I prayed, "I miss my dad. I miss my dad." God, in those days seemed to me to live at the top of the Sacred Mountain, close enough to be petitioned, far enough away that I had some privacy. I wanted and needed God to help me then, and God did help me then. I walked daily and I wrote daily, and somehow the terrible time passed and out of it came books, a blessing I was not expecting. Looking back at that time, I remember God's comfort. It came to me as the strength to go on. I didn't want strength. I wanted my father back. What I got was a sense of my father's continuity. I had the chance to continue to relate to him, even be guided by him, if I was willing to accept God's terms.

"If I am willing to accept God's terms" seems so often to be the nub of it. God's terms feel harsh. They certainly feel demanding. God expects us to be able to live with such intense sorrows. How can we? We can with God's help. The vast cycle of birth, life, and death is comprehensible only if there is a God to help us address it.

When my father died, I needed my God. I needed to know my father had his God too, and that God was big enough to do what was best for both of us—that is, that my father, old and tired, had to go on and I had to remain behind. Still, the loss was staggering to me. For years, by phone, fax, and letter, my father had been my confidant and adviser. Often I flew home to get his advice firsthand. It was to his guidance that I turned in my toughest times. It was to his wisdom that I deferred. He was hardheaded and kindhearted. He had my best interests at heart and he did not mince words. No wonder I missed him. A tiny man, he had loomed huge to me.

In those days I took about a forty-five-minute walk with my dogs, daily, through the sagebrush. I would load the five dogs into the back of my old '65 Chevy pickup "Louise," and I would drive about a half mile from home along an old dirt road, where I would pull off onto a shoulder and unload the dogs. Then we would set out on a trail that looped through the sagebrush and around, back again, to the road. At the midpoint of the trail, there was a small creek. It was always there that I would stop and address God directly. I had a small song I would sing: "I miss my dad. I miss my dad. I miss my dad. I miss my dad . . ."

I believe it was the plaintive and plainspoken nature of my loss that gave God the opportunity to reach back to me. Daily, midafternoon, I would sing from my place at creek side up and out toward the looming peak of the Sacred Mountain, holy to the dwellers of Taos pueblo. I came in from walks always feeling comforted, as if I had taken my loss to the highest place I could and placed the matter squarely in God's hands. I do not know why it seemed to me then as if God could most clearly be communicated with by praying to the top of the Sacred Mountain, but there it was. The mountain rose above the sagebrush, high and wrapped in clouds. There, on that peak, I would picture a listening God who somehow had my father's spirit gently in hand.

Although our culture does not validate this belief, it is important to me to believe in the continuity of life, to believe that there is an afterlife and that the spirits of those we love continue there to love us and to guide us. I have sustained large losses in recent years, my father and two of my closest friends, John Newland and Max Showalter. In the aftershock of their deaths, I had to believe these men were somehow "with God." I had to picture that they were being gently cared for, carefully awakened to the life they could pursue after the life in which I'd known them. Connected as we were in life, I could not afford to let them go without a trace, and so I devised a spiritual practice: I write to them and listen for their replies.

Believing them to still be alive and still be loving, I go to the page and ask them to speak to me. I take them my problems and dilemmas. I take to them the situations where I feel in over my head, out of my depth and floundering. I listen for guidance and write down what I hear. They seem to me to speak in their true voices. The advice they offer is as hard-headed as any they proffered while on earth. My mentors, they were always older and wiser. They seem older and wiser still, and possessed now, too, of what might be called a longer overview. When I write to them and listen for guidance, I get real wisdom back. They say things that I do not yet know, and I have learned that I can trust their guidance through the trickiest of worldly matters. It is as though the afterlife gives them a certain detachment that makes them even wiser than they always were.

As a result of my experiences, I believe that it is possible that we are reached to from the other side. I don't just believe this. I know this firsthand. My life has been touched, and touched repeatedly, with a higher counsel than my own. I think that as we expect to be guided, we are guided and that this collective wisdom is a part of what we get when we humbly address a higher power and ask to be brought to clarity. All those interested in us incline to our aid. We are given insights, intuitions, promptings that seem to, and do, come from a higher hand. We are well and carefully led.

Ours is a peculiar culture. Unlike many more ancient cultures, the Japanese or the African to name just two, we do not believe in the wisdom of the ancestors or in their guiding hands. We do not set up household altars to honor our predecessors and to assure them of an ongoing place in our consciousness. We do not seek their guidance with any faith or regularity. We seem to be primitive in this regard.

One more time, we are back to being what my friend calls atheists. Defensively, we place ourselves outside of any comforting belief. We do not want to be gullible, and so we rob ourselves of what is our intended heritage. Rather than open our minds to the possibility that life continues after life and that we, too, can continue to have a relationship in some form with those who have departed, we try to cut our losses. "He's gone," we say without trying to see "how gone" and whether, in some form, some essence of him doesn't remain—and remain open to us. In my experience, the realm of spirit is open to those who seek it. We have available to us mentoring of the highest order, concern of the most genuine kind. We have this available to us, but we do not use it, not often, and we do not speak of it easily, if at all.

I recognize that my beliefs may strike some people as wishful thinking. I know that it does not sound sophisticated to believe in what might be called spirits. Still, I do believe in spirits, and I do believe that believing in them has given me the strength to go onward where I might otherwise have quit. Much of my encouragement over the past decade has come from the realm of spirit. To deny that is to deny my own experience.

In the ten years in which I have worked on musicals, I have routinely sought the help and guidance of musical elders long deceased. It was to my friend Max Showalter that I owe the openmindedness to try this form of guidance. Max was a theatrical legend, an actor's actor, who numbered among his friends many famous people, Mary Martin chief among them but also Rodgers and Hammerstein, especially Hammerstein, who was for Max a personal mentor. It was Max who advised me to ask directly for help and guidance from those notables who had crossed over. "After all, they were the real experts."

And so, egged on by Max, I would take my problems to those who had faced them earlier. On the page, I would ask Oscar Hammerstein how to deal with a difficult director, a tricky workshop production. I would listen and write down what I "heard." Many times, the wisdom and sheer canniness that came to me far outstripped my own experience at the time. To believe Max, I was either in touch with Oscar Hammerstein himself or with someone else very knowledgeable who spoke of the theatrical world with an intimacy and expertise from which I could benefit—but never claim as my own.

"I do it all the time," Max would assure me. "I have script problems and I go to the Spevaks. I have musical problems, I go to Rodgers or Kern. Before I go to bed at night, I tell them what I am going to be working on in the morning, and in the morning, when I wake up, there they are with me."

Often rising at four A.M. to keep his appointment with spirit, Max believed in letting spirit work through him and on him. He wrote memoirs, plays, and musicals, always claiming the help of higher realms. "Sweetheart, I just do what works and I am telling you, this works for me. Maybe it's not for everyone, but for me it's the best way. I like to keep things simple. I just ask for help by name and I believe that I receive it. The proof is in the pudding."

I, too, could say to you that "the proof is in the pudding." I could tell you that many of my nineteen books seemed to me to be practically dictated, that my job was to simply show up at the page and take down what seemed to want to "come through." After working in this way for a while, I would often pause and go back to read over what had been "written." Very often, the tone and authority with which I wrote seemed to me to be beyond my grasp. Something, or someone, seemed to be writing through me—and they certainly seemed to know what they were talking about.

I think many artists have this experience. We call it being inspired. We call it being visited by the muse. We call it many things, but what it is is the opportunity of the artist to touch higher realms. It used to be more commonplace to speak about this.

Both Brahms and Puccini credited God with being the source of their flow of musical ideas. For both men, the term *Creator* was quite literal. God was the Great Creator. They were the channel through which he worked. It was for them that simple and that workable. It can be that simple and that workable for us, if we will allow it.

When artists speak of being the servant of their art, this is what we mean. Something larger or grander than ourselves seems to be working through us. Our job is to cooperate. That is, to co-operate, to work with the intentions of the higher force that wishes something to be expressed. We may conceptualize this higher force as Art or Writing, Music or Painting. It really doesn't matter what we name it. What matters is that when it touches our consciousness, we yield the right of way. There is a sort of inner door that we alone can swing open. This door, once nudged open, can allow us to perceive a great deal of what we might call higher realms.

I see that in writing about death, I have written a great deal on other matters of faith as well. Nothing challenges our faith as death does. This is why 9/11 spoke to so many of us so clearly. Here was death come to our very doorstep. Here was the death of innocents. How could God allow it? Could there even be a God if such atrocities could occur?

For each of us, 9/11 was something to be worked out in our own way. For me, it came back to the question of free will. God might be grieved by our use of it, but God would not interfere. God would be there as a comfort and a resource in the aftermath, but the freedom to act as the terrorists acted was a part of God's larger plan, that as independent human souls we had the right and the freedom to choose either evil or good. This was a part of our human dignity, our spiritual DNA.

In the wake of 9/11, many people turned both to God and

from God. We all had the blazing images to deal with—the horror of the towers crumbling to earth, the terrible poignancy of people jumping to their deaths, one couple jumping hands intertwined. Some were angered that God had allowed so many innocents to die. Their faith was shaken. "How could God?" they wondered and raged. Others believed that the only way to make sense of all the innocents dying was to find God and locate a higher meaning in the slaughter. Each person came to their own resolution regarding God and 9/11. For me, it all ultimately came down to allowing. God allows us to make our own path. When we suffer, God allows us the grace to come closer to him. In the great suffering in the wake of 9/11, God was ready to receive us and to help us piece together some sense of mercy out of the carnage that had occurred. God was the Great Comforter.

In order to find a silver lining, we must be willing to look for one. At the very least, we must be willing to recognize one when it appears. We must be willing to be comforted in order to be comforted. We must maintain an openness to spiritual realities. We must be teachable in order that we may be taught. It is for this reason that the great prayer is "Thy will be done." The surrendering of our independent spirits to a higher good makes it possible to find a path through darkness. "Thy will be done, O Lord. Thy will be done." This is the prayer of the dark night of the soul. This is the prayer of surrender.

There are those who fear surrender—perhaps we all do. Perhaps we all wonder if we give ourselves over to God, if all that will remain of us will be the hole in the doughnut. No one wants to be a nonentity. No one wants to be a cipher. Surrender is difficult. Without effort, it can be impossible. In Alcoholics Anonymous, surrender is one of the twelve steps, step three. Alcoholics seeking sobriety surrender their lives to God only when cornered by the prospect of an alcoholic death. But even when they are faced with a disastrous alternative, surrender is hard.

Who will I be if I seek only to do God's will? Will I become homogenized, somehow diluted? A look at the natural world is reassuring here. Each flower—the crocus, the lotus, the delphinium, to name only a few—has its own unique essence. Roses, daffodils, daisies, peonies, chrysanthemums—each has its individual beauty. Dogs, too, come in all shapes and sizes: Rottweilers, cocker spaniels, Rhodesian ridgebacks, Pomeranians, German shepherds, Irish setters, Jack Russell terriers, golden Labradors. The natural world, surrendered to God from the very beginning, is filled with diversity. Each creature is its own imprint, a unique manifestation of the glory of God. So, too, we are unique. That uniqueness does not diminish as we move toward God in surrender.

As we move toward God, our natural individuality becomes more vivid. Think for a moment of a monastery or a convent, where all the religious dress the same. Does this make them resemble one another? No, the sameness of the garb makes the individuality of each face shine forth. Brother Thomas looks nothing like Brother John. Sister Carmela looks nothing like Sister Rose.

When we pray "Thy will be done," we are really praying "Make of me my best self, my truest self." The truest, most vivid self is not necessarily the self most known to us. We may hunger for one thing, only to find that God provides us with another, more satisfying form of sustenance, a form that is a surprise to us, not what we would have expected or requested. When we ask God to fulfill us, we have a notion of what it is we think might best serve, and that notion is not always God's intention for us. It is not that God fails to hear our prayers, rather that the prayer God hears may be a deeper prayer than we are able consciously to make. When we invite God to shape us, we are yielding our notions of what our best shape may be. We are entering a new territory, a world of openmindedness, where God's decisions become those we abide by and God's blueprint becomes the plan for our own unfolding. This can be frightening. What are you turning me into? Will I recognize the person that I become? Perhaps not.

After all, God's idea of what is good and what is bad may differ from my own. Let us say I have a difficult relationship, one that tests my patience. I may try using prayer, asking God to give me more patience. God might answer my prayer by giving me more honesty. "I hate it when you do that!" we might exclaim. So much for our plan of patience! God has other ideas for us, and they may not be dull ones at that.

One of the most attractive elements of a spiritual life is its capacity to bear witness. The God-centered life need not be harsh and joyless—to the contrary. My exuberant friend Elberta bears witness to the power of God by her optimism and her grit. The matriarch of a large family, the driving force behind a fiscal empire that includes a flourishing horse ranch, she is an example of what it looks like to live a life by spiritual principles. A beautiful woman in her mid-seventies, with diamonds glinting on her fingers and a sparkle glinting in her eyes, she has courage and good humor. With her ready laughter, she has a power of attraction that radiates strongly from her. Her generous hospitality draws a steady stream of visitors to her door. They are always welcomed. There is always a place at Elberta's table. No matter what hand she is dealt, she turns to God for her strength and she does find it.

For Elberta, God's power is an indwelling power. "You have the power and the strength within yourself, Julia," she will tell me when my faith pales at some challenge.

For Elberta, God's will is all benevolent, despite her being fraught with challenges as intense as her daughter's cancer. She is an expert at finding the silver lining, a past master at counting her blessings. In the days of her daughter's brain tumor, she looked daily for the tiniest signs of improvement and she found them. Where others might have seen only exhaustion, Elberta found hope. Where others might have seen only discouragement, Elberta saw the power of perseverance. In time, where others saw miracles, Elberta saw merely the power of God displayed in the everyday matter-of-fact way that she had expected it. To watch Elberta's life in action is to see by example her belief that faith without works is dead. Traveling to Russia, Australia, and South America, family in tow, she is very much alive, bringing her faith to bear in all situations of her life, all corners of her ever-expanding world.

Faith is attractive. Far from having the joyless, resigned quality that we may fear from it, faith brings to the believer a renewed vitality, a sense of camaraderie and adventure. Seen through the eyes of faith, the world is a safe place. Life is a great unfolding adventure. Strangers are friends that we have not yet met. Optimism prevails. Seen through the eyes of faith, there is nothing to fear in this world. When challenges arise, we will have the inner strength to meet them. Walking through the valley of shadows, we will have the confidence in our God's benevolent protection. We will not, perhaps, be shielded from all harm, but we will be given the wherewithal to meet any adversity.

The question arises: "How, exactly, do we manage to see through the eyes of faith?" This is where the daily work comes in, the daily choice to believe. It is possible to either believe or disbelieve. It is possible, too, to want to believe and to have difficulty in believing. This is when we must reach out. Belief is contagious. Morning reading that posits belief is a positive way to begin the day. The prayer, always, is "Lord, I believe. Help my disbelief."

For each of us the path to a daily belief will be different. I begin my day with three pages of long-hand morning writing. This tells God where I am and what I am needing his help with. Some of us will read the *Daily Word*. Some of us will read the *Twenty-four Hour's a Day* book. Others of us can start with a favorite prayer. It matters less what we do than that we do something. We are trying to hook our consciousness to God's. We are trying to make conscious contact. This begins with the acknowledgment that there is something greater than ourselves to which we wish to relate. We begin by acknowledging our place in the scheme of things. God is the Creator. We are the creation. We owe a debt to God for life itself, and this is perhaps the place to begin: "Direct my thinking. Show me what you would have me be."

We ask God to put his idea for our unfolding into our minds. We ask that our will begin to be aligned with God's will. We are asking here for humility, for the understanding that we do not run the show, however much we might wish to. The day stretches ahead of us. There will be tiny choice points in which we are free to move closer to God. We can be kinder, more generous, more good-humored. The choice is ours. We can act as we believe God would have us act. We can again say our prayers of surrender. "I am willing for you to have all of me, good and bad." When we make God a conscious part of our day, the day begins to unfold differently. We are not nudging for our own way. We are listening, trying to hear what path God would have us take. It begins to seem possible that we are in the right place at the right time and that our unfolding is happening according to a divine scheme.

"But what if there is no divine scheme of goodness for me?" This world is too large and too complex for everything to be accounted for, and I—and my life—may be one of the things that slips between the cracks. This is the great fear, and it is one that most of us can admit to. God's eye may be on the sparrow, but it is not on us. We are the voice crying in the wilderness and our voice is not heard.

There will always be doubt. Doubt is the shadow side of faith. As we age and we see the unfolding of God's arc through more lives, it is easier to believe that there is a plan and that each life does have an arc to it, an unfolding that is in harmony with God and the world around us. Joseph Campbell remarked that the arc of a life can begin to be seen at middle age, that we can then begin to see a tracery of what might be called destiny, shaping our trajectory.

Speaking for myself, in my middle age, my life has taken on a shape I did not expect—and would not have invited. With the publication in 1992 of my book *The Artist's Way,* I became known as a teacher and mentor. That book was so vastly encouraging to so many—2 million plus readers at this printing—that my voice as a teacher eclipsed my known voice as an artist. This was painful to me. I felt I was one artist among many articulating ideas that many of us had shared. Yet I was perceived as the founder of a human potential movement, a lone voice leading the way. This was not something on which God and I agreed. I wanted to be known for my own creativity, not for aiding and abetting the creativity of others. I simply was not as generous as God made me out to be. I was not selfless. Far from it. I would hear a student's triumph and greet it with great glee and satisfaction only to have a small fearful voice peep up: "But, Julia. What about you and your work?"

When I published my novel in 1999, my hope was that the voice of the novelist would eclipse the voice of the teacher.

Ditto when I published my short stories a year later. Then, too, I hoped for acclaim as an artist that would outstrip my fame as a teacher. I wanted great reviews and a wide readership. I got the reviews but not the readership. I was saddened by this. I took it up with God. "Why not, God?" I asked. "What would it hurt?"

I wanted to be known as a writer of fiction. I wanted to be known for my work on the page and in the theater. My work as a teacher struck me as a by-product of my other accomplishments. Without my work as an artist, there could be no *Artist's Way*. The book would have no legs to stand on. My teaching would be based on air, not on many solid years of creative experience. No, I did not want to be known first and foremost as a teacher, no matter how effective my teachings were.

This may sound thankless—I am sure it is thankless—but I was still arguing, as I often do, with God. God may have the long view and I may have the short view, but my wants were my wants and no amount of gentle reasoning by friends, family, and self seemed to blunt the edge of my desires. Why make me a teacher when I am such a fine artist? I wanted to know. I was troubled by the perception that "Those who can't do, teach" and I wanted to scream out: "But I can! I can and I do!" I wrote plays, novels, short stories, songs. I carefully juggled my teaching and my writing so that my writing always took precedence. Nonetheless, in the public eye, I was known as a teacher. Of course, the very fact that I am an artist is what has made my teaching so popular. There is no rift between teacher and artist, except the rift in my own fearful mind. Artists have always mentored other artists. I just do it on a broader scale. I tell myself this. I tell myself there is wisdom in God's plan, but I fight with it. And I am really fighting with God's plan on the nature of my abundance. How much harder it is to fight God's plan when it involves loss and not gain! I am thinking now of my friend Rhonda and her courage in the face of God's apparent caprice.

Mid-May of this year, while still in New York, I received a phone call from my friend Larry Lonergan back home in Taos, New Mexico. He had sad news to tell me. Paul, the snowy-haired, kindhearted, cherished lover of our friend Rhonda, had just died of a heart attack. It was entirely unexpected. Rhonda was shocked and devastated, as well she might be.

Of all the couples that I knew, Rhonda and Paul were perhaps the happiest and the most compatible. Paul was an inventor; Rhonda, a very fine astrologer. They shared a passion for the environment as well. Many of Paul's inventions concerned solar energies. On this work, Rhonda was Paul's right hand, seeing his many inventions as great gifts for mankind and part of her own mission to help wherever she was able. Paul and Rhonda lived together and worked together for seven years, sharing a tiny rustic cabin on the edge of the wilderness and ownership of an Alaskan husky named Starlight. Starlight was desolate over Paul's demise, a sudden and to him inexplicable disappearance. Outside the tiny cabin, he waited nightly for Paul to come home. Rhonda could hardly bear to call him indoors. Rhonda could hardly bear anything, her heart was so ripped asunder.

I might as well begin with the walk Rhonda and I took upon my arrival back in Taos. We headed up El Salto road, a steep narrow road that climbs straight out of Taos Valley and up into the rocky slopes above. Our grief was as real as the warm spring day. Paul was both very with us and very gone as we walked.

Rhonda and I have walked together often over the years. We have walked through my painful nervous breakdown, through my divorce, and through the death of her son. We have walked in seasons of sorrow and of joy. Our strides were slow this morning and measured, as if the road could lead us to answers that we could not find ourselves.

There was, of course, the great unanswerable question, "Why?" Paul was an inventor and he died just as his inventions were coming into fruition. He worked for years, and as success came to him, he left. Rhonda has boxes full of patents and a vision of trying to help his work still come to light.

As we walked up El Salto, the water in the acequia flooded past us in icy cascades. Last year was a drought and this year's water seemed like an abundant blessing. The earth survived its season of drought and Rhonda will survive her season of heartache. But the pain is large and real and there is no easy answer, no simple Band-Aid to put on so huge and fresh a wound.

"He wasn't done," Rhonda fretted. "His work was just coming forward. I am hoping that his company will continue to go in the direction he laid out for them. Of course, you can never know. Without Paul to lead them . . ."

At root, Rhonda was both griefstricken and faithful. "I am mad at God, but I get the sense from Paul that it was also God's timing that he go when he did."

Rhonda said she was grateful that the veils between the worlds were thin just then and that she had an ongoing sense of Paul, of a continuing relationship with him being possible. I was dazzled by Rhonda's spirituality, her faith in the face of the unfaceable. Paul had died, but Rhonda's faith in a greater benevolence lived on. She was shaken but resolute.

"I know I have to come out of this larger, if I am going to come out of this at all," she said. "I cannot be the person I was before this happened. I cannot be the person I was before Paul. I am not that person after all. I will simply have to become someone different, someone much larger than I feel myself to be."

Let me describe my friend Rhonda. She is white-haired and tiny. Her hair spirals alarmingly in all directions. Her face is a map of life, with deep lines etched from living and living deeply. She wears tiny dresses that go to just above her knees. The dresses are made of cotton or silk and they are light lilac in color. Lilac is Rhonda's favorite color and it is her signature. The slender dresses are belted at the waist, and some tiny purse hangs from the belt, so small it seems a fairy purse. And Rhonda does look like nothing more than a fairy.

Although she has the face of a still-pretty crone, she has the body of an adolescent. Her gestures are light and quick.

Her voice is high and sweet. Her tone is kind and curious. She wants to know *how you are*. When you tell her, she listens deeply. Rhonda is a paradox, at once very light and very deep. Looking at you, her eyes twinkle. They are tiny bits of blue sky, like topaz, like a doll's eyes. She purses her mouth and murmurs *"Mmm-hmm"* as she listens. Her hands dance in her lap. Those hands are lean and supple. Like her lithe body, they haven't aged. Sometimes, when she is thinking deeply, her hands will fondle a piece of quartz. She loves rocks of all kinds and will stop on our walks to scoop up some new bit of treasure. She stopped several times on our morning walk, crouching to earth to examine what she had spotted.

"I want to write a book about God," I told Rhonda. "But I think, 'Who am I to write a book about God?' I want to read a book that says that God is safety."

Saying this to Rhonda, I wondered if she was able, still, to feel safe with God, but she did not argue with my idea. I told her I felt we needed to be reassured.

"No one has really felt safe since 9/11," she posited. "People have gone forward under half steam since then." She cited her friend Frank who lost his "whole social circle, all his friends" in 9/11 and who had come out to Taos to heal. He is, Rhonda said, a lovely man who is "only just beginning to thaw."

We talked for a while about my experience living in New York during 9/11, the resiliency and great kindness that I found amid New Yorkers united by tragedy.

"Maybe it felt safer being there right at the epicenter," Rhonda suggested.

"Maybe it did."

"Maybe there was a sense of safety in the solidarity," Rhonda ventured.

"Yes, maybe so. There certainly seemed to be a safety in the way the city came together. Suddenly we were a community, a town. There were shrines in the streets, signs on the elevator bulletin boards for where you could donate clothes. There was a feeling, 'We're all in this together.' I guess that felt safe."

Rhonda murmured, "Yes, I suppose so. I am sure it did." Then she was struck long silent. I fell silent too. The only sound was our shoes crunching against the narrow dirt road as we climbed. This walk was the first of many.

All summer on our near-daily walks, we worked to see if Rhonda could make a faith large enough to take in Paul's death. We walked, and as we walked, we talked. There was always the question of *why*? Why Paul? Why when he was doing so well? Why when their life together was so happy?

"Why didn't God take someone mean?" Rhonda wondered. "Why Paul, who was so kind?"

I did not have an answer for Rhonda, but I knew I believed that she could find one if we just walked long enough, listening carefully enough. God does respond to our questions. We do not pray into an unresponsive void. There is something or somebody that answers us back if we are just patient enough in our listening. I know this from experience.

Rhonda was with me during my first breakdown. She sat with me under a tree in my yard and listened to my looping thoughts as I strove to put a picture together of what I was seeing. And I was seeing a great deal. With great kindness and delicacy, Rhonda listened as I tried to piece together reality again. Now, in the wake of Paul's death, I was simply seeking to return the favor. There had to be a view large enough to hold the shattered pieces of Rhonda's world. There had to be a "reality" large enough and yet kind enough to hold tragedy without despair.

I knew that if we walked long enough and got quiet enough, we would find it. We might find it only for a moment or so, but we would find it and once found, it could be found again. I see the word *safety* has come up repeatedly. What do we mean by *safe*? There are so many things we cannot guard ourselves against. Rhonda lost her Paul to an early and untimely death. He left for California for a brief business trip and died of a heart attack. Could she protect herself against this? Could her faith encompass it?

That first day we walked for an hour, perhaps a little longer, and when we headed back home, I thought, "This is how we will get through this, a footfall at a time."

It is now months since I had that thought, but the truth of it has held firm. Rhonda's faith has been reaffirmed a footfall at a time. This afternoon I spoke with her from New York. She was having a hard day, as she had had many hard days since Paul's death.

"I just do it a day at a time," she told me, although her friends report that she is seeming better—a smile here, a laugh there, some small amount of the joy of living has come trickling back to her, so slight as to be imperceptible to her own eyes.

Starlight, the dog, realized the difference. He began "inviting" Rhonda on early morning walks, long rambles down by the river where Rhonda could stop for a while and meditate. The walks were healing for both of them. "And sometimes, at twilight, Starlight and I go again. These really long walks are good for me and I think for 'us.'" By *us* Rhonda means her household with the dog, as stricken as she was by Paul's sudden departure.

"I realized Starlight was worried that I was going to go away too," Rhonda told me. "I had to say to Starlight, 'No, I will be here for you. You can count on me that I am not going anywhere.' After I told him that, he seemed to relax."

Although Rhonda doesn't cast it in those terms, her speech to Starlight was a statement of faith: she would go on, come what may. In the wake of Paul's death, Rhonda had questioned the worth of going on. He was, after all, the love of her life, and what was her life going to be like without him? What would make it worth going forward? How could she? Heartbroken was a literal term. She felt crumpled and defeated. Feeling that way, she could only go forward a footfall at a time, and that is what she has been doing. Faith makes the unbearable bearable. It renders the burden that is too heavy to be borne alone a burden that is shared. It brings the help of God to our side, and once it is there, that help becomes the walking stick by which we move forward. Rhonda has been moving forward with the help of faith.

"I am still not the same with God," she told me on our phone call. "My faith is still shaken. I do not trust God in the same way that I did. I used to wake up happy, grateful for my life and my circumstances. Now I wake up and I think, 'Another day of this.'"

One day at a time, Rhonda is surviving "another day of this."

One day at a time, despite her misgivings, Rhonda is going forward with her life. She cannot see or imagine her life without Paul, and yet she is living it. She has chosen to side with life itself and to allow the gentle propulsion of life to move her forward—not that it feels gentle to her at this time.

"I think in the past I survived by getting busy," Rhonda mused. "I am consciously not doing that right now. I am trying to let the healing come from the inside. I am trying to not build again until I feel I am building on something solid. If that takes a while, so be it. It seems important to me to be present to what is actually unfolding right now, not to hurry ahead to someplace I think I ought to be."

Rhonda has put her finger on the pulse of faith: the ability to be where we are and to accept that where we are is where we are supposed to be. This is not easy. It is easier to think, "Oh, I should be . . ." and to conjure up an imaginary life in which we are happier and more fulfilled. It is difficult to be with God in the trenches of reality, in the exact center of where we actually are—right now. And yet, all great spiritual traditions teach us the power of the now. We are always told that if we practice living in the now, we will find God there.

Right now it is late at night and I am typing as I look

out at a cityscape of lights. I myself am undergoing a test of faith right now. Last night I learned that my close friend of two decades plus, actress Julianna McCarthy, had suffered a massive heart attack. As I write, she is recuperating in an intensive-care unit in California. News of Julie's near death brought me squarely up against my own faith, or lack of it. I found that when I tried to pray for her, all I could pray for was for her to have peace and the comfort of conscious contact.

"Pray that God's will be done for her," a friend of mine advised me. I didn't want to hear the advice. What if it was God's will for Julie to die? Was I prepared to accept that? No.

Often when we face a test of faith, it is because God's will may run counter to our wishes. We want what we want, and we are unable to take the longer view that God's will entails—for that matter, we may be unable to see the longer view. This is when we are being asked to demonstrate blind faith, that is, a faith in a larger benevolence, even though we ourselves are unable to see the higher wisdom at hand.

"God, I believe; help my disbelief" is the prayer for times of blind faith. We are asking for the grace to go along with the joke, and the joke may seem to us to have a very harsh punchline. We are asking, often, to accept an untimely death or the shattering of a cherished dream. We are asking for the courage to believe, in the face of our own human disappointment, that a silver lining might just exist and that if we stay faithful we might eventually come to see it. So much of what happens to us seems in cozy retrospect to have been designed for our best good. So little of what happens to us feels that way at the time.

"Thy will be done" is a workable plan for living, but it is a plan for living that requires a supreme effort at openmindedness. We are not able, often, to see what God's objective may be, and so we resist the very changes which in the long haul turn out to have been for our good. It is easy, looking at the lives of others, to see the hand of God in practice. The job they didn't get, the girl they didn't get to marry—these things have a way of working out for the good. And yet, how much harder it is when we are the ones who fail to get the job or fail to get the girl. "Thy will be done. If not this, something better," we are taught to pray.

"If not this, something better" presupposes God's benevolence. We are asking for the faith to hold on long enough to recognize the silver lining. And yet, that silver lining can be a long time in coming. Job went through many trials before one more time returning to the comfortable ease of God's grace. We, too, may be asked to endure many "no"s before we get a "yes," and this is why the wise pray for knowledge of God's will and the power to carry it out.

Praying for knowledge of God's will is a way to move our own will closer to that of God. It is a prayer that invites us to have a peek at the longer view. It is a prayer requesting inspiration and the fortitude to take a backseat to God's driving. It is in this that many of us have such a difficult time.

"Thy will be done, God," we pray, "but in the meanwhile, let me try this." It is difficult to allow the timing of God, the moving of other gears into play. We forget that God is orchestrating a much larger whole, and we tend to think of and want God's will for us to be an instantaneous release from all that troubles us. We want our spiritual life to be a product, not a process. We want to be finished, solved, soothed—and sometimes it is our discomfort that is drawing us toward God. That is the case with me right now.

Right now, I am not comfortable. I have unresolved problems that trouble me and cause me to worry. I am worrying about money, about whether to sell or keep my property in Taos, about whether to teach more or teach less. I am not getting out of the house enough. My walks are too infrequent and too short. New York is crowded. I miss God and the voice of God that comes to me from longer and lonelier excursions. Seated at my desk, overlooking my familiar Manhattan rooftops, I am seeking God and God is elusive. I write about God and in writing about God begin to find some small part of what it is I am seeking. God is an itch I cannot quite scratch. My friend says, "Pray for faith. What you need now is more faith." And so I pray. I pray from a place of discomfort. This discomfort is what drives me to the page. On the page, I begin to discover some small sight of God. I catch a glimpse of the hem of his garment. I grab for the hem.

God wants us to want God. No one has ever made easy terms with God. That is a fantasy. Even Christ prayed, "Why hast Thou forsaken me?" Even Christ prayed, "If it be possible, take this cup from my lips." The cup that God offers us is not always the cup that we would choose. Perhaps it seldom is. We want the Kool-Aid. God insists on giving us the life-giving water. It does not taste as sweet.

We want God's will to be dates and honey. We want to be able to savor the sweetness of God's will for us, and yet at times its taste is as bitter as ashes. We long for something and it is denied us. It is denied us for no reason that we can see. It is hard to see where this serves our good. It is hard to see where God's will is taking us. We want to fast-forward the action a little. We want to say, "Ah, it had to be this way in order that later it could be that way."

But sometimes God keeps such knowledge to himself. Sometimes we are only given the short view, and the short view is long on rejection and short on what we will only later perceive as God's protection. We want what we want and we want who we want. We may want these things for a very long time. When our desires run counter to God's will for us, we must turn to prayer. Only by the grace of God, only by the power of prayer, can our will be alchemized into something more malleable and God-centered.

I know a woman who spent ten years longing for the husband who had left her. No matter that he was gone and not coming back. She could not accept his loss. She could not accept the many ways in which God was moving her onward. She refused to pray, "God, grant me the serenity to accept the things I cannot change." She did not want serenity. She wanted her husband back. She was angry with God for not granting her wish. She fought God every day on the road her life had taken. She turned a blind eye to the many gifts God was trying to give her, the many compensations that were available to her. No, her will was set, and rather than take comfort in God during her loss, she blamed God as the cause of that loss. To the observer's eye, this was a tragedy. She lost not only her husband but her God by assuming this posture. She suffered greatly.

It is now twenty-five years since the marriage dissolved, and it is now possible even for the grieving ex-wife to see the wisdom of the marriage dissolving. In the years since their separation, both wife and husband have become very different people, following two distinctly different and utterly incompatible paths. "I could never have had my life and done my work if we had stayed together," she now says. "There simply wasn't any room for me to grow in the directions that I needed to grow in." She doesn't add that her husband needed room to grow as well and that their marriage had become claustrophobic for them both. The seeds of their growing differences were the initial cause of the divorce. There was a wisdom in their separation that God could certainly see.

When we prolong a fight with God over God's will, we are bound to suffer. We lose not only the object of our desire—the man, the job, the career victory, the healing of a sick child— we lose our connection with God himself. This is not to say that God abandons us. Rather, we abandon God. We do not see where his will is taking us, except perhaps over the brink. Not seeing the wisdom of God's will for us, we fight that will's unfolding. "There must be some mistake," we think at first, and then, as it becomes clear that there is no mistake but instead a very large difference of opinion, we begin to feel victimized. God holds all the cards. God could change things if God would—if only God would! Very often we blame God for things that really fall into the arena of free will.

It may not be God's will at all that we are not loved back, but our lover has free will and is using that free will to walk away. God, like ourselves, can only wish that it were different. Free will is part of the package. It is the gift God made at the beginning. It gives us the power and the dignity of choice.

All of us are at liberty to shape our own destinies. We have free will and we can use that will to follow God's will or to stubbornly insist on following our own. When we stubbornly follow our own lights without asking that God shape our goals and desires, we often run counter to God's will for us and all sorts of havoc is the result. That havoc is caused not by God's will but by our refusal to go along with God's will. Whenever we or anyone is in violation of God's intention for us, strain is the result. Too often we blame that strain on God.

When strain occurs, there is a prayer that is the shortcut back to sanity. That prayer, simply, is this: "Please give me knowledge of your will for me and the power to carry that out." God's will can be surprising—and not at all what we expect.

A woman I know tells the story of getting pregnant by a man who told her he had had a vasectomy. He had not. Already the single mother to one child, she was proceeding with the pregnancy, assuming that was God's will for her. The man felt cornered and went so far as to demand to know how

he could be certain the child was his. Not only had he gotten her pregnant, but he was now questioning her integrity.
That question was the final straw. Not only could the man not
be trusted, he was cruel as well. In desperation, the woman
prayed to God for knowledge of God's will and the power to
carry it out. To her surprise, a great calm and clarity settled
over her. She knew with absolute certainty that an abortion
was the right option for her, that she could not tie her life and
that of her child and that of an unborn child to a man who
was a pathological liar.

"Until I prayed for God's will, I was confused and con-
flicted," she recalls. "I just assumed it was God's will for me to
have the child. I never even prayed to find out. I guess I was
doing God's will as told to me by the Catholic Church, which
I grew up in. I was shocked by the solution that God seemed
clearly to offer me when I prayed. I prayed and prayed again,
and the answer remained the same: have an abortion. That
was the wisest choice for me and the daughter I already had. I
felt great calm and certitude. I was able to make arrangements
quickly and effectively. I had the abortion. In the years that
have passed since, I have often wondered what would have
become of me, my daughter, and that child if I had not had
the wisdom to pray."

There are probably those who would say that an abortion
could not possibly be God's will and that the woman must
have prayed wrong—or heard wrong when she prayed. To
my eye, the sense of peace and lack of conflict that overtook
the woman when she prayed is the surest sign that it was
God's will that she was hearing. God's will is not always

what we imagine it to be. God holds the longer view and is far more able than we are to take in complex variables. Juggling the multiple negative variables that the woman faced, God was able to see her path clearly and to give her a sense of direction.

So often faith comes down to having a sense of direction. Faith requires believing that we are headed in the right direction for our lives. When we feel lost and abandoned, when we feel that God is not beside us, we are always mistaken. God is with us every moment, in every circumstance, in all places. We may lose touch with God, but God never loses touch with us. God is the Great Creator. We are the beloved creative children, never out of sight and out of mind, watched over and cared for at every instant. All that is required is for us to one more time avail ourselves of God. "Lord, I believe; help my disbelief," we must again pray. We must claim that God is with us always. We must seek to touch God and to allow God to touch us right where we are.

Sometimes we do not want God to see us and find us "right where we are." We may feel that our circumstances are beneath God's dignity. Like the woman with the unexpected and unwanted pregnancy, we don't pray. We are embarrassed to stand in front of God. We may assume that God's will for us is something that it is not. We may be afraid to pray. We may feel that God "wouldn't want to know" what we were up to. This view of God is actually patronizing. We have anthropomorphized God into a doddering parent who must be protected from the facts of our lives.

We have it backward. God does not need our protection. We need God's. There is no fact, no detail of our life too sordid for God's intervention. God has seen murder. God has seen rape. God has seen drug addiction's and alcoholism's utter degradation. God is available to us no matter what our circumstances. God can find us in a crack house. God can find us crumpled in a doorway or cowering on a park bench. We need only reach out to discover that God reaches back. We are led a step at a time even when we feel we are alone. Sometimes God talks to us through people. Sometimes God reaches us through circumstance or coincidence. God has a million ways to reach out to us, and when we are open to it, we begin to sense the touch of God coming to us from all directions. At our most abandoned, we are often at our very closest to God. We reach for his hand and do not feel it. Why? We are being cupped in the palm of his hand.

If that image is too anthropomorphic for you, realize this: God is intimate. There may be no celestial hands, but there is a celestial being that infiltrates our lives and our very beings. We are a part of God. God is a part of us. When we pray, we tap an unsuspected inner resource. That resource is God, God dwelling in the last place that we would seek him, within our very beings.

"Julia, the answers are within yourself." I have a friend who often tells me that when I tell her I am seeking God's will and feel confused, dazed, or lost. "You have the answers right within yourself," she will assure me. "Pray and you will know the right thing to do."

We may not know the right thing to do two weeks from now, but we do know the right thing to do next. There is always some small something that is available to us as a next right step. Sometimes it is simply to keep praying. Other times it is to take some small action in the direction that our prayers have led.

Make no mistake, our prayers do lead us somewhere. We may think that we are praying into the great void. We may feel as though there is no one listening, but we are listening and within us lies that divine spark that does know where it is we must go and what it is we must do there. If God is within, we can always find at least that spark of God to make contact with. In the darkest night of the soul, when we feel the most alone and most hopeless, there is still a witnessing God that knows that we do pray.

Many times what we are seeking from God is a sense of witness. We want to know that someone, somewhere, is paying attention to us and to our struggles. We do not even necessarily want God to intervene for us. But we do want to know that God is paying attention. We do want to know that God understands. This is the juncture where we often get derailed. Many very spiritual people can have a tinge of righteousness. They may see our struggles, but they do not understand them and they give us the uncomfortable feeling that God does not either. Ah, but God understands.

It was Christ who said, "Let he who is without sin cast the first stone." He knew that no one was without sin. (Sin being defined as "missing the mark or falling short of the target.")

God has seen sin since the beginning of time. He knows the reasons that we sin and the ways that we try not to sin. He knows our sorrow and our need for forgiveness. He knows our very natures: dragged downward by our fears and upward by our aspirations. Yes, God understands.

And if God really understands, then there is no place at which we cannot meet him. We can say, "Dear God, I am jealous, envious, angry, tired, afraid." God is the solution to all of those conditions, and the grace of God is what allows us to forgive ourselves when we fall short. One more time we are brought back to prayer as the greased slide to our own heart's desires. "Dear God, this is how I am right now." We really yearn for union with God. Prayer is making the phone call that says, "Dear God, please answer."

And God does answer—just not always immediately and in ways we can instantly decipher as coming from God. A friend of mine was experiencing a thoroughgoing depression. She prayed, "Dear God, I am depressed. Please help me." In short order, she had three separate friends tell her they thought she was taking the wrong medication and that she should get her medication checked. Hearing it the first time, she resisted the input. Hearing it the second time, she still resisted the input. Hearing it the third time, she reluctantly took in the input as possible guidance and made an appointment to see a psycho-pharmacologist. His evaluation? She was on the wrong medication for her depression. There were many symptoms that her current medication left untreated.

Sometimes, as in this story, God's answer to our prayers

is so practical that we do not see it as God-ly. My depressed friend was enduring a prolonged bout of sexual uninterest. In theory she still found sex interesting, but that was in theory only. In practice, she had no sexual appetite, and because it was sex that she was talking about, it did not occur to her to pray about it. "Maybe that's all just over for me," she mused. "Maybe I have reached a stage where sex really doesn't matter so much."

"And how is your sex life?" the psychopharmacologist asked her, working his way through a list of symptoms of depression.

"Why, I don't really have a sex life," she found herself explaining. "That just seems to have gone by the boards for me."

"You might find your new medication very interesting then." The doctor gently laughed. "A lack of sexual interest is yet another symptom of depression. You may find getting treated quite a treat."

Telling this story six months into recovery, my friend laughs a lot. "God was very thorough with me," she explains. "I asked for help with my depression and I certainly got that, but I also got a real makeover sexually. I felt like I was waking up from a long sleep. Suddenly I found myself thinking, 'Oh, he is really attractive.' I would have thought matters like that were outside of God's area of expertise; I am not sure why I thought that, but I did."

God hears not only our spoken prayers but also our unspoken prayers. We may have a certain agenda in mind when we pray, only to discover that God has a wider, deeper, and better

agenda in mind for us. We may pray for help with our loneliness, and what we have in mind is a new significant other.
God may answer the prayer by an influx of nonsexual friends
so that our social life broadens and deepens and our loneliness
becomes less acute. God may set about fixing up the life that
we have got rather than having a single person come along
dressed as "the solution to all your problems."

Ellen is a single woman in her mid-fifties. She has a fulfilling career, interesting friends, and no significant other in
sight. At her friends' urging, she signed up for a computer dating service. Filing her data on-line, even using a pseudonym,
she felt suddenly very vulnerable—especially when two men
"bit" and wanted to get to know her.

"I realized that I wasn't really ready to date," she tells me.
"I was almost ready. I was ready enough to date on paper, in
the abstract, but not when it came down to sitting across a
table sharing a few cocktails and the intimate details of my
life. When it came right down to it, I decided I didn't really
want a boyfriend yet. What I wanted was devotion—a good
dose of unmitigated adoration. Reality need not yet apply."
She pauses to laugh at herself. "So I got a puppy. This may
strike some people as hiding out and ducking the issue. I think
it was taking the steps in the right order for me. The puppy
is so delightful. It's a godsend, and I don't have to ante up my
sexual history to a relative stranger."

Conversely, another friend of mine prayed for a relationship, and then got—for her—the radical notion that *she*
should sign up for a computerized dating program. Writing
down her likes and dislikes, really spelling out what it was she

dreamed of finding, my friend experienced a sense of calm and excitement. Maybe there was somebody out there looking for somebody like her. She received a flurry of responses to her "hopelessly picky" ad. One of them stood out to her, and they began exchanging e-mails. Within a few weeks, they were brave enough to meet face-to-face. Within a few months, they were brave enough to admit exactly how well matched they truly were to each other. In short order, they got married. (Although they sometimes didn't care to explain to friends exactly how they'd met.) At this writing, three years in and counting, the marriage continues to thrive.

"I really think it was divine guidance that got me to place that ad and to be so honest in it," my friend recalls. "I think I figured, 'What have I got to lose?' In any case, I prayed for guidance, and once the notion of the computer service came to me, it just wouldn't go away. The more I prayed, the clearer I got that this was some footwork that I myself could do. I wasn't just a helpless victim. I had options and choices, and the chance to see where those could take me was just waiting for me to muster up the courage. I am so glad that I did."

Very often when we pray for knowledge of God's will for us and the power to carry it out, a notion will float in that seems to us radical and even unconnected to our prayer. We might pray, for example, to have a new significant other only to have recurrent guidance to take a master's degree in poetry. We might pray some more, believing that certainly our prayer has been misunderstood—only to receive the same guidance all over again. At this point, it is best to be openminded. God may be up to something on our behalf.

I am friends with a person who prayed for a new signicant other and was directed to take a master's in poetry. Unable to see quite where it was going to take him, he dawdled over committing to the degree. "I thought I knew what I wanted," he explains. Finally, after more prayer and more firm guidance, he undertook the master's program.

"What a revelation! For two years I was too busy working on my poetry to think very much about how I was all alone and poor, pitiable me. I began to be really interested in my own thoughts and insights. I began to feel I might have some genuine talent as a writer and some genuine worth as a person. I was a year into the program before I realized I was now attracted to a completely different type of person than I had been previously. I say 'different,' but I might as well be blunt and say I was attracted to healthy people for the first time in my dating life. I was no longer looking for someone to fix me or someone whom I could fix. I can see now how the answer to my dating prayer really was, 'Get a master's degree in poetry.' The shift in my self-worth led me to very different choices. I hesitate to say this, but I actually like myself and like the person I am now dating. That is what I would call an answered prayer."

It is always easier to see God's will for us in cozy retrospect. My friend who sought a master's degree told me he thought he was "crazy" to be seeking it. He tried to add up its worth in linear terms. He wanted to know "Where's it going to get me?" and the answer did not seem obvious. Would he make more money with a master's degree? Oh, possibly, but maybe not. And yet the guidance was gentle and insistent. He was to take a poetry master's. That was God's will for him.

According to noted psychic Sonia Choquette, the voice of true guidance is always gentle and insistent. "The voice of the soul is not abrupt or harsh," Sonia says, "although it may be surprising. If you pray for guidance and the guidance that comes startles you, wait and pray again. If the same guidance comes, you must begin to be open to the possibility that the suggestion might well be God's will."

The ingenuity of God is often startling. We think that we can see God's will coming—and that it will be either A or B. Arriving, God's will is often—as a friend of mine says—H, heliotrope, something that never would have occurred to you. It is for this reason that prayers for God's will are best kept a daily and doable practice. This doesn't eliminate surprises, but it does keep surprises a little more to the minimum.

"I used to receive large course adjustments from God," a friend of mine relates. "I would pray very seldom and only in times of real emergency. I would pray when I had drifted far off-center, and the answers that I would receive to my prayers seemed very shocking to me, very radical. Now that prayer is more daily for me, the course adjustments are smaller and more doable. My answered prayers are no longer such a bucket of cold water in the face."

It is perhaps in the realm of human relationships that daily prayer can bring us the greatest relief. A woman recalls praying for knowledge of God's will for her and the power to carry it out regarding her husband. "The answer came back very simply. I would pray, 'What should I do about him?' meaning, 'Should I get a divorce?' and the answer would come back to me, 'Just love him.' That seemed like such insurmountable advice. 'Just love him!' Didn't God know what a cad I was dealing with? How could something as simple as 'love' be the answer?"

But the simplicity of love was the answer. The more she tried to simply love her husband, the less of a cad he suddenly seemed to be. "I was transforming me and my attitudes, but what happened was that somehow I was also transforming him and his attitudes," the woman ruefully recalls. "I went from being married to this monster to being married to this lovable monster to being married to this lovable man, and all I did was try to follow the advice I got in prayer, 'Just love him.'"

"All I did was try to follow the advice I got in prayer"— that is so often easier said than done. So often the advice we get in prayer seems beyond our reach, and often not because it is too complex but because it is too simple. "Just love him" seems like advice that only a saint could take to heart. Surely there must be some advice more designed to help fallible me! But no, the answers that we get in prayer often seem intended to stretch us and to stretch us in ways that we would not have foreseen.

I live in New York where God can seem very elusive. Unlike in New Mexico, there is no easy looking to nature for the assurance of God, the Great Creator. New York is filled with monuments to man and his accomplishment. The skyscraper seems less an invention of God than a concoction of man's ingenuity. The crowded streets filled with the bustling and hurried crowds do not seem like evidence that God is in heaven and all is unfolding as it should be here on earth. All seems to be unfolding pell-mell, without divine assistance. And yet, can that be the case?

God is everywhere. God is in everything. This means that God is in New York and right there in the very crowds that seem so bent on ignoring him. God does not need to be merely a beautiful cloud formation or the darkly folded purple velvet of a mountain's flank. God can be in the crowd at the subway platform. God can be pressing up the escalator. God can be flagging a cab. God does not need to match our romanticized notions of God. God is more intimate than that. Far more intimate. God is aware of the farmer in Iowa struggling with his fifty pounds of overweight, and God is aware of the actress in Los Angeles who must be fifteen pounds underweight to look good on camera. There are no secrets from God.

If there are no secrets from God, then we can safely think about what it is we are trying to hide from God and reveal that thought to God now. There are so many things that strike us as unseemly. For some of us, ambition is a dark secret. We do not want God to know exactly how much we care about our career and the lengths we are willing to go to try to ensure its proper unfolding. For others of us, the deep secret is our longing for an intimate personal relationship, a love match that would truly involve both "love" and "match." We do not want to bother God with our dating dilemmas, although we are often the first to say "It would take a miracle" to meet someone.

When we hide from God our true goals and agendas, we cannot really hide them, but we can prevent ourselves from enjoying the comfort of knowing that God is "on the case" and working on our behalf. We can rob ourselves of the comfort of an ongoing collaboration with God, in which we both try to work to meet "our" goals. The problem, of course, is that we often assume that our personal goals and God's goals for us are at opposite ends of the table. We do not trust that our dreams come from God and that God has the power to accomplish them. Instead, we act as though every idea we have is born out of self-will, and even in the most willful of us, this is never the case. God inspires us with desires and dreams. God gives us goals and agendas. God is able to help us to meet those goals and fulfill those agendas. God is prepared to help fulfill our goals and dreams. One more time it comes back to the questions of prayer. When we pray, "Please give me knowledge of your will for me and the power to carry it out," we are often shocked by the fact that what is clarified for us is some very personal intention. We pray for God's will only to discover how sharply we long for a partnership of our own with another human being. We pray for God's will, thinking we will be pointed toward heaven, only to find that we are pointed squarely back into our career with a clear idea of what it is that we must do next to move ahead further.

God is not otherworldly. God is not flaky and airy-fairy. God is grounded in reality, and as we pray to God, we become more grounded, not less. As we ask to have our life run by God, we become more comfortable, not less, with the actual details of that life.

God has his eye on the sparrow, but he also has his eye on the Dow Jones. God might find us taking the step of establishing a prudent financial reserve rather than trusting to the fates that all will be taken care of. God, after all, invented the acorn and the squirrel and knows a thing or two about savings. When we ask God for help in our financial affairs, that help may show up in very practical forms. We may discover that God puts in our path the precise advisers we need. There are those who are "good with money," and God may choose to introduce us to a few such people. Once we become willing to involve God in all arenas of our life, there is no arena too worldly for God to be involved in.

It is the idea of God "being involved" that is often the sticking point. Many of us prefer to think of our relationship with God as being unrequited. Most of us are not really comfortable with the idea of a personal God, one interested in all our affairs. We think that there are areas beneath God's concern, and those are the areas, particularly finance and romance, that we tend to try to run ourselves. Very often it is the area that we declare beneath God's interest where we could use the most divine help. Stubbornly isolationist, often more than a little self-pitying, rather than open our eyes to the help all around us, help that has been divinely sent, we try to go it alone. In so doing, we shut out many of the intended helpers sent in our direction.

When a gift horse is sent our way, we not only look it in the mouth, we slap it on the rump to get it out of our vicinity as soon as possible. "It's just a coincidence," we say when something transpires that seems an answered prayer.

A woman writer of my acquaintance began to feel claustrophobic in her work. She was too much alone at the computer.

There was little in her life that seemed to accompany her as she made her daily trek to the page. "What I need is a friend," she told herself, but she was hard-pressed as to where she would meet such a friend. On her once-daily dash out to Starbucks? At about the time that she was realizing her need for a friend, she read a very good romantic novel. The writing in the book was delightful. So was the sensibility of the writer that it seemed to reveal. On impulse, she wrote out a fan letter—not something she had ever done before.

She e-mailed the letter off into cyberspace, expecting to hear no more of it. But no. The writer of the fine romance sent a short letter back. My friend sent a letter responding to that letter. Again, the writer sent a letter back. Of course she answered—and that letter was answered as well. Before she quite knew what had happened, my friend found herself in a daily e-mail relationship. Claustrophobic no longer, now she had someone to tell her daily tale to. She could say "I got to the page for a little while today, and it was uphill believe me," or "Hurray, hurrah. Today I had a good writing day. I actually managed to put in several hours and they were well worth the effort. For once I had ideas and the words to clothe them in. I am ecstatic."

When I mentioned to my friend that her new e-mail relationship was clearly an answered prayer, she frowned at me. "I wouldn't go that far," she all but snarled. "Haven't you ever heard of coincidence?" If I was selling God, she wasn't buying, but did that mean God was absent?

God dwells in coincidence. God dwells in serendipity. God dwells in synchronicity. God dwells in lucky breaks.

God, the Great Conductor, cues many of our entrances and exits—if only we are willing to be cued. It takes faith to act "on impulse," to follow "a hunch." (Not to mention "to listen to guidance.") And yet guidance, the impulse, and the hunch are the inner promptings that keep leading us where we are meant to go.

My friend the writer listened to an impulse that said, "Write a fan letter." She had never written one before in all her years as a writer. The impulse led to a friendship that answered her need to put an end to her writer's isolation. Like it or not, the friendship was an answered prayer.

What is it about answered prayers that we find so threatening? Is it that we don't really want the collaboration that such a response seems to imply? It is easier and more familiar to play victim than it is to throw open the gates and declare, "With God's help, anything is possible to me." And yet, with God's help, anything is possible and the nature of that "anything" can be more and more to our authentic liking as we become willing to invite God into our life.

"Please give me knowledge of your will for me and the power to carry that out." It is in the knowledge of God's will for us that we begin to discover our true nature. God's will and our will are not at opposite ends of the table, although we may fear that they are. It is God's will for us to be happy, joyous, and free and just what will make us that way is what we are out to discover. Things may make us happy that we do not credit with the power to give us happiness. Things may make us unhappy that we falsely believe will make us happy. When we turn our will and our life over to the care of God,

the key word there is *care*. In God's care, we discover ourselves and our true nature. We learn to see which of the many
things on life's menu might be appropriate to our own genuine appetites—and as we pray for knowledge of God's will,
we may find our tastes shifting. We can cooperate with where
and how we are being led. The chief means by which we are
able to cooperate is through our gratitude. Gratitude leads us
to alertness to God's involvement with our lives.

Gratitude is not an attitude that comes to most of us easily.
It is a learned skill. It is the ability to see and say thank you for
the many gifts in our life as they are unfolding. In order to have
a grateful heart, we must be willing to open the lens of our
vision far enough to take in what is actually being given to us.
We cannot just stay focused on the one thing we demand and
seem to be denied. No, gratitude involves looking at our lives
more holistically. There is always some small thing for which
we can be grateful—and often many larger things as well.

Thank you, God, for my health. Thank you, God, for my
means of earning a livelihood. Thank you, God, for my friendships. Thank you, God, for my family. Thank you, God, for
my creative outlets. Thank you, God, for my home. Thank
you, God, for my pets. Thank you, God, for my mode of
transportation. Thank you, God, for my interest in getting to
know you better. Thank you, God, for my faith—and for my
hope of having more faith.

Gratitude lists can range, like this one, from the general to
the very specific.

Thank you, God, for my weight finally coming off after
so many years of trying. Thank you, God, for my nice flannel

sheets that feel so good to snuggle into on a cold winter's night. Thank you, God, for how well my new computer works and for my having the openmindedness to learn how to use it. Thank you, God, for giving me a market nearby that has decent vegetables. Thank you, God, for my car holding up for another season without needing to have major work done on it. Thank you, God, for my managing to discover such a great new mascara. Thank you, God, for helping me finally get a good haircut. Thank you, God, for my newfound stores of patience with the dogs. Thank you, God, for my notion of rereading Raymond Chandler and finding him just as good as he ever was—even better!

Gratitude shifts our focus from the negative to the positive. Gratitude says, "Thank you, God, for giving me such a large and sunny apartment." Not: How long will I be able to keep it? Gratitude says, "Thank you, God, for my having views that I can enjoy. Thank you for the tree right beneath my window." Not: Soon it will be winter and the leaves will all be gone. Gratitude makes us conscious that life is made of thousands of small variables and that many of those variables are already good. "Thank you, God, for bringing me to a really good dentist." Yes, I need to have a tooth pulled, but I do know he will do it carefully. "Carefully" is perhaps the thing we most yearn for and that can be found, if we are willing to look for it, in the care of God.

"If we are willing to look for it" is a key phrase in talking about faith. Most of us could enjoy far more faith than we do if we were willing to look for it. "If we were willing to look for it," we might see the hand of God in God's "no"s to us as well as in God's "yes"es. With an open mind, we might be able to see where our life is being shaped and guided. We might be able to see that those things we have been refused have often not been in our best interests. I can speak to this question myself from my direct experience.

When I was in my twenties, I was married to a man I was very much in love with—whose values differed almost totally from my own. Despite our love, the differences in our values worked to drive us apart and, after several years together, we painfully separated. I wanted nothing more than to put the marriage back together again, and yet it was clearly not God's will that we do so. Every time we thought of reconciling, too many differences would rear their head. When I would pray for knowledge of God's will for me and the power to carry it out, I would receive the guidance that I was to just let the relationship go—difficult advice to follow when you are young and in love as I was.

For the better part of a decade, I kept trying, one more time, to glue the marriage together again. There was no putting Humpty Dumpty back together again. The marriage was over, and my job was to learn to accept it. This I finally did. As I worked to put time and distance between me and another futile reconciliation, my career began slowly and gently to take off. This was a career I could not have pursued if I had stayed married. The values my career embraced were antithetical to the values that my husband's career embraced. Reluctantly, I had to conclude that God's will for me was a life without my husband in it—and a better life than I would ever have managed had we stayed together.

It is now more than twenty years since my last reconciliation and in those two decades I have had ample opportunity to gauge exactly how much more wise and in the long run how kind God's will for me really was. God's "no" to me was actually a "yes" in disguise. I needed only to accept the clear direction I was being given in order for me to start to feel relief.

When we surrender to God's will for us, we often feel relief. We intuitively know we have been fighting a war we couldn't win, and when we say, "Enough! I will do it your way!" we can almost hear the synapses of the universe snapping into place as our good starts to move toward us. It is not God's will for us to be miserable. It is not God's will that we should suffer. Many times when we oppose God's will, we are actually in the process of selling ourselves far short.

I can see now that had I stayed married to the man I so loved I would have had a claustrophobic life, one in which many freedoms were curtailed and a great many friendships declared off-limits as well. I was in love with a man who was both possessive and territorial. I was not only his wife, I was his property, and straying too far into my own interests was a real threat to him. I was willing to pay this price, but God was not willing to have me pay it. Whenever I prayed for knowledge of God's will, I was firmly given the sense that I was to pursue a separate and equal course, which is what I did do—but not until I had fought with God for the better part of a decade.

On Tuesdays, for dinner, I often see a friend who was my friend during the time I was struggling to remain together with the man I belonged apart from. She will laughingly remind me of how willing I was to put up with difficulties all in the name of love. "What can I say"—she laughs now—"you wanted what you wanted and whom you wanted. It didn't matter to you that your whole life was being thrown out of kilter by his demands. I don't really think you had a life in those days. Certainly not the life you have managed to have now."

The life that I have managed to have now is not a life of my own choosing. It is the life that God put together for me almost behind my back. It includes a form of fame I wouldn't have chosen, money for work I didn't know that I could do, respect as an expert in my field, and respect from myself for doing something that I myself value. None of this was on my agenda when I was insisting "Just give me back the man, please, God." Thankfully, God did not listen—or if God listened, God chose wisely not to give me what I longed for. A far more loving hand than mine was shaping my destiny. All I needed to do—and I mean this literally—was cooperate. My job, a day at a time, was to not sabotage the good that God was unfolding for me. I had to post a note on my telephone: "Dial this number for pain and rejection."

It is often not easy to refrain from sabotaging God's will. When something lovely begins to unfold, we often want to uproot it. We become volatile and restless. We become irritable and discontent. We yearn for drama—and we often allow ourselves to cause it. We chomp at the bit in the job that suits us, the one where we are paid well for doing what it is we do well. Or, let us say we are finally moving into a loving relationship that is going where it ought to go one day at a time. This is too much for many of us. How tempting it is to pull the relationship up by the roots, to demand that it go faster or in a different direction.

God's will is the temperate and organic unfolding of our good. Our will is the self-centered histrionics that keeps our good at bay. Is it any wonder that twelve-step programs urge us to live one day at a time? Just for today, I can tolerate letting goodness happen to me. Just for today, I can resist the temptation to sabotage God's will with my own.

Can't I?

Often I can't. And this is where prayer enters the picture. We often say, "It would take the grace of God. . . ." What we seldom realize is that there is such a thing as the grace of God, and it can be actively invoked in our behalf. "My Creator, I am willing for you to have all of me, good and bad. Please remove from me now whatever defects of character stand in the way of my usefulness to you and my fellows." This prayer goes a long way toward tempering our self-destructive impulses.

It is difficult to pray for God to run our lives and to continue to act out in our lives with the same freedom as before. God is a tempering agent, which isn't to say that life with God is dull—far from it. With the help of God, we might find ourselves speaking up for ourselves but with dignity. We might find our formerly white-hot temper being newly under control. We might find our tendency toward extreme solutions—those in which our solution to a problem is actually worse than the problem itself—abruptly curtailed. All of this makes life interesting, far more interesting than havoc. The idea that God can be invited to co-create a life with us gives us a vested interest in the life we are making. We are not the victim any longer. On the other hand, we are not the sole creator. We are the collaborator. We are involved with God in a partnership, and this is where it gets interesting.

If God's will and our will are not at opposite ends of the table, they may be said to be in communication with each other. We may find, as we pray, that what we pray for becomes more and more what we have. This is a neat trick. Which came first, the chicken or the egg? Which came first, God's will for us or our will to do God's will? We are endowed with freedom, and it is our perfect right to use that freedom to pursue an understanding of God's will for us. That is to say, we can entrain our own will to a higher will and in so doing experience more freedom, not less.

"How can I best serve Thee? Thy will be done"—that is a prayer that gets us results. We begin to see in each day's march a higher hand, and that higher hand does shake our own. Today might seem like a dead end until we say that prayer and begin to discern some purpose in it. There is nearly always some small, selfless something that we can do to move us an iota closer to God's will for us. "Relieve me of the bondage of self" we pray—and then make the brief phone call inquiring how the day went for someone else. It is a spiritual axiom that it is in self-forgetting that we find ourselves, that is, we find a version of ourselves that is comfortably without the hunger for more. It could be argued that God's will is characterized by the sense "This is enough," whereas the human will is characterized by the nonsense "There has to be something more."

Wanting more—and doubting that we will get it—is a human condition as banal and painful as a toothache. We want more money, more prestige, more friends, and in wanting more we often fail to have gratitude for what it is we do have. Thus, we are always operating on the basis of unsatisfied desires. We are always hungry, for one thing or another. This chronic hunger creates a sense of desperation. "I *must* have more." That desperation sets up a demand, and a demand is nearly always counter to God's will for us.

It is God's will for us to feel satisfied, fulfilled, filled. When God is what we want more of and not some other lesser thing, we stand a chance of having our appetite sated. When we pray "Thy will, not mine" be done, we bow ourselves out of the driver's seat and into the passenger's seat. Suddenly, we are free to enjoy the ride. The scenery that whizzes past may be beautiful. Freed from squinting at the road, we may actually take in the sights and enjoy them.

Ours is an abundant world, but it seldom seems that way when we are demanding more. When we say "Thy will, not mine," we are saying "This is enough," and in saying that, we may actually have that experience. This is an experience of acceptance, and acceptance is usually the sticking point when it comes to our will versus God's. We would accept God's will for us if we could just see where it was going. If God would just give us a glimpse of what we were being prepared for, then we would go along with God's preparations. If we are all indeed being brought along like fighters, then there is nothing random in what we are given. We are given just what we need at all times to further our spiritual growth, fund our spiritual development.

It is perhaps the dominant human experience to always think "This is not enough." We want more of all good things, and we ignore the fact that what we have is already enough, always. We want heaps of faith. We want heaps of worldly possessions. We want . . . It is the wanting that keeps us off-center and it is here again where prayers of gratitude begin to satiate the hungry heart. If we are saying "Thank you God for exactly what I have right now," then we are less likely to be mentally demanding more. When we are focused on the abundance that we do have, then we are able to let go of needing always to have more. What we have is actually doing us quite nicely—if only we can see it, which we so often cannot.

We cannot see the benevolence of God's will for us because we do not expect benevolence. We expect God's will for us to be niggardly. We so often see God as a miser, doling out the least possible benefit just to keep us quiet. We do not expect God to be generous. We do not expect God to fill our cup to overflowing. And yet, when we begin to work with prayers of gratitude, this is often the experience that we get: abundance. It is by counting our blessings that we begin to be able to see our blessings. It is by seeing our blessings that we begin to fathom the possibility that God could actually intend for there to be more of them. Gratitude gives us a glimpse of God's good intentions.

God's good intentions are so often what we doubt. We are

afraid that what we have will be ripped away from us. We see God as an Indian giver, a capricious and often withholding deity that doesn't much care about us and our feelings. We do not see God as a builder, working to give us a foundation on which more can be built. Jesus was a carpenter. Carpenters build things. It can perhaps be just that simple with our lives. We are the raw materials with which God works. As we strive to cooperate with God, he is able to erect sturdier and more lasting edifices from our lives. This is what we need to know: God is a builder. He wants us to have safety and security. It is a builder's nature to provide those things. God does not want us on the street. To the contrary, God wants shelter for us from the storm. We are always being taught: God is the shelter. We continue to fear: God is the storm.

What does it take to have an experience of God as safety? First and foremost, it takes a grateful heart. By enumerating the many ways in which God has already served us, we begin to be able to see that God's will may continue to serve us well. "Thank you for my health, for this sturdy body. Thank you for the roof over my head. Thank you for the bedding on my bed. Thank you for my bed itself. Thank you for letting me rest in you, O Lord."

When we rest in God, we begin to have a different experience of God. It becomes less about our striving and more about our receiving. God is the great giver, and too often we are too busy and too self-driven to be able to receive. We ask for help, but then we hurry blindly on, and when our help arrives, we do not pause to acknowledge its source; we just grab for it and keep on moving. "God help me" we pray, but when God does, we are often too preoccupied to say "Thank you."

A friend of mine is worried about money. She is afraid of ending up out on the street. Each month she worries about where her rent money will come from. Each month her rent money does come. God opens some new door to her, and the flow enters where least expected. My friend does not thank God for this continued support. She is focused, always, on her notion that the support will soon stop. In this way, there is no way that God can ever do enough for her. No matter what miracles occur, she always wants more. Wanting more, she is blind to the fact that what she has been given time and time again is enough. We do not want enough. We want *more*.

The divine flow is inexhaustible, but we do not conceive of God in those terms. We think of God anthropomorphic-ally. God is a celestial Sugar Daddy. God is Santa Claus. We think of God as doling out a limited amount of goodness, a finite amount of abundance. We see others as competitors for God's bounty. We are afraid that our good may take away the good of another. More to the point, we fear that another's good may take away our own. We do not see God accurately as all and the source of all. We see God as the benefactor of some—and we may doubt our own worthiness. If we doubt our worthiness, then it is only a matter of time until God reaches the same conclusion and the source of our bounty dries up. No wonder we are fearful.

How much better we do when we do not make our God so human. If we see God, perhaps, as a flow of energy, a divine electricity that goes just where it is needed, we begin, then, to be on a better track. If God is a source, an energy, that enjoys giving and we are recipients for God's gifts, then we are on somewhat surer footing. If God likes to give, if it is God's nature to give, then we are on better footing still. If we have a faith in God's nature as giver, we do not need to be so concerned with our own worthiness as receiver.

It is one of the burdens of our culture that we feel ourselves to be so unworthy of God's care and attention. We give lip service to the idea that God is the Great Creator and we are his children, but we do not feel ourselves to be beloved children. Far from it. We have taken the mythology of the Garden of Eden deep into our hearts and we know that we are not worthy to receive God's focused care.

Let us think for a moment how different our lives would be if only our creation myth was different. We all know the story: It is a very nice day in Paradise and then Eve, uppity Eve, reaches for the apple. She offers it to Adam, a hopeless codependent, who does exactly as she bids and takes a bite. Then what happens? The sky parts and we hear a loud, booming voice of displeasure. Adam and Eve are expelled from Paradise and told they will bear their children in pain and suffering. What if the story had ended differently?

What if when Eve reached for the apple, the skies parted and we heard a voice filled with pleasure and warmth, exclaiming, "Took you long enough! I made those apples red for a reason! What do you two think about seeds? I thought they were pretty groovy, but if you can come up with something even better, just let me know. . . ."

In other words, what if our aspirations, hopes, and dreams—

our reaching for the apple—were met with understanding and encouragement? What if God was supportive instead of competitive? Nurturing instead of punitive? What if we could expect God to encourage our growth and expansion, instead of discounting and condemning it? Wouldn't we have a very different attitude toward God? Wouldn't we have a very different expectation regarding God's support? Wouldn't faith be easier to come by?

Of course it would.

And so, it falls to us to reeducate ourselves. We need to look at the crippling ways in which we have been raised to understand God. We need to tell ourselves new stories and teach ourselves new lessons if we are to have an adult faith that works. We must ask ourselves: "What kind of God *could* I believe in?" Very often, even in observing the natural world, there is at least as much support for a benign God concept as there is for the punitive one with which so many of us have been raised. So often, many of us outgrow certain stories of childhood, Santa Claus and the Easter Bunny, but do not outgrow the God stories of our childhood. It simply doesn't occur to us that we are *allowed* to rewrite our concept of God. As a result, we are ourselves adults, but our faith is still infantile. We have not allowed ourselves to redraw the lines of our childhood faith in order to find one that works for us as adults.

What kind of God could I believe in?

Most of us know intuitively when we are hearing the truth. We can believe in a God that is all-powerful because such a God makes sense to us. God *is* all-powerful. We know this in our bones. God is not threatened by us, by our dreams and our schemes. Far from childishly competing with its creations, this is an adult God, a generous God. We can believe there is one source, one Divine Mind that runs through everything and is everything. We can believe this, again because we intuitively know this to be true. The truth resonates within us. The truth causes celebration in our very bones.

So, too, we can believe in a God that is co-creative with us, that gives us the freedom and dignity of free will and yet the opportunity to align our will with divine will. We can believe that God is love, and we can know that love to be a love beyond our imaginings, all-accepting, all-forgiving, all-knowing. We can know God as our one true source, the locus of all of our good. Our very heart sings "yes" to this concept.

Beyond any anthropomorphic notions of God, we can sense that there is one divine energy that infuses all of life that is in all and is all. We can accept and believe that God is the One Power. Our whole being resonates to the truth that this is so. God is ever-expanding, ever-growing, ever-outflowing itself into all the forms that it has made and will make. God is creativity, pure creative energy. The term *Great Creator* is accurate. We are God's creations and we are intended, in turn, to be creative ourselves. All of this we can accept to be true because we "know" it as true. On hearing the Word, we accept it. There is nothing in us that resists or resents this God concept. We are born accepting it. When we hear it, when we come to it for ourselves, we feel the peace of alignment.

Faith, then, is a form of common sense. We can come to believe what it makes sense to us to believe. We can outgrow the stories of our childhood that do not match our adult experience of God. And the key word there is *experience*. All of us have a personal experience of God, and we can build upon this to make a firm foundation for our lives. There are moments, in every life, when God is clearly present. There are times when we know God and we know that we know God. These moments can be built upon. Each life contains them, and they can be made into building blocks for a personal faith. When we divorce ourselves from superstition, from ideas of God that are old and scary and unworkable, we begin to have an idea of God that is optimistic and trustworthy. God can be trusted, we come to realize. This is the basis for all faith.

But how do we know God can be trusted? We intuitively feel that in our moments of connection but those moments can be fleeting. It can be difficult to recall them to mind with sufficient clarity, and it is here that our culturally induced cynicism sets in. Believing is "gullible" we fear. It is too easy to take the short view and to say that based on our personal experience—and our fears—God feels capricious. It is here that the natural world serves us as the great teacher. In the natural world the overweaning wisdom of God is apparent. Who can observe the seasons without seeing God's wisdom in their timing and perfection? So, too, we have our seasons, and we must learn to trust God regarding our own unfolding. As with all things, there is a time of dormancy, a time of germination, a time of fruition and harvest. We must be patient with these things in our heart. We must develop patience and an open mind—a very open mind.

God is making something of us. What we are to be remains

to be seen, and we must cooperate in order that we may be made what it is God desires of us. It is here that our impatience often catches us up short. We want to know what God's plan for us is, and we want assurance that God's plan is sufficiently in sync with our own. We may say, "Thy will be done," but we add, under our breath, "and tell me what it is."

God does not always tell us what it is that God is up to. We may go through seasons when we are blind to what God's will for us may be, try as we might to see it, striving our best to do God's will yet we are baffled as to just what that will is or just where that will is leading us. We may not be able to see the longer view, and not being able to see it, we may doubt that it exists. It is here that faith must become active. We must make a decision to trust. We must renew that decision daily. We must pray that prayer that is at the root of all faith, "Lord, I believe; help my disbelief." It is in the humility of this prayer that we are led to a greater and firmer faith. We are led to be able to trust when things do not *feel* certain.

When things feel certain, it is easy to believe—and sometimes things *feel* certain. Sometimes we are given the knowledge of more than a day at a time. We get a quick glimpse of the overview, of where we are being led and why. We see what God is doing with us. We get a glimpse of how it is we are being made larger and better. We even agree with God's methods. Sometimes this happens, not often, and when it does, it is a blessing. When we get a glimpse of God's will for us, we are often filled with gratitude. We are being made something with beauty and dignity. We are being made more than we dreamed of. We see ourselves as a part of the greater whole, and it is magnificent. God's will has both ingenuity and grandeur to it.

If we could just see where God is leading us, we would all cooperate more of the time. All of us like to be made something larger and better, and we are willing, when we see what is larger and better, to go along with the temporary discomfort we may feel as our growing pains. The problem is that we so often cannot see where God is taking us. We hold such a small part of the larger picture. We do not see how our temporary discomfort is leading us to anything worthwhile. Feeling uncomfortable, we blame God. We feel abandoned and trifled with. We do not trust that God has us in his care and that in that phrase *care* is the operative word.

Care is the operative word—infinite, tender care. This is what we doubt and also what we dream of. It is God's nature to care for us, and it is perhaps human nature to doubt that care. We know all too well the human failings that come to bear when we promise care. We may, as parents, be too tired or too stressed to give our best care. We tend to project these same attributes onto God. We tend to worry that God is tired and God is stressed and that somehow looking out for us is something that has somehow slipped between the cracks.

But God is not tired. God is not stressed. God is the infinite caregiver. Our well-being is God's priority. We are urged to trust this, to become "as little children." We are asked to be wholehearted, to go back to a time before we were cynical and doubtful. God wants us to have faith. "Suffer the little children to come unto me." We are the little children. How do we become the children that we are?

Faith asks us to believe in our own goodness. Faith asks us to believe in our own worthiness to receive. For very many of us, this renders us straight back to prayer, where we again must pray, "Lord, I believe; help my disbelief." We are praying now to believe that we are worthy of God's love, worthy of God's generosity. One more time we are thrown up against our creation myth in which God expels us from the Garden at the first hint of our "uppity" nature, our reaching for that apple in a show of human curiosity. We are faced with having been raised to believe in a vengeful God. How can we undo this conditioning and come to accept a God who is actually accepting of us?

Here the Scriptures are valuable to us. We go again back to the story of Christ saying, "Let he who is without sin cast the first stone." This story tells us that in God's eyes all of us are both flawed and perfectly acceptable. None of us is without sin. Sin is to be expected—and accepted. If God can accept our shortcomings, why then can't we? "My Creator, I am willing for you to have all of me, good and bad. . . ." That is the prayer that says to God "I know I am flawed. Work with me as I am. I give myself to Thee."

It is in giving ourselves to God that we become like little children. It is in taking that step of faith that says, "Here I am. Make of me what you would." We hold out a hand to our Creator. Humbly, we say, "Help me that I may serve you." Voluntarily, we reach for that humility. We offer ourselves for a partnership but acknowledge that God is the leader in that partnership. Children do not try to be the parent. They are happy to be protected and guided. The parent is allowed to be the parent and the child, the child. We must work to allow God to be our parent. We must consciously curb our desire to run the show and say, "Thy will, not mine, be done."

Humility has a bad name among most of us. We associate it with its cousin, "humiliation." Who wants to be humiliated? No one. But humility before God has no negatives. It is the simple acknowledgment of facts as they are: God is greater than we are; we bow before God's greatness. We open our hearts to what God would show us. We ask to be teachable. When we do so, we are taught.

One of the first things that we are taught is that we *are* like little children. It is with emotional relief that we can let go of our need to run the show. There is something very refreshing about choosing to be right-size. When we admit "I do not know what is best here; Thy will be done," we often feel a comforting sense of letting go. We have tried to run the whole show and to shape our lives according to our own dictates and it has left us feeling alone and isolated. We crave companionship. And the companionship we most crave is God's. But we cannot play God, edging God out, and be God's companion simultaneously. If we want to feel God, we must get our roles into proper perspective. We must let God be God, the Creator, and we must take our place as creations. God must call the shots.

As I write, a friend of mine is struggling to let God call the shots. My friend is a writer. She is ambitious and wants a career success. She has been writing for many years and to a great deal of encouragement but no huge success such as she envisions. Her books sell modestly. Her plays meet with moderate acclaim. She always gets enough encouragement and financial reward to go on but not enough to declare herself once and for all at the top of the heap. God is offering many things to her, but a worldly triumph does not seem to be among the gifts on the table. My friend is fighting with God, insisting, "I must have my way." God does not fight back. God simply asserts, "Here is what is really in your best interests."

Keeping her success moderate, God is rendering her a worker among workers, a friend among friends. My friend doesn't like what God is offering her, and so she turns a blind eye to the many gifts her situation allows her. She is angry with God, and so she turns her back on the routines that would make her will and God's will more compatible. She refuses to pray. She will not go for long walks for fear that God will try to join her there and whisper to her of the life they could be sharing. She doesn't want to share her life with God. Not really. She wants God to do what she wants when she wants it, and when God has other plans for her, she feels bullied.

When I say to her, "You think God is a bully," she denies it.

"Let's just say I think God is stingy," she phrases it.

If asked, God might say, "I think she is stubborn," but no one is asking God for God's two cents' worth. Asking God to chime in is to risk being openminded. To risk being open-minded is to risk being teachable. To risk being teachable is to risk being taught, and my friend does not want to be taught the lessons that God is now trying to teach her. She is in rebellion and God allows us to rebel. Our rebellion becomes its own teacher as we rail until exhausted and, finally spent, turn back again toward God. Or, we do so if we are lucky enough to be willing.

But we do not have to wait to turn toward God. We can do it more and more quickly. At the first nip of malcontent, we can pray "Thy will, not mine be done." Asking to be shown God's will, we can often get a glimpse of where it is God is taking us. We may not be able to see far down the path, but we can see a little and often that little is enough.

My friend the rebellious writer cannot see for certain that her next book will be a best seller, but she can see enough to know that she is intended to write it. Knowing that much, she can begin, and in beginning, she can feel a certain easing up of her argument with God.

"Just for today, I know I am supposed to be writing," she tells me. "I resent it, thinking that it will be the same old thing—good but not good enough—and yet I think I am only asked to do the best that I can and to hope that that is enough." Telling me this, her tone still holds a grudge. She would like more of a guarantee from God, more assurance that if she just plays ball, she will in fact "win." But God is not offering such assurances. God is asking her to have faith and that is a demand that she resents.

"God's terms are too hard," she tells me. "Does God think I am a grownup or something?"

She has hit the nail on the head. God's terms with us are paradoxical. We are asked to become like little children, and then we are expected to be grownup, to do our part. The paradox becomes clearer if we realize that it *is* grownup to become as little children. It is a realistic assessment of our actual position in relationship to God.

"Faith is everything," another friend of mine, a therapist, declares. "I am always being asked to have enough faith, and when I try to have enough faith I do have enough faith. Or I have so far."

"I have so far" is one way that we can extend our faith. We can look at how far we have come and we can remember the growing pains we underwent to get there. This is another form of counting our blessings. We can count our occasions for faith, and in so doing, we can see that we have never been led astray. A case in point:

My friend the therapist is also a writer. Some years ago he wrote a very fine script that kept getting optioned and almost done—almost, but not quite. Frustrated by the near misses, my friend prayed for the faith to accept the situation and was led, a step at a time, into becoming a therapist. "But what about my writing?" he wondered, even as the steps to his new career unfurled smoothly before him—if he just found faith enough to take them. To his surprise, he did find that faith— and a deepened faith in God overall. Still a writer, he now has other sources of money and self-worth besides his writing. And as I write, his script is optioned once again.

"Once again" is an important phrase here. To have faith is to have faith in process. God is not finished with us. We are works in progress, and as much as we would like to know the end point of all the growth we are asked to undertake, we often do not see an end point—or any point at all. At any given time, we may be able to sense only a fraction of God's intention for us. Frightened by change, my friend the writer thought he could be either a writer or a therapist—God intended that he be both.

If, as it has been suggested to me, God does bring us along like fighters, then nothing we do or have done is ever wasted. "God is efficient," my friend actress-poet Julianna McCarthy tells me. Apparent detours are later revealed to be shortcuts. Take Julianna's own story. Her son, Brendan, is an estimable poet. For years, Julianna attended Brendan's poetry events, read his drafts, listened to him as he forged new work. She followed his progress with enthusiasm, little realizing that he was taking a path she herself would soon follow. And then one day she wrote a poem. "Just a little poem," but she liked it. In fact, she liked writing it very much, so much that she tried another poem and then another. Next, she tried a poetry workshop, liked that, and tried another. Before she knew it, she was working near daily at her poems, and then after that, she realized she was carrying the poems with her as part of her constant consciousness.

"You're a very fine poet," friends told her. At first she turned the compliments aside, thinking and even saying "No, Brendan is the poet." But Brendan-the-poet joined voices with the rest of her readers to say, "You can really do this." Eventually, the penny dropped. "I can really do this," she found herself thinking, and so thinking, she acted upon it. Julianna, at age seventy-five, is pursuing a master's degree in poetry.

Another friend of mine is now a filmmaker. She did not set out to be a filmmaker. She set out to help her husband, the filmmaker. In trying to assist him as he made his way, she learned the ins and outs, the trials and the difficulties, of independent films. And then one day she caught herself thinking, "Someone should make a film about that." And then, "Why 'someone'? Why not me?

"I would never have had the courage to approach film-making directly," she tells me. "I did far better to approach it obliquely, through my husband. I was comfortable playing second fiddle, and I really played it very well. It was only when a topic came up that I couldn't interest him in that I began to think, 'Wait a minute. This should be a movie.' Even then, I didn't think it should be 'my' movie. That thought came later. First I had to be convinced of the worthiness of the topic and face the sad fact that no one seemed to see it except me. I really had to be brought along very gradually. I had to think, 'If I like this idea, other people will like this idea.' I had to think, 'What a pity that no one is going to ever see this idea on film.' Then I thought, 'What the hell. Maybe I could try.'"

"Maybe I could try" was the doorway of faith. It was tentative. It was shy. It was anything but blowing its own horn. God had given my friend exactly enough courage to try, no excess for braggadocio. And so, led along indirectly, coaxed into it a step at a time, my friend moved from filmmaker's helper to filmmaker. God had brought her along like a fighter, and she was in fact ready to step gingerly into the ring.

If God is efficient, we can try to get a glimpse of just where

God's efficiency is bringing us. We may be being rendered something we admire but fear. Julianna was made a poet. My friend "the filmmaker's wife" was made a filmmaker. There are many other things we may be being rendered as well, not all of them creative or professional.

"My husband was always the one who spoke up for us," another friend of mine says ruefully. "He was the loud wheel, and if you offended 'us,' he would be the one to say something. This was true until the day that I suddenly spoke up. I had been watching his good example, admiring his courage and wishing for some of my own, and then one day I suddenly had it. I spoke up. No one was more surprised than I was."

But did she just speak up out of nowhere? I asked my friend.

"Actually, I think I had been praying for courage," she told me, laughing at herself. "At the very least, I was thinking, 'Dear God, why can't I be more like he is.'"

God answers our prayers and sometimes we only know that they have been answered when we start behaving differently, trying things that we had previously considered beyond our reach.

"Make no mistake. Prayers are answered," a minister friend of mine tells me. "People think that prayers go out into a vacuum. But they actually go out into the great receptivity that is God. If you pray for courage, you will be given courage. If you pray for nerve or daring, you will be given that. You may not get a massive dose of it. You may get just a little, enough to move forward but not so much you'd really notice, and then one day, you do notice. You see that you have been led a step at a time, first one baby step and then another, and now you are here where before you were there."

"Now you are here where before you were there"—that is a good description of how God works with us. We are not often shoved into the limelight. More often we are edged forward; we are nudged and coaxed and encouraged until we take the step out of the shadows we have been balking at. Often we see a huge step and we say, "I cannot take that" and we are right. But what we can take are the many little steps that make up the one giant step. We can take each baby step because it is "only" a baby step and we do not let ourselves think too much about where such baby steps are leading us. Taken cumulatively, baby steps work just as well as giant steps at taking us where we want to go. In fact, they may work better, since they allow us to keep our equilibrium while taking them.

Take the matter of this book. I am writing it slowly and carefully, one page at a time. I do not write "everything I know about faith." I write "a little more than I think I might know about faith." And then I write a little more than that. The "little mores" add up over time until I have not two pages or three pages, not a dozen pages, or several dozen pages, but a hundred pages, more than a hundred pages, all arrived at one page at a time, gently and cautiously.

"Gently and cautiously" is how most of us approach the matter of faith. We may see that we need it in order to go forward in our lives, but we may not know how to get it, even though we do need it. And so our first steps toward faith may be exploratory. "I wonder what it would be like to have more faith." And "I wonder if I would have more faith if . . ."

For most of us there is some small something that we would "have more faith if." We may know we would have more faith if we tried writing Morning Pages, as I do. Or we might know that walking brings us more faith. We might know that a little spiritual reading could bring us more faith. Or we might know that there is a small risk that we are avoiding because we lack faith, and we might see our way clear to mustering just enough faith to try that tiny risk. For most of us, we would have more faith if we tried to have more faith. Our need for faith is always slightly larger than the amount of faith we feel we have.

"I think faith is dead center as the issue determining the quality of our lives," one friend of mine posits. "If we have 'enough' faith, then we are willing to take 'enough' risks to respect ourselves. If we are shirking our faith, we are not taking risks and soon we feel we can't respect ourselves."

To hear my friend tell it, either we expand or we contract. There is no staying the same. When we try to stay the same, the shoe begins to pinch. We are not the size we once were, even if we are not yet the size we long to be. For most of us, the act of expansion is an act of faith. Faith requires risk. Risk requires faith. In order to be faithful, we must move beyond what feels to us like our safety zone. We must move out on faith.

The risks we are asked to take are always personal. For some people, the risks are career-oriented: making the difficult phone call, sending out the résumé, calling about the job.

For others, the interpersonal arena is where the risks lie in wait: telling a friend we find their questions intrusive, asking another friend to strive to be more prompt, offering an apology for our own brusque behavior. In the quiet of our hearts, we all know which risks are ours for the taking. We know that to take those risks requires us to summon our courage.

Courage is a side effect of faith. When we ask for more faith, we are automatically given more courage. Faith is an act of the heart, not the head. We may be able to reason our way into seeing that it is faith that we need, but we cannot reason our way into having the faith that we need. We must, instead, take leaps of faith, some of them blind. Our leaps of faith can be small, but they are very real. We must muster the courage to dial the phone, to clear our throat and to speak. There are risks that no one else can take for us. But there are also risks that we can take piggybacking on the courage of others.

In twelve-step talk, there is the sandwich call. This is where a difficult action, a risk, is sandwiched between two other calls. For example, "I am going to call and see if I can rent a small theater space" is a call made to a friend. Next comes the frightening action, the call to try to rent the space. And then, back to the friend whom I call again, saying, "I just tried to rent a small theater space."

Piggybacking in this manner, all of us are able to demonstrate more faith than we may be able to muster alone. We may call a friend or a sibling to say, "Stick me in the prayer pot. I am about to undertake X." Then we undertake X. Next, X having been undertaken for better or for worse, we then call back, "Thank you for putting me in the prayer pot. I did it!"

"I can't believe I did it!" is the often-exclaimed prayer of relief for risks undertaken. There is a pride in the exhalation. There is a sense of accomplishment. There is a feeling of job-well-done. The "I" did it is actually usually a "we" did it. Either we have piggybacked with a friend or we have piggybacked with God himself, asking for the courage to take a risk and then discovering that we do, in fact, have the necessary courage for the risk at hand.

The "risk at hand" is a good way to look for the next small step we can take in faith. We do not need to reach for something far beyond our grasp. That may strike us as too large and undoable. What we need the courage for is the very next small step, the very next small risk. We usually know just what that thing is. Asked to name it, we can. We can say to ourselves, "I know what's next and I just wish I had the courage to do it." The wish to have the courage is actually a modest prayer. Very often, we no sooner wish for courage than we find we have the courage. Our prayers are answered, even when they are almost unsaid.

"I didn't *really* pray about it," we will sometimes say, meaning that our inner heart seemed to be listened to before we had the chance to articulate its yearning with language. "I mean, I was hoping that something would happen, but I never really thought I would find the nerve. . . ."

"I never really thought I would find the nerve" is another telltale comment that tells us we have again been operating on faith. Like, "I can't believe I did it!" the phrase flags for us the fact that perhaps "I" did not do it alone. Perhaps there was a helping hand, even God's helping hand, involved. Very often we prepare the way for God to help us, and then we miss it when he does. We do the footwork of morning writing, for example, but then when our days seem to line up with more synchronicity and good humor, we forget that we invited God to have a hand in our affairs. We "just" wrote Morning Pages. We "just" took a walk. We "just" did something that improved our conscious contact with God, and then, armored by that increased contact, we took a risk that we previously couldn't take.

"I just called him," we say, as if we took an action out of the blue. We fail to give ourselves—or God—credit for the preparatory steps that led up to the fateful call.

The phrase "I just" is a flag that indicates we can look a little more closely at our behavior. Very often we will discover that we have taken many small steps before we "just" did X. Those many small steps are steps of faith. We may feel we have none but we are demonstrating some, "just" in small amounts. When we worry about lacking faith, we can remind ourselves that we do have faith, just faith in tiny increments. Those tiny increments are enough. They add up over time to large risks taken, giant steps moved forward.

Often, when we think about needing faith, we picture that we need a vast swath of it. But do we? Let us say we wish we had the faith to try a trip to France. The idea feels overwhelming to us—but we can get on the Internet and "shop" fares just to see. Knowing that there are seven fares available to us and that three fall within our price range is a step closer to Paris without really leaving our comfort zone right at home.

Through the magic of the Internet, we can use our computer to browse through Paris, a site at a time.

Our keyboards can take us to the Left Bank. We can find our way to the Louvre. We may not yet have the courage to visit the Eiffel Tower in person, but we can do it on the page. We can learn that there is a restaurant at the base of the tower and that it is most romantic to go up the tower at night as the lights of Paris sparkle below. In short, we can begin to know our way around without taking the actual risk of going. We need only enough faith to explore the possibility. Possibility has a way of gently becoming probability. We need only enough faith to be openminded. When we actually take the trip, it will be also done in small increments. We will need enough faith to book a ticket, enough faith to print out an itinerary. Eventually, to our surprise, we will find we do have enough faith to travel to France and that that faith has been given to us almost without our noticing it. *Un peu* at a time.

Faith often comes to us gently. We discover that we have it, but we don't know quite when or how it arrived. We picture its arrival as being far more dramatic than in fact it often is. Let us say that we wish for enough faith to take a master's degree in poetry. Our search for faith begins with the whim-whams of "I am not worthy." Just who *is* worthy isn't clear.

"Oh, I couldn't!" we gasp as the idea for the master's degree comes to us. But there is a part of us that realizes that we could. Then we think "I wonder what's out there?" and we begin to explore. We tell ourselves that our explorations don't mean anything, that we are just looking. But when we look, we find. We discover that there are programs that are tailored to students like ourselves, adults with work lives that cannot be neglected—although the twice-a-year residency of two weeks at a time might just be budgeted in. It's worth asking about, and when we do ask, our supervisor is surprisingly empathetic. There is a way to make it work.

Next we learn the price of the various programs, and we learn the available loans that can help us with that price. Before we realize exactly what we are up to, we have narrowed the field down to three schools that seem workable to us, and the next thing we know we are working our way through filling out the paperwork. We do have enough faith after all. It just took doing a little footwork to reveal our faith to our self. This is why we say "Faith without works is dead." We might just as well say "Faith with footwork is alive," for that is the way the scenario generally plays out for us.

Faith comes to us a day at a time. Faith comes to us a risk at a time. As each day unfolds, we are able to see the risk that faith has brought us to and whether or not we have the gumption, yet, to try taking it. Sometimes when a risk still feels too large, we will need to piggyback our faith on the faith of others. It is time to say again, "Put me in the prayer pot. I think I am going to try X." Or it is the time to say "I am calling you now, and the next call I am going to make is the call to the admissions office. Pray for me until I call you back."

Faith is contagious. We can borrow the faith of others to

support our own. It is not always easy to take a risk, but it is always far more possible if we are willing to share our risks. We can make the "sandwich call" to lower the risk of a high-risk action. We can say to a friend, "I am talking to you now and then I am going to try X, and then I am going to talk with you again. So pray for me!"

Before I go in to teach a large workshop, I often ask friends to pray for me. As I move into my work, I can feel the support that their prayers have garnered for me. Difficult presentations become easier. Lonely career actions are now shared. Part of having faith is that it makes us more independent, but another part of having faith is that it gives us the courage to be more interdependent as well.

"Thanks so much. I really felt your prayers" is a phone call I often make to thank my sister Libby or my friend Elberta, two people who often pray me through a set of creative rapids. "No problem," they frequently respond, and it is true that what felt like a problem to me myself alone often gets miniaturized into "no problem" when I take the step of sharing my risk with others.

There is no area of our life that is immune to the healing power of faith. It is not just career maneuvers that require increased faith. Often it is in the interpersonal realm that we most need help and must learn to ask for it. "Please give me the courage to talk with James," we might say about a difficult co-worker with whom we are having a conflict. Here, too, we can ask for the faith of friends to see us through. We can call and say, "I need to talk with James. Could you put me in the prayer pot so that I will be able to do it lovingly and effectively?" It takes faith to initiate a difficult conversation. It takes faith to try to work things through.

"James, I often feel that when we get into meetings, I don't get enough credit for the work I have done. I feel as though you make everything sound like your solo effort. Can we do something about this? I do not mean to be overly sensitive, but I don't want to be self-destructive either. Could you share a little more of the credit?"

James may or may not be able to be more generous. The fact that you have taken an action on your own behalf will nonetheless shore up your faith in a proper outcome. It may be that you will need the courage to speak with a supervisor and that courage, the daring to take that risk, is something that can also come to you through shared prayer.

The courage to take a risk may start out as "God, please give me the courage to try X." If we are still afraid, more prayer may be needed and perhaps the willingness to reach out to another. "Put me in the prayer pot," we may say. Or some risks may involve a sandwich call. "I am calling you now because I am afraid to call my supervisor, whom I am going to call next, and then I will call you back."

"And then I will call you back" are words of faith. Faith is not always without fear. Sometimes it is through a fear that we nonetheless have the courage to act in our own behalf. We dare a risk despite our misgivings.

"I don't want to try to talk with James. He is only going to be hostile. But I am going to try to talk with James anyway and see where that gets me. So, yes. Stick me in the prayer pot. I am going to try to catch him as we change shifts so that's about four o'clock your time, five o'clock mine!"

The net of God is farflung. Our allies are sometimes close, sometimes distant. We may be connected to likeminded souls through e-mail or on the phone. Our friends may be as close as our own family or as far away as the next hemisphere. It matters less where our friends are than that we know we do have them. One way that we discover our friends is through daring to be vulnerable to them and with them.

We may wish for faith to make us fearless and invulnerable, whereas in reality faith may render us fearful yet willing and very vulnerable. We are given what we need when we ask for help, but just what that may mean is often surprising. "I put you in my prayer pot while you were talking with James and I lit a candle for you too. Could you feel it?" The prayer shared, the candle lit, the help offered may not be felt immediately in concrete terms. What we may experience is "enough" rather than "a lot." We may have enough faith to talk with James and to tell him, as openly and gently as we can, our grievances. We may have enough faith to listen to what James has to say back. We may be able to set aside our defenses long enough to give him a hearing, and what we hear may surprise us.

"You're the one that everyone thinks of as so competent," James may shoot back. "I am barely in the room when both of us are there together. If I mention you any more, I will just be erased and I can't afford that, can I?"

Faith opens a dialogue and it takes faith to continue it.

Very often we ask for faith to start something without realizing that we will need to draw on further faith to see the
situation entirely through. This is again where prayer comes
in. "Send me more help," we can pray. And with our friends
we can say, "Keep me in the prayer pot. This is going to take
a while."

"This is going to take a while" is one of the earmarks of
growing faith. Faith unfolds through time. We need faith
over and over again, not just once in a great while. Faith must
be our constant companion. God must be a partner for us,
not merely a spiritual pinch hitter to be called in at the bottom of the ninth. By saying "This is going to take a while,"
we begin to acknowledge that life is a process and that we are
given what we need to undergo that process. "Not I but the
Father doeth the works" begins to become our lived experience. We feel the hand of God acting not only on us but also
through us. We begin to have confidence that God's power
will flow where it is needed, that we can ask to be tapped
into that power and expect that our request for power will be
honored.

Faith builds upon faith. As we ask for help and help is
given to us, we begin to be more confident that we can ask
for help and that help *will* be given to us. As we pray to God
for more help and we experience more help, there begins to
be a sense that we have an unexpected inner resource, that
God is not somewhere out there but much more imminent,
even *within*.

If God is within us, then we do not need to reach for

faith or strive for faith. It is always at hand, as close as our breath, closer. *Faith, then, becomes analogous to the working of a previously undeveloped muscle.* Faith is latent in all of us. It lies within us waiting to be developed. We develop faith by asking for it. As we reach for faith, we find it. Faith waits within us. It is the secret treasure hidden in the cave of our hearts. We are the ones who must say "Abracadabra" and swing the door open.

Faith can be reached for before we reach an emergency. Faith can be an everyday matter of simply striving to find and do God's will. For most of us, however, faith is something that we come to out of a sense of urgency. Our lives feel bankrupt and we say, "There must be something more than this." The "something more than this" is faith.

"Please give me a sense of meaning," we pray—and we are led. We are not always led easily. Many times we take step after step in the darkness. The dark night of the soul is well named. We grope for God blindly. We feel we are clutching at straws, but what we find is the hand of God—God as a spiritual experience, not a theory.

An inkling at a time, just as we asked so desperately, we are given lives that have meaning. As gently as a flower unfolds, the meaning of life unfolds within our questioning heart. Our prayer is answered, even if it feels that it is answered in foreign ways. God is subtle and comes to us unexpectedly from many different directions. Bereft and frightened, we want a light to dawn, but when it comes, it is often so gradual that we fail to realize that it is dawning. Slowly at first, and feeling at first that we are straining, we begin to make spiritual connections. In our pain, we begin to look to others, wondering if they, too, carry pain. "How do they do it?" we ask ourselves, meaning, "How do the masses that inhabit this planet manage to find a meaning to it all?"

Catalyzed by loneliness, we begin to see that we are not alone. We start to see how our lives have roots in a great interconnected life. We start to see that we are not alone, even in our questioning. Searching for a sense of meaning, we are led to humility. Our pride is leveled. We find our heads no higher than any other's. Rendered teachable, we are shown how to interrelate to one another in kindness and compassion, in ways that reinforce the benevolence that lies behind all and among all. Moved by our own personal discomfort, we begin to experience empathy for the universal discomfort that is life as it is frequently led. We see that life without a higher purpose feels devoid of meaning.

"There has to be something more," we conclude, desperately cornered by our pain. That pain springs open the inner gate. We look within ourselves and discover, waiting there, the seed of belief. Our anguished inward glance activates this seed, *seemingly automatically*. Humbled by our pain, we receive the rudiments of a spiritual awakening. Abruptly we are shown that we are a part of God and God is a part of us and that all of us are in this together. Even if only for a moment, we know this to be true. Often, how we are shown all of this is through the crucible of what might be called existential pain. Agonizingly, we suffer our anxious pangs of aloneness, and as we do, we come to realize that all beings do. That first awakening sense of "My God, we all suffer" is an awakening to the human condition. Abruptly we realize that it is a part of the human condition to hunger for connection, to strive to find that connection first with each other and later, next, with God. God, we realize, is the great matrix that holds everything together. We must rightly relate ourselves to God in order to rightly relate ourselves to anything else. Faith is no luxury. It is the cornerstone of a meaningful life. This realization is the great gift of the dark night of the soul.

If, as many have posited, God is everything, then God must be involved in every nook and cranny of our life. Our entire life must be an open book to God, an arena in which the action of God is welcome. There is no room for holding back. There is no corner for reservations, for areas of life beyond the reach of God.

Most of us, faced with the magnitude of surrender required, discover that we have pockets of inner resistance, areas of our life that we are reluctant to surrender to divine control. It may be finance. It may be romance. It can be any area in which we have an agenda and are afraid to let go.

In this regard, the suffering newly sober alcoholic has an advantage over most people. The juggernaut of self-will has already brought a rapacious form of spiritual bankruptcy. Faced with the ruin of life as he has led it, the newcomer is open-minded in spiritual endeavors. He has everything to lose if he continues to try to run his life as he has been doing. He has everything to gain by allowing God to run his life for him.

The great surrender has already been made when he faced the fact that without spiritual aid he was unable to conquer his addiction. "Either God is everything or God is nothing"—he is faced with deciding which one it is going to be. The leap of faith opens up as a welcome way out of the jaws of death and sure devastation.

Most of us are not cornered quite so neatly. We know we *should* give our lives over to God, but we wonder if we can't wriggle out of a wholehearted commitment. We wonder if we can't hedge our bets just a little. We wonder if we can't invite God in part way and part time. Surely that is better than nothing, and surely that must be enough.

It is enough.

The beauty of faith is that we can always increase our commitment. We can start by opening the door just a fraction. We can think, "I wonder what it would be like to let God into my life a little." And we can act on "a little." God is generous and God doesn't make terms too hard for those who seek him. "A little" is more than enough.

We might want to begin just by starting our day with some ritual that includes God as part of our consciousness. It might be as simple as saying, "Good morning, God," before our head leaves the pillow and we are up and about into our day. I myself use three pages of long-hand morning writing as my welcome-to-God ritual. I write exactly how I am and how I am feeling and I find that if I start off very blue and far down in the bottom of the barrel, by the time my pages are finished, my mood has lifted and I see where, with God, my day can be headed toward the good.

There are others who start their day by reading spiritual books and using the uplifting thoughts they find there to alter their own consciousness. There are those, too, who start the day with a period of meditation. Some people both read and meditate. It matters less what you do than it matters that you do something. God does not seem to be picky about the something that we choose. We can make our own choice, and in choosing to include God in our day, we find that we seem to be included in God's. Events open up to us that might otherwise have passed us by. We become braver and bolder, fueled by a power greater than ourselves. As we connect ourselves to a higher power, we find that the higher power, in turn, connects us to others. We begin to experience urges and inklings. We begin to think, "I could try . . ." And we do try.

Try is the operative word when it comes to faith. We "try" to have faith. We "try" the faith idea out a little bit. The entire notion of faith is an exercise in openmindedness, a scientific experiment in which we try and then note the result.

Many of us are afraid to try faith because we do not know quite where it will lead us. For this reason, God lets us start with the smallest possible amount. We can experiment with "the God idea" and see where that leads us. The smallest bit of experimentation often leads us to experimenting further. We try more God reliance, and when we don't meet with any baleful results, we try more still.

For many of us the notion of any dependency at all is distasteful. We have seen too many examples of wrongful dependency. We have seen people who are overly dependent on others—family, friends, parents, significant others—and we are resolved not to be like them. We can see clearly how their overdependency has warped their personalities and robbed them of dignity and autonomy. We don't want to be anything like them. Not to be too flippant, the word *soul* implies *solo*. Rather than using our connection to other people or even to our job as a crutch, we want to be free agents, able to move freely in the world. Where does this put us in regard to the idea of faith?

The truth is that reliance upon God renders us far more independent. Reliant upon God and God alone, we are freed from overreliance on people and institutions that may harm us. In the Alcoholics Anonymous Big Book, God is referred to as the "new Employer." This is a handy way to think of the relationship. Our job is to serve our Employer, to be the best employee possible. Why does this rankle with some of us? Why is it that being subject to God's dominion seems so distasteful to us? It is at least in part due to our assessment of the world's affairs, which we tend to blame on God and not on the human misuse of free will. We simply do not feel we can trust God. There are too many warring nations in the name of God. We are wary of aligning ourselves with religion's abuses. We want to seek God, but we want to seek God on our terms. Fair enough. God seems to take us on whatever terms we come.

If God takes us on any terms, why even talk about such absolutes as turning our will and our life over to God? God allows us to approach at our own speed and distance. Once we have arrived, however, once we have actually made conscious contact with God, we ourselves begin to crave more. We ourselves begin to sense that half measures avail us half measures. We start to hunger for a deeper and more full-bodied commitment. Like lovers, we want to go all the way.

What does it mean to "go all the way" with God? It means that our relationship to God deepens and becomes passionate. It means that we, like all lovers, surrender control. We are willing to be taken where the tide of the relationship moves us.

But how many of us are ready to abandon ourselves "utterly." It takes courage to make such a surrender, and without the courage born of desperation, many of us balk. What will become of us we wonder if we give our lives utterly to God. We often have images of what a godly life means, and very often it means giving up things that we hold dear. We may have many ideas about God that say "God does not do business," and so there goes our career. Or we may believe "God does not do sex," and therefore there goes our love life. Very often our idea of God is otherworldly. We think of God as a monkish sort, disapproving of our involvement in the world. In short, we forget that God made the world and that nothing in it is really foreign to God. We forget that God is worldly.

God does do finances. In fact, turning our finances over to God's care has often been a route not to poverty but to prosperity. God is an expert at husbanding resources. God is an expert at increasing the worth of what we hold. To involve God with our finances is to ask the source of all abundance to have a hand in our affairs. This is not folly. This is wisdom. But how seldom do we see it that way. For many of us money is somehow "dirty" and not something we think God can attend to. We think that ambition is something to be ashamed of, a secret that we can keep from God. We forget that there is no secret that we can successfully keep from God. God knows our worldly dreams and desires. Is it possible that God can help us to have them? That seems too good to be true. Instead, we act as if any success that we may have achieved has somehow been achieved behind God's back and that the last thing we want to do is draw God's attention to our finances. Our finances are nearly as secret as our sexuality. Most people have a hard time talking about God and money or God and sex. There is God, and then there is the rest of it. But where did the rest of it come from, if not also from God?

God created sexuality. Our sexual natures are a part of God's design for us. God does not intend us to be celibate, long-suffering, frustrated. To think of God as antisexual is to think of God erroneously. And yet we are often certain that it is God's will for us to be alone and asexual. We are reluctant to turn our love life over to God's care for fear that God just won't want us to have one. Rather than believe that divine guidance could go a long way toward straightening out our tangled affairs, we tend to want to keep God out of this arena. We tend to think that God's plans for us here are bound to be punitive and not any agenda we could go along with. Rather than say to God, "Lead me here. Direct me to my best match," we often unconsciously pray, "God, in this area, let me go it alone. Thanks but no thanks on any input here." We do not want God to know who it is we'd like to go to bed with. For that matter, we do not want God to know that we'd like to go to bed at all. Somehow we think that in order to be spiritual, we should be above and beyond all of that. We believe that God is above and beyond all that, and we don't really want to show him any dirty laundry lest it get us on his wrong side. And so we lie by omission. We just don't mention sex in our relationship with God.

"What God doesn't know, can't hurt us," we seem to reason. And we strive to keep God in the dark about the very areas where we probably could use the most support and guidance. Who couldn't use more financial security? Who couldn't use an improved love life? And yet it is radical for most of us to really think that we can have faith in God in these arenas. Rather than try, we shrink back.

Shrinking back from God, we begin to harbor secrets. We have our reservations about God—based on our feeling that God would have reservations about us. We treat God in a second-class way because we are sure that to God we are second-class citizens. We lack the self-worth to see how it is that we can really have an open relationship with God. Openness implies honesty, and honesty requires a certain amount of self-respect.

For many of us, that necessary amount of self-respect is hard to muster. Without meaning to do it, we sell ourselves short and we sell God short. We deny ourselves the comfort of true intimacy. We are saying, in effect, it takes too much faith to have faith. Rather than risk a rejection by God, we hedge our bets and go to God on only those matters where we feel it is appropriate. And our notions of what is appropriate for God may be pretty narrow.

"I've spent the past several years counting God out," Curt says. "When my life was a complete basket case, I was good at letting God step in and take over. I was desperate. My life was a wreck. I had no real alternative. Then, as my life began to come together—and it was coming together because of my letting God run it—I began to edge God out. I began to try to force my will on situations. I could see what I wanted, and I wanted to have it whether God wanted me to or not. I began to try forcing square pegs into round holes. Let me tell you, the wood went flying. I was determined! I was also pretty sad. I have been pretty sad for several years now. I was much more comfortable in the days when I let God run things."

Curt is a sober member of Alcoholics Anonymous, and he is trained by his program in the art of self-inventory. "I have seventeen years of sobriety," he says, "and a number of those years were pretty comfortable. When I am willing to let God run the show, I am not filled with fear. I am not demanding something I may not get or holding on ferociously to something I have already got. But somehow, as my life began to work better and better, I began to want the reins back. I met this woman I really liked. I couldn't let God decide for me whether or not I got to be with her, could I? I also had a job opportunity that seemed too big and glorious to let pass by. I grabbed for it. I was frantic that I might not get it. I couldn't remain detached and say, 'Thy will be done.' I wanted that job!"

Wanting who and what he wanted, unwilling to see if God wanted him to have these same things, Curt edged God out in both the arenas of romance and finance. "A day at a time, I got more and more uncomfortable. Instead of letting go and letting God deliver to me what God chose, I held on tighter and tighter. I made the job my higher power. My relationship to it gave me my worth and my dignity. I made the woman I loved into my higher power. Instead of seeing her as a gift God had given to me, I saw her as the end in itself. I had to marry her. I had to 'have' her for myself alone. Naturally, this didn't work out too well. She could tell I was desperate. I tried to hide my desperation behind a façade of nonchalance, but then I was just being a phony and that didn't get me anywhere either."

Curt got both the woman and the job, but he found himself wanting a way to "give back" both of these things and to once again let God run the show. "Face it. My clutching at things had not made me happy. I needed to find a way to get back to God and to ask God to take over my life for me. I didn't want to drink again and I knew that too much misery could head me straight back toward a drink. I needed to find a way, without drinking again, to become utterly willing to have God run the show. I was a case of self-will run riot, and I needed to change that if I was to stay comfortably sober."

What Curt is talking about with his phrase "comfortably sober" is what many members of Alcoholics Anonymous define as "emotional sobriety." Emotional sobriety could be defined as the state of being comfortably ensconced in God's will, not wanting to run the show ourselves. When we are emotionally sober, we are willing, one day at a time, to let life unfold for us. We are willing to see what God has in store for us. We are less inclined to push the river or, in Curt's phrase, to try to drive square pegs into round holes. "Thy will be done" becomes a prescription for adventure. We are willing to let God control the ebb and flow of our life. God will put people in where needed. God will take people out where needed. God will give us meaningful work and God will move us on to other work when that is what is called for. In all arenas, including romance and finance, we allow God to call the shots.

"I have been reading the AA Big Book again," Curt says. "I have been trying to nudge myself toward the proper steps. I have read the description written here so brilliantly by the first sober alcoholics, and I see that I want the life they are talking about. Long-term sobriety doesn't mean much without emotional sobriety as well. Unless I am careful, I can become nearly as crazy a 'dry drunk' as I ever was crazed while I was drinking. I want to surrender my life back to God and let God run it for me. I am hungry for the quality of life that I enjoy when I let God run the show."

Notice that Curt is not saying that he wants to abdicate his life. He still wants to be a full participant but on God's terms. Not his own. He is back to wanting God to be the Principal, the Director, the Father, the new Employer. He is back to wanting to take a role in life that is as God dictates it and not as he himself wills it. Curt is lucky. He is reaching for surrender without reaching for a drink. He is voluntarily groping his way toward humility rather than holding on to his own "dignity" which is the ego's way of justifying a hard and fast position it is unwilling to relinquish.

"I want to give it all back to God," Curt says. "Without God in charge, the job is too much for me. The marriage is too hard for me. I can't really handle any of it, even though it is all exactly what I said I wanted."

Very often, when we get "exactly what I said I wanted," we need God more than ever. We now have something we really cherish, and our tendency is to want to hold on to it too tightly. This is when we need the faith to "let go and let God." We need to be able to allow God to control our lives and to participate in our lives rather than run them.

"I can see that my relationship to God has to come before everything else," Curt says. "I need to place my relationship to God before the marriage and before the prestigious job. If my relationship to God is right, my relationship to everything else will fall into its proper place. If my relationship to God is faulty, I will have faulty relationships and dependencies." Curt speaks from bitter personal experience. His tone is rueful and chastened. He has had his turn in the barrel, trying to run the show.

God dependency corrects all other faulty dependencies. God keeps us right-size and allows us to go through the ebb and flow of our work day without overreacting. We are able to see our co-workers as separate and equal. We treat them with dignity, and we behave with dignity ourselves. God is our source. We remember that, and it draws everything to scale. We are able to see our true employer as God and our boss as a stand-in. We perform our work well because that is doing God's will for us. We do the best we can and let the chips fall where they may.

God allows us, too, detachment in our love relationships so that every shift of our partner's mood is not an indictment of our lovability. As our relationship comes to include God, the ebb and flow of personalities becomes far less personal. We lead our life each day in relationship first to God and then to our partner. We treat our partner with loving courtesy, but those attributes are grounded in our relationship to God. Secure in God, we turn less to our human companions to supply something they are not able to supply. God is the source of our emotional security. That established, we are able to love others with a less-demanding neediness. This is attractive to people. We have an inner compass, a personal gravitational field that circles us back, always, to God. Our partners may love us, but they cannot supplant God for us. We may love our partners, but we cannot supplant God for them. When this is clearly understood, when God is the primary relationship and all others, however cherished, are secondary, then we begin to have right dependency. "Thy will be done" we pray, and we include our relationships within the range of the prayer.

The range of our prayers to God is in direct ratio, always, to our willingness to have God be central. As we move ourselves out of the center of our consciousness, as we move God toward center, we begin to experience a new openness with God and, as a result, a new freedom and a new happiness.

We experience the transformative power of God. We do not regret the past or wish to shut the door on it. We see how God can use our experiences to benefit ourselves and others. This brings us to a great mystery.

When we turn our will and our life over to the care of God, we begin to experience the "care" of God. With a tender solicitude, God reaches into our past, transforming its wounds and wreckage. Many things we deeply regret and feel certain cannot be changed *are* changed by the grace of God touching them. Miraculously, God has the power to act not only in the present and the future but also in the past. God's healing is not bound by time. As we watch with wonder, old relationships are gently repaired. New understandings are reached. Where once there was only ruin, we are given the opportunity to mend broken relationships and forge new ones. We see that the care of God embodies a gentleness and tact that we can only marvel at: "Let everything that breathes praise the Lord! Praise the Lord!"

When we turn our will and our life over to the care of God, we are putting ourselves in right relationship to the Universe. The jagged edge of our self-will is blunted. Where before we were almost always on a collision course with something or somebody, now we are coming into accord. Before, we had tried to live by self-propulsion. If only people would do as we wanted, everything would be great! Now we are less interested in the behaviors of others. We are more interested in seeing that our own behavior is in accord with what we take to be God's will for us. We release others to their destiny.

When we release people to God's will for them and stop forcing agendas of our own, people feel it. They are often surprised. Our coercion had often been subtle but palpable. Now we truly are giving more than lip service to the notion of free will. "You are free to behave exactly as you choose"—our new attitude permeates the air. Where before we sought to wrest happiness and satisfaction from people by their doing as we saw fit, now we are coming to them open and vulnerable. We are dependent on God for our happiness and satisfaction. People can do as they please.

Freed from our agendas for them, people often surprise us by behaving with great generosity. No longer resentful of the subtle and not so subtle forms of coercion that we indulged in, people approach us with a new candor. We are able to meet them with a new openness as well. God is doing for us what we were unable to do for ourselves. God is forging relationships that are based on equality and respect, on dignity and autonomy. In our hearts, these are the bonds that we always hungered for but that always seemed to elude us. As we move toward God in good faith, good faith extends into the realm of our relationships. We begin to experience the heady excitement of seeing people as they truly are and not as we "need" them to be to fulfill our agendas. No longer merely ingredients in our self-willed recipe for happiness, people are exuberantly, magnificently, themselves. Seeing them in all their glory, freed from the cloak of our projections, we experience other people as far more genuinely lovable. They experience us that way as well.

Janice and Mitchell are a married couple in the throes of reevaluating their relationship. For thirty-five years they have been together in every format imaginable. They have lived together and they have lived separately. They have had outside lovers and they have had monogamy. They were together as unmarried hippies when their daughter was born. They share a daughter and now a grandchild. They have been legally married a half dozen years now, and always Mitchell has had the compulsion to cheat on Janice. For her part, Janice has had the compulsion to stay with him and to force him to stop cheating. A staunch Buddhist, she has prayed, chanted, *willed him in every possible way to do as she wished.* Mitchell has resisted all of her persuasion, all of her coercion, all of her righteous anger and her pain. She has sought to control him and he has sought freedom from control. Their exhausted friends have counseled divorce, but Janice and Mitchell are not ready for divorce. They are addicted to the dance that they are doing together: bad, bad Mitchell; virtuous, long-suffering Janice. There seemed to be no way out of their dance short of death, and even then one imagined that the dance could somehow go on. *Enter God.*

Long familiar with twelve-step programs, Janice and Mitchell were unexpectedly told of a new one, "Couples in Recovery." In this program, each partner made a commitment to put God first, ahead of the relationship. Each partner was asked to release their partner to the care of God and to focus on their own behaviors. For Mitchell and Janice, long used to focusing on each other, this was radical stuff. Put God first? How could they? Their tortured relationship had been the deity before which they offered all of their prayers. Dubiously, little expecting much change, both Mitchell and Janice committed to put God first and their relationship second. Immediately, they both experienced an inrush of freedom and self-respect. With God in first place and their relationship in second, they found that a new candor and openness was suddenly possible.

"We are communicating in a way that we have never managed before," Janice reports to me. "We are able to actually talk, and this is miraculous. Always before, the whole emphasis was on 'Why won't you do what I want?'"

While it is still too early to predict the eventual outcome of their new rapport, Janice and Mitchell are experiencing the sense of wondrous freedom that comes when God is in charge. They are telling each other the truth and allowing the chips to fall where they may. To their surprise, they are experiencing a great deal of sympathy for each other. They are able to see each other's viewpoint and to move away from previously frozen positions.

"We have never talked the way we are talking now," Janice confides. "Before, we were always feeling that we had to say what the other one wanted to hear. No wonder Mitchell felt so trapped with me. There was no room for us to think about whether or not we just plain liked and enjoyed each other. It was all about duty and who was right and who was wrong. Now, with both of us trying to put God first, we find we have a lot of common ground. We are discovering that we just plain like each other and that may have been the invisible glue that held us together through thick and thin. We are beginning to see that it wasn't just pathology and codependency. There was a genuine affection for each other that had gotten lost in the shuffle. With God in charge, our affection for each other begins to be obvious again. We are laughing a lot, and, believe me, for a long time laughter had been absent."

The presence of laughter and lightheartedness is a sure indication that Janice and Mitchell are operating within God's will. When we are aligned with God, our heart does lighten and we do experience the humor that is present in life. Freed from the pressure of trying to make life happen as we think it *should* happen, we are able to enjoy the ebb and flow of emotions and events as they *do* happen. We begin to be able to play more keys on our emotional piano than just the melancholy and dramatic ones. We begin to be able to experience the full range of responses that are part of our human nature.

When we are operating within a false idea of God and God's will, an intellectual construct of God's will, we often feel hamstrung. We are dutiful in our responses, but we are not joyful or full-hearted. We are acting as we feel we *should* act and not as our true natures dictate. In the name of spirituality, we are actually manufacturing a false form of spirituality built on a false piety and a feeling of superiority to the human condition.

When we begin to experience God more directly, less through our intellect and more through our heart, more experientially and less theoretically, we begin to have a more joyous experience. We discover we have access to a broader range of human emotions in our own responses to daily life. We feel the way we *do* feel not the way we *should* feel, and we discover that the way we do feel is acceptable to God who, after all, gave us the full range of human emotions we are now willing to undergo.

"Thy will be done" is not the mantra of a joyless life. We are not signing up for a life that boils down to one long tour of duty. "Thy will be done" has more color in it than that. God's will has a great deal of color in it. Looking at the natural world, this diversity and color should not surprise us—and yet it does. Our idea of God is shockingly drab and colorless. We act as if The Creator has only a few colors on his emotional palette and that they fall into the sensible range—dull grays, browns, maybe olive drabs.

What if God is more colorful than that? What if we look at the natural world and begin to consider the actual power and diversity of what we are dealing with. What if we begin to see that "Thy will be done" is an expansive and not a constrictive concept, what if we start to realize that God's will for us is that we get larger, not smaller?

Most of us have an idea of a dream that falls outside of the reach of what we feel we may be able to attain. We think that something we would love and desire is too grandiose for us to actually consider, too far beyond the scope of what it is we are able to have. "What we are able to have" is often dictated by a faulty God concept. We anthropomorphize God into a stingy and withholding parent. We expect that we will be given little that we want and be asked to get by on less than we actually need. None of this has anything to do with the reality of God. We do, however, tend to imagine our lives as ruled by such a despotic dictator. Our notions of God are often punitive and miserly.

What if we believe in a benevolent and expansive force? What if we consider the idea that our dreams come from God and that God has the power to accomplish them? What if our "grandiose" schemes are actually God's will for us? What if God's will is expansive and colorful and exciting? What if turning our will and our life over to God is an invitation to adventure and not to drudgery? What if God is *for* us and not *against* us?

For most of us, it is radical to consider the idea of a God that is actually on our side. We hope, at best, for a God who will turn a blind eye to our strivings and not nip them in the bud. We tend to think that if we call God's attention to our adventures and agendas, God will disapprove. We think of God as a spoilsport, a wet blanket. We ignore the evidence of the natural world that plainly shows us an exuberant intelligence committed to diversity.

We can take any category of creation and learn a great deal of The Creator through the simplest of surveys. Take dogs: Weimaraners, boxers, Jack Russells, Pomeranians, golden retrievers, Airedales, bulldogs, beagles, Irish setters, whippets, Dalmatians, black Labradors, basset hounds, Irish wolfhounds, Lhasa apsos, Rhodesian ridgebacks. We can see humor and diversity. We can see dignity and grandeur. We can see playfulness and loyalty. We can see beauty, intelligence, curiosity, stamina—more.

Just to drive home the point, let us consider another category, the flower. We have: rose, peony, tulip, lilac, lily, daffodil, aster, delphinium, dandelion, orchid, iris, violet . . . Once again we see infinite diversity and tenderness. We see sheer creative glee. Might not the same tenderness and glee carry over to the creation of humans? Might not human beings bring to God a wonderful opportunity for creation? And how much more exciting, how infinitely interesting when you consider that we, too, carry within us the potential for creation. God just might take a lively interest in our unfolding. God might be easily persuaded to aid and abet us in plans for expansion—after all, God is by nature expansive and so are we.

Perhaps when we say "Thy will be done," we are committing ourselves to a life of adventure. Perhaps God's will involves expansion and not constriction. Perhaps we will be asked over and over again to commit to becoming larger and more generous. Perhaps God views us as capable of endless growth and renewal, endless diversity and creativity. Perhaps God expects us to fulfill our fullest potential and will actually cooperate with any plans that make of ourselves that which we dream of being.

What if that which we dream of being is actually God's will for us? What if we are the ones who hold back, setting an arbitrary limit on what God's power in our life will be? What if we are the ones who decide "this is too good to be true"? What if we turn back God's gifts over and over and over again? It is possible that this is the case.

Most of us do not believe that the sky is the limit. Instead, we have a ceiling that we set, which is the height we think of as God's will for us. Do we consult God when we set this ceiling? No, we ordinarily do not. We set it with the help of parents and friends, well-meaning spouses and therapists. We try to set our ceiling at a "reasonable" height. We do not want to get our hopes up and have them dashed. We fear being too big for our britches, and so we define as grandiose many plans that may be well within our grasp with the help of God.

Unless we are careful and alert, we automatically presume God will be adversarial to our plans, not cooperative, and so we set about trying to accomplish our dreams under our own power, using our own limited resources. And what happens? Our dreams often remain beyond our grasp. For all of our trying, we are not able to wrest success from the Universe. We grow tired and very often we grow bitter. In our bitterness, quite often we blame God. We act as if it is God's fault that our dreams were not fulfilled when we never asked God for help in fulfilling them. More often we may have actively barred the door to any help from God, and yet we seldom see that. We are like angry children who would not allow God to join our game and then are angry at the game's outcome.

Anger with God often lies just under the surface of our seemingly well-ordered lives. We keep to ourselves the great secret that we are disappointed and frightened. We act as if everything is fine. We put up a façade of reasonable adult behavior, and we try to never let on that we secretly feel like heartbroken children because our dreams are unfulfilled. If we have faith in God, we have faith that God will disappoint us. This is all that we have allowed God to do, but we seldom see that. Instead, we act as if God is the one who set out to let us down.

Here we are behaving again like children. God is to know our hearts' desires and to fulfill those desires without our having to lift a finger. We want our dreams to be fulfilled, but we do not want to take the risk of articulating those dreams and we do not want to experience the vulnerability of going to God with those dreams. We want God to come to us. We want God to be like Santa Claus, a benefactor and not a partner. We do not see that in the long run such a notion of God runs counter to our own dignity. We do not want to think in terms of "the long run." What we are after is instant gratification, and we want a God that will snap to and give us, presto, that which we want but haven't even mentioned in prayer.

God does know our dreams, spoken and unspoken, but that does not mean that we are not to speak our dreams. In the act of articulating our dreams for ourselves and for God, we reach a necessary humility. We make ourselves right-size when we acknowledge that there are dreams beyond our reach that we yearn for. When we ask God to expand our lives, we acknowledge that God is an expansive power. We become as the tiny mustard seed, holding a world of potential.

A world of potential is what we have before us when we have faith. We acknowledge that "what is" now can be transformed and that there is no limit to God's capacity to enlarge and transform us. We can lead lives larger than the ones we now lead. We can depend on God to expand us and to support our expansion in concrete and practical ways. God knows our needs and has the wherewithal to fulfill them. Often we have an idea that God is airy-fairy and not practical. We act as if the worldly transactions that we must undergo in our daily march are somehow beyond God's understanding. Nothing could be further from the truth.

God is practical. God is conscious of all of our schemes, plans, and needs. God is the Great Creator and there is nothing that falls outside the realm of his attention. It is not true that banks and corporations are the highest power that we encounter. God is a notch higher than these powers and has the capacity to influence them. When we pray to the Great Creator for guidance, we are talking to someone sophisticated and complex, someone well able to deal with modern life with all its twists and turns. We are not naïve. We are not gullible. God is not simply for the simpleminded.

God is for all of us and for all of our most complex transactions. Dependency upon God is not childish. It is child-like—and we all know how quickly children can grow and transform. When we make ourselves childlike in relation to God, we open ourselves to similar growth and transformation. It is a paradox, but in striving to become as little children, we also become more fully adult. We open ourselves up to the root word *response* in the word *responsible*.

Operating with a childlike faith, we respond to events around us. We do not go numb with denial. Instead, we take in the ramifications of events as they unfold, and we humbly ask the Great Creator's help in dealing with them. We are given that help upon request. This means that we behave in ways that are adult and mature. We do not shirk or shrink back from the implied responsibilities of our lives. We allow God to be manifest in all corners of our experience.

Opening ourselves fully to God, we move through the world without the easing of our defenses. We no longer need our defenses. God is our defense. God in action is what people encounter when they intersect with our life. The experience may mystify them, for God transforms those with whom we interact. "I don't know why I am suggesting this," they may say, "but it occurs to me that we could try. . . ."

There is a new openness and flexibility to human relationships. God is the great balm. Perceived differences are set aside as the Great Creator works to make us a harmonious whole. "Truly I direct my steps by all your precepts," we are told in Psalms 119:128 and we may find that God is the Great Director, easing difficulties that seemed insurmountable.

"God is our refuge and strength, a very present help in trouble" we are told in Psalms 46:1. This tells us that God is pragmatic. God is grounded. God is something that is workable if we will but try working the God idea out. It falls to us to be open to God. It falls to us to pick up the tools of faith and try to build with them. When we say that faith without works is dead, we are saying that faith is better put in practice than kept in theory.

Angela is a young actress. She depends upon her talents and upon God to manifest her talents. She is faced daily with the odds against her success. She ignores the odds by casting her dependency upon God.

"I just try to do the next right thing," Angela says. "I may not be able to see the big picture, but I can almost always see the smaller one and see where, if I have the faith, I can take a step forward. I try to take a step forward, even a very small one, every day."

When Angela takes her small steps in faith, God is free to take larger ones. She and God are moving in the same direction, and their wills are in alignment. "I try to sense if what I am doing next is 'right' for me," Angela says. "I try to keep in mind the prayer 'This or something better,' so that I am open to God's will being different from what I am able to see myself. I have what I think of as the three-knock rule. If I want something, I will knock on the door three times to try to get it. If, by the third time, the door doesn't open, then I will assume it is not God's will for me and that there is something else, something better, that God has in mind for me."

Angela's "three-knock rule" is a handy way of trying to keep our will in alignment with God's. It is a checkpoint for Angela to correct any self-will, if she finds herself with her heart set on an agenda that may not be in God's plans for her.

"Sometimes I will say to myself, maybe God doesn't intend me to be an actor," Angela says. "But always, just as I am about to give up, another door will open, and I will walk through it. So far, the message that I am getting is that God does intend for me to act. I also think that there are other things God intends for me, and if I am openminded, I get a glimpse of those things as well. Take directing. The times that I have tried directing, the doors have flown open for me. This tells me that it is something that God intends for me to be doing and so, even though I feel intimidated by the degree of responsibility that it entails, I am meant to show up and try it—and so I do. I find that God seems to plan for me to be bigger than I think I am, and I have to bear in mind as I try to become bigger that it was actually God's idea, not just mine."

Many times when we pray for knowledge of God's will for us and the power to carry it out, a notion will come to us that seems too large to be carried out. We will strive to know the next right thing, and we will be shown something that seems beyond our grasp until we try it. The "until we try it" part is the measure of our willingness. Very often we pray for knowledge of God's will, get a glimmering of something we could try, and then shrink back. "Not that! That's too much!" we think. But is it too much?

God has unlimited resources. When we are in alliance with God, working in conscious partnership with God, those resources become our own. Many things that seemed beyond our grasp are actually well within our means when we begin to operate in accord with God's will for us. All we have to do is be openminded enough to cooperate.

Claudia is an aspiring playwright. She worries that she has no representation for her plays and that she is not doing things properly, "by the books." She has tried to get representation, but all her efforts have always fallen short. Agents have admired her plays, but for one reason or another they have been unable to take her aboard as a client. Meanwhile, without an agent, Claudia's plays have attracted the attention of two estimable directors. She has been awarded prestigious readings at good venues. She has moved steadily ahead in visibility and credibility. None of her progress has looked the way it *should* look. It has all been the inky finger of God and not what is written in the how-to-get-ahead books on her craft.

"But I need an agent!" Claudia sometimes thinks in panic, and then she catches herself thinking, "Maybe I don't need an agent. Maybe God is doing for me exactly what an agent would be doing for me. Maybe, for right now, God is my literary agent and a darned good one."

If it is God's will for Claudia to be recognized as a playwright, no small thing like the lack of an agent will stand in the way. God is all-powerful. That power extends into the world of theater. Where there is a will, there is a way, and where there is God's will, there are a million ways.

"Let me tell you how I came to the attention of one prestigious director," Claudia recalls. "Our introduction came through an old theater teacher of mine, a man now in his eighties. I got in touch with him through our college alumni group, and he said, when he heard I was writing plays, 'Why, you must contact X.' X was a highly touted director I had gone through college with but not seen since. I would never have had the nerve to call him if it weren't for my old professor saying that I should. When I did call, X the director remembered me from our long ago undergraduate days. He was delighted to hear from me, asked what I was up to, and when I told him I was writing, he said he wanted to read whatever it was I was up to right away. I was flabbergasted and intimidated, but I sent my work over to him. He read my work and he liked it. Before I knew what had happened, we were collaborating together on a new project."

With God as our primary collaborator, the door to all other collaborators is ajar. God is able to make introductions for us that we would not dream of. God truly is all-powerful, and as we begin to trust this, we get more and more of an opportunity to see this at play.

Alan is a writer who has long worked successfully in books, television, and film. An idealist, he has long wished that his scripts of social activism could be a reality. "I can write how it should be, but that doesn't mean I can get people to do what they should," Alan says ruefully. He dreams of making a large change in the way people think and of their waking up to the potential within them, courtesy of reading one of his "wake-up-call manuscripts."

"I see society and I see shifts that we could make as a people. I see that there are whole arenas where we are sleeping and causing great harm by our lack of awareness. I write in order to alter people's awareness. I am hoping to make a difference."

Used to being frustrated, Alan was shocked recently when one of his science-fiction scripts became the actual blueprint for some scientists seeking to make social change. "I wrote what I thought of as a dream scenario. I invented scientists who were openminded and willing to tackle large issues— little did I suspect I would actually meet them."

Alan wrote a script in which the scientists he described were able to see themselves. They called Alan to prestigious Los Alamos Laboratory in New Mexico to discuss how they could make his blueprint work as a part of reality. Alan was shocked. His ideas were being taken to heart—and by the very people that he had long hoped to reach.

"I had to pinch myself," Alan says. "I had to get a grip on myself and say to myself, 'Alan, this is real.' The men I was meeting were the men I had always hoped to meet, although I barely believed that they existed. I made up a prototype, the scientist as humanist, and they came along and filled in the outline of what I had written. The political actions that I outlined in the script were actions that they felt ready to take. I found myself and my ideas being taken far more seriously than I ever imagined possible. It seemed like the hand of God—and I suppose it was—getting my script to the precise right people who could actually actualize some of its ideas."

Alan now commutes from his home in Hollywood to Los Alamos Laboratory. Instead of just toiling alone at his computer, he works with think tanks that support his political views. He is taken seriously as a thinker and as an artist—an outcome that seemed far beyond his reach as he sat at the computer keys "hatching" a storyline that seemed beyond possibility. We are told in Psalms 85:12–13, "The Lord will give what is good. . . . Righteousness will go before him, and will make a path for his steps."

Alan found a path for his steps and he has followed it now for two years. During that time, he has shifted his identity from writer to political consultant, and he is able to watch with satisfaction as the societal changes that he is proposing begin to nudge their way toward reality.

"God is practical," Alan says now. "I was a pie-in-the-sky dreamer and God moved my dreams into the realm of the possible. For this I am deeply grateful. I love my life now and the feeling that what I think and see can actually make a practical change. I have God to thank for moving my ideas out of the realm of theory and into the realm of practice. Left to my own devices, I think I would have written forever and never stepped forward to implement my ideas on the real plane. That wasn't good enough for God, and I am grateful that it wasn't. I cannot tell you the degree of self-respect I feel now that I am actually working to implement what I see."

"Faith without works is dead," and what Alan now experiences is a living faith.

"God called my bluff." Alan laughs. "God took me seriously, more seriously than I took myself."

God does take us seriously and often far more seriously than we take ourselves. God is all-powerful and many plans that seem pie in the sky to us, from God's perspective appear quite doable. Like Alan, we may be called upon to step up to the plate. We may think that we are in the realm of theory, whereas to God's eye we are well within the realm of practice. Nothing is impossible to God, and God may indeed look to us to dare to dream so that God's plans can move forward. God may dream through us, counting on us to be conduits for a larger and higher plan than we may imagine.

"Let your light shine before others, so that they may see your good works and give glory to your Father in heaven," we are told in Matthew 5:16. In order for the power of God to be made manifest in this world, we must cooperate. We must open ourselves to God and give him an arena in which to operate. There is no area of human life that is beyond the reach of God, but we are the tools by which God reaches into human endeavors. When we refuse to be tools for God's will, the higher plan is temporarily stymied. We must open ourselves to being useful. When we are useful, we are used, and it is in being used that many of us find our deepest fulfillment.

"I don't want to be used," the rebel in us may say. "I want God to be useful to me, not vice versa."

It is one of the ironies of the spiritual life that as we are most deeply useful to God, God is most deeply useful to us. Take Alan, who had no plan of being genuinely of service. Now that he is actively working in real-life political arenas, he can see the shortsightedness of his previous position.

"I was settling for half measures," Alan tells me. "I was telling myself it was good enough to contemplate change when in my heart what I longed for was the power to accomplish it."

Alan's desire to actually move in the real world was a desire that he kept hidden even from himself. It was the wisdom of God that uncovered that desire in Alan and invited him to act upon it. Often, our deepest dream is an unspoken dream. We are unable to articulate it for fear that we are asking too much. God, listening with ears of the heart, is able to hear our unspoken prayer. Hearing this soul prayer and acting on it, God often seems to catch us by surprise. We do not expect to be taken as seriously as God seems to be taking us. When the Universe opens a door or two for us, we shy away.

Jules is a composer who has been at work for five years on an opera concerning a great explorer. He has heard glorious music in his head, and he has labored to put that music on the page. Working alone, he has managed to wrest from the heavens a large and beautiful work. Out of nowhere, or so it seemed, he was offered the opportunity to put his opera forward. He was offered singers and a marvelous musical director—all available to serve his vision.

"God caught me completely off guard," Jules says ruefully. "I was used to laboring alone and thinking about how steeply the odds were stacked against me. It never occurred to me that there might be someone as eager to see what I was writing as I was to write it. What happened was that we met through mutual friends, a little bit of cultural matchmaking. When the musical director said he wanted to move forward with my opera, I thought, 'Wait! There must be some mistake!' But there was no mistake. The musical director told me he had been praying to be guided to a large new piece of work that he could help introduce into the world. He had a genuine calling to help people such as myself. All that remained was for me to be willing to let myself be helped."

To his consternation, Jules discovered he had a great deal of inner resistance to letting himself be helped. Every time the musical director made a suggestion, Jules immediately came up with several "good" reasons why the suggestion would not work.

"I had to laugh at myself," Jules says. "I was the worst collaborator you could imagine. He would suggest we go north and I would stubbornly think, 'No, we must go south!' Fortunately, I had friends who could see my resistance as exactly that—resistance. They practically had to muzzle me so that I wouldn't blow things out of proportion. With the help of my friends, I learned to say 'Yes' and to go along with the flow of the work as it was intended to unfold. I practically needed a broom to sweep myself out of the way. The funny thing was that what I was being offered was truly an answered prayer, just a prayer I had been too cowardly to articulate. When I look at it now, I see that I was tempting God all along. I was ready for the proof that there was no friendly God. That all of my work was in vain. When it turned out not to be in vain, I almost felt God was expecting too much of me."

For many of us, the answering of a prayer feels as if God is expecting too much of us. It is too good to be true, and if we are not careful, we will work to make certain that that is so. When Alan got his first phone call from a legitimate scientist interested in his ideas, he almost didn't call the man back. When Jules got his phone call from the musical director, he found himself being curt and abrupt. "If there was such a thing as a charm school, I acted like I had attended its opposite," he recalls. "Here was this famous man calling me, and I was acting like it was a big imposition to take the time out to talk with him."

Fortunately for Jules, the musical director was quite seasoned. He knew the vagaries of the creative temperament and he was able to weather Jules's apparent indifference.

"Luckily for me, he knew it was just a defense." Jules laughs now. "I was really a jerk, and I am very lucky that the man I was dealing with had dealt with other timid artists before me. He knew that my arrogance was just a mask. He knew it before I did, and he was able to act in a way that was so even-tempered and reasonable that eventually I calmed down. When I did calm down, I saw what he was offering me as a miracle. I wonder how many miracles are scuttled at the last minute by people like me?"

Jules asks a good question. Very often when God delivers a miracle, we look the gift horse in the mouth and pat it on the rump to get it out of our lives. "It was too good to be true," we tell ourselves—but was it? All too often we are the ones who determine what is too good to be true, and we may set the limit far lower than God would. "I sought the Lord, and he answered me, and delivered me from all my fears," we are told in Psalms 34:4, but often, when something good is happening to us and we are seized by the fear that it is too good, we do not seek the Lord. Rather than go to God asking for the acceptance of the good things that are coming to pass, we withdraw into ourselves, rehearsing our fears and taking them for reality.

"When the musical director took an interest in my opera, I didn't say a prayer of gratitude," Jules recalls. "In fact, I stopped praying altogether. I just went into fear and I guess that fear was first of all that I wasn't good enough and, second, that somehow the help I was being offered wasn't good enough. In other words, something had to be wrong, with me or with him. It simply seemed beyond the realm of the possible that everything was unfolding exactly as it should have been."

But perhaps everything does unfold exactly as it should—if only we will let it. If we just stand aside, maybe the words of the psalmist are true: "You bestow upon him blessings forever; you make him glad with the joy of your presence." Perhaps there really are, as Joseph Campbell assured us, "a thousand unseen helping hands" that rush to the fore the moment we begin, as he advised, to "follow your bliss." In order to find out, we have to follow the route that Campbell has suggested. We have to begin to follow our bliss. This isn't as easy as it sounds.

It takes courage to follow our bliss. We must first convince ourselves that it is permissible. We must have the faith that our will and God's will can coincide, that doing what we wish and pursuing what we love is all right with God, not counter to his intentions for us. We may discover that we unconsciously believe in a God concept that is lethal to our happiness. We may believe in a stingy God or a capricious God. We may believe in an Indian giver God who dangles the prize before us only to snatch it away. We must sometimes do a little sleuthing to see exactly what kind of God we believe in and whether that God also believes in us. The results of our sleuthing may surprise us.

"I believed in God," Jules reveals, "but I didn't believe that God believed in me. God could work miracles but not where I was concerned. There, I expected the worst. I expected to be teased and then disappointed. God was sadistic and I was God's victim. I am not sure where I got this concept, but I had it. Believing this, no good could come to pass for me. I would sabotage it to make it match my beliefs and expectations. I had to realize that I was putting a limit on God by not allowing God to work on me and through me. That was an eye-opener. I thought that God was all-powerful, and yet when it came to helping me with my career, I thought God had better things to do.

"To be specific, when the music director said he felt my opera tackled important themes and deserved to be heard, I simply couldn't accept that someone as important as he was taking a genuine interest in the work I had done. It seemed too good to be true, and yet all the time I was working away in isolation, I had told myself the work was important. My low self-worth almost sabotaged my project. I had to pray to be openminded and not self-destructive. I had to pray, 'Thy will be done and keep me out of the way!'"

"Clap your hands, all you peoples; shout to God with loud songs of joy. For the Lord, the Most High, is awesome," declares Psalms 47:1–2. Instead of hearing it as exaggerated, we need to take this advice to heart. We do need to be able to rejoice with God. We do need to be able to shout with joy. Many of us are far too emotionally guarded to actually be able to do so. We carry ourselves as though braced for the worst. We are ready to be good sports about God's will for us, but we are not ready to really revel in the joy of what God is unfolding for us. We are prepared to accept the negative but not the positive. The positive sends us reeling. We feel out of our depth, but are we?

Perhaps, with a little help from God, we can become accustomed to God's generosity. Perhaps we can become accustomed to God's will and our will coinciding. It's worth trying. We need to remain calm and centered as great good comes to us. We need to respond to life with a spirit of exuberance. We need to anticipate and accept the new opportunities that await us. We need to stay as close to God in times of joy as we do in times of sorrow. We need to pray with the words of Psalms 3:3, "You, O Lord, are a shield around me."

If God is a shield around us, God can keep us from deconstructing our good. It is a little like altitude adjustment. The goodness of God's will for us takes getting used to. When good things first start to happen, we can fear suddenly that they will stop. Rather than rejoicing in our newfound good, we can fear losing it. For example, after months of looking, we get the ideal apartment and worry suddenly that God will not help us any longer with making the money to pay the rent. Out of nowhere, we are believing in an Indian giver God, one who delights in hurting us. We are waiting for the other shoe to drop and for the goodness that we have experienced to prove itself temporary and a lie. We do not expect that God will continue to support us. We are worried, unconsciously, about being too big for our britches and we are expecting God, like a punitive parent, to take us down a peg. Something is too good to be true, and we just "know" it. And why do we know it?

One more time, our poisonous creation myth is having its way with us. We are convinced that we have reached for the apple somehow and that God, a jealous and vengeful God, is about to expel us from Paradise. And do we ask God if this is God's intention? No. We keep our fears to ourselves—right where we are keeping our prayers. Faced with the goodness of God, we often find ourselves going numb, fearing the worst and expecting it at any moment. The kinder God is to us, the more we expect a trick. God is suddenly the enemy. Is it any wonder we may cease trying to pray?

As we are moved higher, closer to our dreams and goals, we must move closer to God. We must ask God to give us the grace to go along with divine will unfolding. This means we must pray to be able to pray. "I will sing praises to my God all my life long," Psalms 146:2 instructs us. To take this guidance to heart, we must learn how to pray in good times as well as bad.

As I have mentioned, I have a friend who says that God brings us along like fighters. This means that no good comes to us before we are ready to receive it. We are able, with God's help, to accept God's help. Listen to Scripture on this very point. "Very truly, I tell you, the Son can do nothing on his own, but only what he sees the Father doing; for whatever the Father does, the Son does likewise. . . . He will show him greater works than these" (John 5:19–20).

"The greater works than these" can come in many forms. It may be a new apartment, a new job, a fine and sustaining relationship. Whatever the form God's good takes, it is up to us to accept it, and to do so we must be openminded. The Psalms tell us, "Truly I direct my steps by all your precepts," and we must do precisely that. When God shows an intention to expand us, we must be obedient to that intention. As God moves to expand us, we must allow ourselves to be expanded. As God brings us blessings, we must allow ourselves to be blessed. We must accept the goodness that God intends for us. We must not turn aside the generosity that God bears on our behalf. We are told by Deuteronomy 31:6, "It is the Lord your God who goes with you; he will not fail you or forsake you."

What could be more clear? Despite our fears, God is no Indian giver. God is with us always and not less so when he is abundant to us. This is a promise, one of many promises that Scripture makes to us. We must be openminded enough to accept the promises Scripture offers us. We must be willing to receive the abundant goodness of God.

The Psalms tell us, "God is our refuge and our strength, a very present help in trouble." When we are refusing to believe or receive God's goodness, we *are* in trouble. In troubled times we must turn to God. Now is the time to try affirmative prayer, to calmly state the spiritual truths that we know to be true, even if we are temporarily having difficulty accepting them. We can pray, "I am led beyond my doubt and constriction." We can pray, "I am able now to accept the abundant good of God."

As we pray affirmatively, our faith strengthens. By declaring ourselves the recipients of God's good, we are able to allow ourselves to actually receive God's good. "He has made everything suitable for its time," we are told by Ecclesiastes 3:11. This assures us that nothing is too good to be true. If something good is coming to pass, it is because it is right and appropriate for it to come to pass. It is a time of harvest. It is a time to celebrate God's blessings. We can pray, "I accept the abundant blessings of God." We can pray, "I accept God's timing in the unfolding of my good."

A season of harvest may appear as necessary in the progression of my spiritual growth. It may represent the culmination of a long-term project. When we allow God to prosper us, we are giving full rein to God's powers within our life. When we release our fears and allow God to act through us, we are cooperating with God's nature, which is expansive and generous. As we cooperate with God, we begin to sense a feeling of well-being. The fears that first beset us begin to abate. We start to celebrate, and this is as it should be. The Psalms tell us, "Let everything that breathes praise the Lord! Praise the Lord!"

When we praise the Lord, we are able to cooperate with our own unfolding. This is a spiritual law: what is praised increases. If we wish to prosper, we must thank the Lord for our prosperity. We can pray, "God prospers me." We can pray, "Thank you, God, for my abundance." We can be specific, "Thank you, God, for my new and beautiful apartment." We can pray, "Thank you, God, for my solvency."

Our lives are a collaboration of ourselves and God. If we wish our lives to be transformed and made ever more perfect, we need to acknowledge God's role in our lives. God is the Great Architect, the Great Creator. Whatever good we experience, God is the source of our good.

With God as the source, our lives come squarely back to being a matter of faith. We will experience the life we have the faith to experience. We can live in fear or we can live in faith. Fear can be transmuted to faith if we will ask God for help in that transformation: "Thy will, not mine, be done."

Resting in our faith, we begin to feel a life of comfort and security. We begin to feel a sense of safety. We begin to feel that God is doing for us what we cannot do for ourselves. Living one day at a time, we have faith in our life's unfolding. We are given what we can handle and never more than we can handle. God is vigilant on our behalf. God is indeed our shield.

And yet, even if we turn to God as our everlasting rock, difficult things will come to pass. A life lived in faith does not mean a life lived without difficulty. It does mean a life in which difficulties are accepted and overcome. A life lived in faith does not mean a life immune to the human condition; rather, it means a life lived fully accepting the human condition. It means a life in which we see through adversity to the opportunity that it holds for us. To the eyes of faith, every difficulty has a silver lining, a way in which we can grow still closer to God through our acceptance.

Our comfort level, at any given time, is in direct proportion to our level of faith. To the degree to which we can accept life on life's terms, to the degree to which we can believe that what is happening is supposed to be happening, we are able to meet calamity with calm, chaos with serenity. If I am able to believe that God's will is what is happening to me, I can accommodate myself to it or not. I can fight God's will or I can accept God's will. In the accepting of God's will lies spiritual mobility. I am able to make myself comfortable in uncomfortable circumstances.

Proverbs 1:5 tells us, "Let the wise also hear and gain in learning." This Scripture advises us that no matter what level we have reached in our faith, there is always another level that we can go to. There is no limit on how close we can get to God. God is always ready to be still more intimate with us. God is always ready to be even more our companion and our mentor. There is no upper ceiling on our relationship with God. There is always room for more growth, more tranquility, more faith. Scripture tells us, "Call on me and know that I am here for you always." This is a promise.

"I am here for you always"—those are a lover's words. They seek to calm the fear that lurks at the heart of every lover, the fear that one day we will be abandoned and again alone. We can celebrate these words. We can hold to them. It is God's promise to us to never abandon us. It is this promise to which we must cling when we are in times of darkness.

Psalms 25:5 tells us, "Lead me in your truth, and teach me." Sometimes we are led through a dark night. Sometimes we are taught through darkness. At such times we are not able to see or feel God. Like Christ, we call out, "Father, Father, why have Thou forsaken me?" And yet we must believe, despite our disbelief. We must have faith, despite our lack of faith. We must throw ourselves on the mercy of God and ask for his presence to comfort us. We must pray: "Our Father, Who art in Heaven, hallowed be Thy name. Thy kingdom come. Thy will be done. On earth as it is in Heaven."

This is a prayer of acceptance. It does not ask God to change circumstances. Rather it asks God to give us the grace to attune ourselves to circumstances: "Thy will be done." When we pray as Christ taught us to pray, we are acknowledging that there is a higher plan. We may not be able to see it, but we know that it exists. We ask to believe that God's will is unfolding "On earth as it is in Heaven." This is a prayer of humility. We are asking here to be led. "Our Father" we pray, putting ourselves in the position of a little child.

"I sought the Lord, and he answered me, and delivered me from all my fears," Psalms 34:4 tells us. So, too, we can go to God with our fears and ask that we be relieved of them. It is truly possible to have these fears removed. Jesus assured us, "Ask, and it will be given to you."

Sometimes we do not know what to ask. We come to God with our hearts full of pain, but we do not know where to begin to ask for help with our burden. We want more faith, and yet we do not know what having more faith would feel like. We are used to suffering. We are used to feeling abandoned and alone. It is news to us that there is a God who is with us always. This is the God to whom we now turn and who does answer us according to our need.

"Search and you will find," Christ told us. "Knock and the door will be opened for you." We must bring our fears to God in order that God may answer them. We must search and we must knock. We must come to God like little children. It is a relief to come to God in this way. All too often we try to come to God as an adult. We mask our fears and our needs. We do not want to appear foolish before God. We do not want to admit what is truly troubling us. Putting on appearances before God is dishonest, and it leaves us feeling alienated and alone. We are told to pray with more candor.

"I call upon you, for you will answer me, O God; incline your ear to me, hear my words," advises Psalms 17:6.

"Cast all your anxiety on him, because he cares for you," states Peter 5:7.

God is able to withstand our anxiety. God is able to stay calm amid our turmoil. God is able to know the fear of our heart and yet remain steady in the unfolding of our good. We are the ones who vacillate. God is an unchanging good. God is a constant, an "everlasting rock." As we rely on God to be that rock, our own fears quiet. We find ourselves once again faithful because we are renewed. Listen to Romans 12:2, "Do not be conformed to this world, but be transformed by the renewing of your mind, so that you may discern what is the will of God—what is good and acceptable and perfect."

Too often, we cannot discern the will of God. We cannot see what is good and acceptable and perfect. We have our heart set on some shortsighted objective, and if events do not appear to be unfolding as we think they should, we are disquieted. As 1 Corinthians 13:12 tells us, "For now we see in a mirror, dimly, but then we will see face-to-face. Now I know only in part; then I will know fully."

Until we can know fully, we must accept things on faith. We must make the effort to believe that things are unfolding as they should be, that God has a higher plan of which we can know only a part. Psalms 73:24 promises us, "You guide me with your counsel, and afterward you will receive me with honor."

When we affirm divine order, we are able to see beyond the haze of negative appearances. Affirming divine order, we are able to claim and to know that God is present in every circumstance. Divine order is at play both in the universe and in my life. As I clear my vision of negative thoughts, I recognize what is always true: God is omnipresent, guiding and ordering my existence. The wisdom that surpasses all understanding is in charge. This is true whether I am able to see it or not. All is in divine order.

To believe all is in divine order is to rest in confidence in the benevolence of God. We are told in Proverbs 3:26, "The Lord will be your confidence and will keep your foot from being caught." Yet many of us still fear that it is naïve to believe in God. We are afraid of being gullible. We are afraid of being "caught." Rather than embrace a childlike faith, we think it is somehow more worldly and intelligent to doubt God. "Who wouldn't?" we ask.

Taking our worldview from the nightly news or daily headlines, we pride ourselves a little on our cynicism, telling ourselves that it is realistic. Exactly how powerful can God really be if the world is in such a sorry state? We blame God for human shortfalls. We think it is sophisticated to have our reservations, little realizing that in holding on to our reservations, we actually cripple ourselves. We are stuck with one foot in each world. We speak of taking a leap of faith, but it is difficult to take a leap if we are not fully committed and agile in our faith.

"Now may the Lord of peace himself give you peace at all times in all ways," we find in 2 Thessalonians 3:16. Who is the Lord of Peace? Can we believe in him? What would it be like to have peace "at all times" and "in all ways"? Peace at all times would mean no more restless insomnia as we rotisserie in our problems in the netherworld between waking and sleep. Peace at all times would mean no more waking with a feeling of dread, no more living with anxious activity designed to block our awareness. Feeling peace, we would feel clarity. We would sense the counsel of God. Trusting in that, we would be able to look over our options with the confidence that we would have a healthy choice available to us. Grounded in the Lord of Peace, we would trust our ability to make that choice. We would know and feel ourselves to be guided.

Feeling peace at all times, we would no longer feel divided between our will and God's. We would have confidence that the two were in harmony. Genesis tells us "God created humankind in his image." This is astounding information. We are God-like this tells us. This means that we have an inborn capacity to choose as God would have us choose. We do not need to strive to imitate God. We are already like God. Knowing that we are like God, affirming that we are like God, we can experience the promise of peace in all ways. "The peace of the Lord is with me," we can pray.

"Do not worry about how you are to speak or what you are to say . . . for it is not you who speak, but the Spirit of your Father speaking through you," states Matthew 10:19–20. When we are fully aligned with God, when we are committed in our faith, we become channels for good. God acts through us without obstruction. We are freed of the bondage of self. We are no longer self-seeking. We are conduits for God's grace to move into the world. God acts through us and we act through God. There is no friction, no discord. Job 22:21 tells us, "Agree with God, and be at peace; in this way good will come to you."

When we agree with God, we agree with the unfolding of his will for us. We no longer fight circumstances or events. We are open to the idea that everything is in divine order, unfolding just as it is intended to unfold. In Exodus we are told, "My presence will go with you." We can practice experiencing the presence of God. We can remind ourselves that at all times in all circumstances God is present. Bearing this in mind, we can learn to see through apparent negativity. We can remind ourselves, "God is present even if he doesn't seem to be present." As Job asks, "How small a whisper do we hear of him?" There is always present the whisper of God. In fact, there is always present what Job calls the thunder of his power. God is both bold and subtle.

Like God, we are both bold and subtle. Faith makes us both bold and subtle. We dare to undertake many things that seem at first to be beyond our capacity. "Do you not know that you are God's temple and that God's Spirit dwells in you?" 1 Corinthians 3:16 asks us. Many of us need to affirm that we are God's temple. We need to remind ourselves that God's Spirit dwells within us. It is too easy for many of us to focus on the negative. It is too easy for many of us to be aware solely of our shortcomings. We strive for an objective, and when we fall short, we castigate ourselves rather than applaud our courage in trying. We feel distanced from God, having somehow conceived the idea that God loves us only insofar as we approach perfection, not in our frailty. But the truth is, God loves us just as we are. We are told in Scripture that the Lord "understands every plan and thought." This means that God embraces our attempts and not just our successes. God meets us more than halfway.

"Above all, clothe yourselves with love, which binds everything together in perfect harmony," we are advised in Colossians 3:14. When we seek an experience of faith, we are seeking an experience of harmony. This means we must look in every situation for the undergirding of love, which is always present.

Adam was a poor student with an even poorer self-image. He had struggled through grammar school, fought his way through high school, barely made it through college. He was, therefore, dismayed when his persistent spiritual guidance indicated he was to go back to school and attempt a master's degree.

"Every time I prayed for knowledge of God's will for

me, the answer was the same: 'Go back to school.' I thought God was expecting too much of me. I thought it was highly unlikely that I would even make it into the program that seemed appropriate."

Goaded by his consistent guidance, Adam did apply to graduate school. To his shock, he was accepted in not one but two very fine programs and he had his choice about where to go.

"I thought the best program would probably be too hard for me, but my guidance was one more time very firm that I should try for the best. Against my better judgment, thinking, 'I'm only going to flunk out,' I accepted a slot in the finest program available. 'What do I do now?' I remember thinking. The guidance came through loud and clear, 'Ask for help.'"

A proud man and a stubborn one, Adam did not like being told to ask for help. He prayed a second time and again the answer came back to him, "Ask for help." He decided to be obedient to his guidance, even though it made him feel far too vulnerable.

"I called my faculty adviser and said, 'I really feel over my head in this program. I am convinced I will never be able to meet your standards, do you have any ideas?'" The faculty adviser did have ideas, many ideas, and first and foremost among them was his idea that he and Adam work together to help Adam make it through.

"My adviser was incredible. I found I could bring him any question, that there was no question too basic or too stupid for him to address seriously. He also suggested that I organize a study group, that I go to the best students I could find and ask them if they would be willing to work together. I found the best students. I asked them for help and they were willing. Our study group became something on which I could rely. I actually think it helped all of us."

Reaching out for help, Adam found there was help to be had. People were kind to him as he worked on being kinder to himself. "I always struggled to do everything myself. I found that I didn't need to feel so all alone, and I didn't need to act so much like the Lone Ranger. With help from my adviser and newfound friends, I was able to more than meet the standards of the program that I was in. I now have a master's degree and that's coming quite a long way for someone who considered himself a poor student and a loser."

Psalms 95:2 tells us what Adam now knows, "Let us come into his presence with thanksgiving; let us make a joyful noise to him with songs of praise."

"I learned not to underestimate God," Adam concludes, "and I learned not to underestimate me."

Most of us underestimate both God and what we are capable of with God's help. We call this modesty, but it is actually a form of self-deception. We are more comfortable with a limited definition of ourselves and our powers. We do not want to extend ourselves. We want to cling to our known dimensions, and as we do so, we often complain that our life is not satisfying. Our souls hunger for growth. That is their nature. In order for a life to be satisfying, it must contain a modicum of risk. We must expand in order that we not contract.

Faced with expansion, many of us exclaim, "What an order! I can't go through with it!" And we are correct that left to our own devices, we could not. But we are not left to our own devices. We are given God's help. With God's help, we are able to accomplish many things that ordinarily lie beyond our reach. We are often astonished by what is possible. Listen to Matthew 9:28. "Jesus said to them, 'Do you believe that I am able to do this?' They said to him, 'Yes, Lord.'"

When we say, "Yes, Lord," we are rendered larger and more expansive. Challenges that overwhelmed us prove to be doable. Adam attains a master's degree. He shifts his self-image from loser to winner. All of us have areas that with God's help can be transformed. As this transformation occurs, our image of ourselves begins to shift. Basing our view on God's view of us, we begin to see ourselves revealed as spiritual beings with unlimited potential. Although we may find it daunting, we start to see ourselves as ever-expanding souls, ever ready to experience new terrain with God's help. And God's help is available to us in myriad guises.

Candace is a portrait artist. Quite successful, she supports herself with her art, and yet she always feels that there is room for improvement. She has learned that as she is ready to be taught, teachers appear for her. All that is required is the necessary humility to open herself up and be vulnerable. She believes this vulnerability to be God's will for her.

"I wanted to work on my backgrounds," Candace says. "I went to the Internet and to the library and studied all that I could find on the great portrait artists. Much of the time

I would think, 'I'm already doing that trick,' and I would have to say to myself that I was doing pretty well. Still, I yearned to do better, and that is when I saw an ad that an Old Masters class was being taught in a nearby city. Part of me said, 'I'm too advanced for this class,' but another part of me recognized that possibly that was just a defense. I called the teacher and asked a few questions to give me a sense of what it was she was offering. It sounded like just the ticket to me."

And so, once a week Candace commutes sixty miles round-trip to her new class. She is thrilled by what she is learning. "I could not believe what a difference it made to begin again to be taught in person instead of just through books. I found myself thinking over and over again, 'Now I get it!'"

No one told Candace she had to take the Old Masters class. Her portraits were already selling well, and she could have been content to rest on her laurels, but she experienced an inner imperative that told her she could do better. She listened to that inner voice and it led her to help. She considers her new class to be a spiritual opportunity.

"I know it may sound sort of hokey, but I believe that when I am painting, I am actually listening to God," Candace says. "I do experience inspiration, and that gives me a sense of well-being when I am cooperative with it. I honestly feel my time at the easel is like time spent in prayer. I believe my portraits are my form of service to God. God gave me my creative gift, and my gift back to God is to use it—and to use it as well as I possibly can.

"In the case of the class," Candace continues, "I had an insistent hunch that it was right for me, even though I wanted to say I was beyond it or that it was too expensive. I wanted to say the commute was too much of a hassle, that I was too busy and didn't really have the time. I found I had a whole raft of excuses I had to face down. My inner resistance was nearly as strong as my inner guidance to go forward. I had to pray for help to be openminded and go forward and I am so glad that I did. I found that for me it was money and time well spent. I no sooner laid out the money for the class than I received a flurry of new commissions. I was excited because it meant I would be able to put my new learning to immediate and practical use. I believe it is God's will for me to be a painter and the best painter that I can be. This means that I have to stay teachable. I do my best to do that."

All that God asks is that I do my best and my best is not always fearless. Like Candace with her inner resistance, we may be guided in a new direction and experience a host of inner gremlins that seem determined to keep us from going forward. When we are faced with such resistance, we must turn again to prayer.

The strength to do God's bidding is a strength that comes to us through prayer. Prayer is a practical tool, and we can use it as a lever when we experience our own resistance. Those who have experimented with prayer well know its power. Those who have not experimented with prayer, do well to try. When stuck or stymied, we can turn to God in prayer. Our obstacles melt away. We discover that with God all things are possible. Does this sound overconfident? Our confidence doesn't rest on what we can accomplish alone. Our confidence is grounded on what God can accomplish through us.

When I am a willing tool in the hands of God, great things can come to pass—far greater things than we imagine possible, left to our own devices. Artists well know this. They are accustomed to being the conduits for works far greater than themselves.

"The music of this opera [*Madama Butterfly*] was dictated to me by God; I was merely instrumental in putting it on paper and communicating it to the public," declared Giacomo Puccini. Brahms concurred: "Straightaway the ideas flow in upon me, directly from God." These men are relating their experience, their spiritual experience: God is in me expressing through me and as me. My victories are God's victories.

"Faith without works is dead," we can tell ourselves whenever we are tempted to rest on our laurels. "How can I best serve Thee?" we can pray. Service implies action. Action requires faith. Our world expands as we allow ourselves to place our confidence in God. The Talmud tells us, "Every blade of grass has its angel that bends over it and whispers, 'Grow, grow.'"

We, too, are intended to grow. Expansive creativity is the order of life. Life is energy: pure creative energy. There is an indwelling creative force underlying all of life, including ourselves. When we open ourselves to our creativity, we open ourselves to the Creator's creativity within us. We are creations. We are meant to continue creativity by being creative ourselves. God's gift to us is creativity. Our using our creativity is our gift back to God. It could be argued that faith is the necessary ingredient to living a creative life.

"What we play is life," says Louis Armstrong, speaking of music and musicians, but he could be speaking for all of us. When faith "comes into play," so does a feeling of playfulness. We let go of striving. God is in charge. We are not stretched so thin by the strain of our self-sufficiency. We speak of the "play of ideas," and that, too, is a literal phrase. When we are living faithfully, we are open to an influx of new ideas. We are receptive to the flow of life. When we are not defended and closed, ideas come to us. We experience ourselves as standing knee-deep in the flow of life, the flow of ideas. Out of those ideas, we choose those that resonate with us most strongly. We are open to guidance, which often comes to us in the form of attraction. We experience our good as a magnetic force that draws us toward it. Often the element of fun or delight enters the picture. As Jean Houston remarks, "At the height of laughter, the universe is flung into a kaleidoscope of new possibilities." We experience God's will not as harsh but as benevolent, even playful.

God is the Great Creator, the one Creative Mind. As Carl Jung remarked, "The creative mind plays with the object it loves." And so, yes, God plays with us but not as a cat plays with a mouse. Instead, God plays with us tenderly, affectionately, patiently. We *are* the objects of God's love. As such, we are in a very real sense God's playthings. This is not to say that God takes us and our concerns frivolously. Rather, it is to say that there is a deftness to God's touch upon our lives, a lightness that is at once gentle and enlivening. God's touch upon our lives invites our relaxation. As 2 Thessalonians 3:16 tells us, "Now may the Lord of peace himself give you peace at all times in all ways." If we experience peace at all times, in all ways, then we can stop straining.

We can relax into God's will. We can allow our souls to be warmed and nurtured by God's loving intention toward us. "The Lord is my shepherd," we are told in Psalms 23. As our shepherd, God supports and sustains us through any seeming challenge. Reading this psalm, we can be reassured that we are not alone. The presence of God surrounds and enfolds us. We are not solitary beings striving to wrest our way from a hostile world. We are connected, and the world we move in is friendly to our aims. When we turn to God to guide us, we are led experience by experience to a broader and more gentle world. God gives us a "steadfast love," as we are told in Psalms. We can luxuriate in that love. We can bask in God as in a pool of warm sunlight. The light of God is reflected in all creation. With the eyes of faith, the divine is what I see.

Seeing God in each situation and in each person is a choice that I can make. I can look for the sacred in everything, knowing that all creation is a reflection of God's love. When I look for God in everything and everyone, God is what I find there. Job 22:21 tells us, "Agree with God and be at peace; in this way good will come to you."

There is a divine plan of goodness for all of us. Not one of us is beneath or beyond God's care. There is a great tapestry woven by God of which we are all a part. As we strive to align our will with God's will for us, we can sometimes gain a glimpse of that great tapestry and of the part we play in God's design. Every time we reflect upon divine order, we feel serene. And yet appearances may deceive us. We may not be able to discern the emerging pattern of perfection that is God's blueprint for our growth. We may feel ourselves to be thwarted, and when we do, we must affirm, "Everything is in divine order; all is unfolding exactly as it should."

At any moment, we are free to join God's plan or defy it. We enjoy the gift of free will, which gives us dignity, and yet free will also gives us a means of rebellion. We can turn aside from God's intention for us. Rather than praying for knowledge of God's will for us and the power to carry that out, we can insist on an agenda of our own making. We can pout. We can posture. We can protest. "Dear God, please give me what I want," we can pray rather than praying "Dear God, please help me to want what I am given."

When we ask God to help us want what we are given, we are asking God for the grace to live in harmony. Although appearances may belie this fact, God's will is the harmonious unfolding of the whole. All works toward the good. Colossians 3:14 tells us, "Above all, clothe yourselves with love, which binds everything together in perfect harmony." How do we "clothe ourselves with love"? We strive for harmony.

God is harmony—but we are not accustomed to harmony. We are accustomed to tension and to the false belief that we must fight to win that which is rightfully ours. Attuned to fighting, we are unable to accustom ourselves to receptivity. We are too defended to receive what flows to us easily and freely. Focused on a specific goal that we "must" have, we are often blind to the many other gifts that come our way.

Obsessed with an agenda of our own, we miss God's agenda, and then we tell ourselves that we are experiencing chaos when what we are experiencing is merely not what we would wish. And what we would wish is often quite shortsighted. God takes the longer view.

The longer view is not popular with most of us. We want what we want and we want it now. God's delay feels like God's denial—and, at least temporarily, it *is* God's denial. Most of us do not take "no"s easily. We have an idea of how our life should go and we pester God to have our life go just as we would plan it. There are far more variables than we allow for. God's world encompasses *everything*. Our world encompasses our own goals and agendas. And yet if everything came to pass exactly as we would will it to, how often would we be selling ourselves short?

In cozy retrospect, it is often very clear that the "no" that we received was actually a form of spiritual protection, not merely a deliberate and flippant thwarting of our will. When we receive a "no" from God, it is often actually a "yes" in disguise. Instead of focusing on what we cannot have, we need only turn our attention toward that good which God is moving forward in its stead.

Carl is a world-class pianist. He has for years worked as a duet partner to a very famous violinist, a name whose glory brings in tickets. As the pianist, Carl found that he did not receive the same rave reviews as his concert mate. In the eyes of most critics, the violin grabbed all the attention. The piano was "just" accompaniment. Carl resented his second-fiddle position but felt powerless to change the critics' perceptions. He often stewed resentfully in the shadow cast by his more honored colleague. At times he could grow bitter, feeling what was the use of playing beautifully since no one seemed to notice or care? At times like these, Carl felt shortchanged by God.

"I wanted more glory. I wanted the credit I felt was due me and my musicianship," Carl recounts. "It pained me to get milquetoast, also-ran reviews, but I had to say to myself that not many musicians made their living as I did, playing music that I loved and bringing in top dollar for it too. I also had to admit to myself that there was far less strain on my psyche in a duet career than I would have experienced as a soloist. In a sense I was cushioned, and if I felt my talents were frequently overlooked, I had to say to myself that it came with the territory. It was nothing personal."

When Carl reframed his grievances, looking for the positive, he could see that there was much to recommend his career exactly as it had unfolded. He had worked consistently for more than a decade. He had traveled the world, playing for audiences in places as far-flung as Germany, Italy, France, and Japan. He had played a repertoire that he cherished, and he had played it well enough that he enjoyed an impeccable reputation among other musicians if not with the public at large.

"I don't really think that I had the ego strength for any other type of career," he admits as he summarizes his thoughts. "I am not a performer who is comfortable putting myself front and center. I put my focus on performance, not presentation. That may not be good salesmanship. Given that, I may have received more attention than I otherwise could have expected."

"My presence will go with you," we are told in Exodus 33:14. When Carl allows himself the luxury of gratitude, he can see that God's presence has indeed accompanied and blessed his career.

"Sometimes I just get greedy," he says. "I hunger for things that I am not really emotionally well equipped to handle. What I have got is probably precisely what I should have had. I have had a very fine, even a distinguished career. I should be grateful, and when I am vigilant with myself spiritually, I am."

As Carl accurately points out, it takes spiritual vigilance to see and appreciate the will of God when it runs counter to our own all-too-human desires. "Thy will, not mine," we can pray and in the surrendering of our will, we are often able to begin to see the silver lining. We become openminded. We become teachable. As we desire to grow and evolve spiritually, we are ready to learn what we can from each experience. Opening our hearts and our minds, we welcome each experience for the wisdom that it contains.

When troubled by our rebellious reactions, we can remind ourselves that we are on a spiritual quest, a journey of self-discovery. This may seem thankless, but it's not. Sometimes slowly, sometimes with insulting speed, we can become aware of God's great wisdom on our behalf. As God's plan unfolds, we can be ironically, gratefully aware of ourselves as partners in his higher wisdom.

Praying to accept God's will, we can become openminded, able to discover more of ourselves and our world. Striving to accept our daily lessons, we find ourselves enrolled in a divine curriculum: That divine curriculum is priceless. As we read in Isaiah 2:3: "Many people shall come and say, 'Come, let us go up to the mountain of the Lord, to the house of the God of Jacob; that he may teach us his ways and that we may walk in his paths.'"

God does teach us his ways. As we pray for acceptance of God's will, we are actually praying for the grace to be teachable. Although we seldom single it out for comment, one of Christ's chief roles was that of teacher. A wise and gentle teacher, he taught through parable and through example. It might be said that in his ascended state, he teaches us still— sometimes by his "yes"es and sometimes by his "no"s.

Andrew is recently engaged. Fifty-nine years old, single all his life, he did not expect to fall in love or to have that love lead, as it has, to marriage. "We're both in shock," Andrew reports. "We're both older, and neither of us has ever been married before. I had accepted my bachelorhood. I had thought, 'Well, God, it's just you and me and that's OK.' I knew what to expect of my life, and then along came this tremendous surprise."

To hear Andrew tell it, God's newly revealed will is a tremendous challenge. "I am not complaining. In fact, I am thrilled, but I was comfortable before. I knew that if I put something down, it would be there when I went to pick it up. With two of us, that's not true anymore."

Andrew is grateful to have met his fiancée and believes

that she is the perfect woman for him. He looks back on his years of loneliness when he pined for relationships that didn't come to bloom and he feels that God was saving him for the relationship that he has now. God's delay was not his denial. God's delay was simply God's delay while he readied everything for the perfect unfolding.

"Timing is where we most often fight with God," reveals a longtime AA member. "That is why the slogan for AA is 'Easy does it.'"

Many times when a prayer is not answered immediately, we conclude that it will not be answered at all. Many times when it is answered with "Not now," we fear that it is being answered by "Not ever." One way to think of it is as if God were preparing a feast. We keep saying, "The roast is ready. It's time to eat!" but the vegetables aren't done. God is the Master Chef, timing everything to perfection.

"Unless and until they work on their spiritual condition, sober alcoholics are restless, irritable, and impatient, especially impatient," says the AA old-timer. "The AA slogans evolved because they represented simple ways of dealing with complex issues. 'Easy does it,' means 'slow down' and 'calm down,' but it means much more than that. 'Easy does it' is a promise. It means 'Easy accomplishes it.' It tells us that if we just take our foot off the accelerator, God will do just fine at setting the pace at which our life unfolds."

"I have been sober for thirty-five years," confides Jessica. "I have learned that the will of God moves at its own pace and that I cannot hurry it along with my self-will. I always want things right now, and I find that I often get frustrated that God seems to move so slowly. On the other hand, the minute something does come true, I always think, 'If this had happened any sooner, I wouldn't have been able to handle it.'"

Jessica is an actress who has enjoyed considerable fame during her career. She has worked consistently in television, film, and theater. She has always wanted God to give her more and other than what she has received, and yet she ruefully acknowledges that what she has gotten has proved to be quite right for her.

"When I was doing a daytime soap opera, my face was familiar to millions. I couldn't leave the house to go shopping or have a dinner out without being recognized by the public. I found this disconcerting, yet I always claimed I wanted to be more famous, which would have meant more intrusions and more necessity for living in the spotlight. I think on balance the amount and type of fame that I got was just about right for what I could actually handle. It wasn't emotionally sober of me to always want more and always want it faster. I had many a 'dry drunk' fighting with God about God's timing. I had to work at my emotional sobriety, which meant I had to work at being willing to accept God's timing."

Faith is the key to accepting God's timing. We must believe that we are being cared for and very carefully. We must believe that we are being watched over, that there is a divine plan of goodness for us. God's will unfolds for us one day at a time. We must be willing to live life at that pace in order to reach a comfort level with ourselves and our circumstances.

God cannot be hurried, no matter how hard we push. In pushing, we only exhaust ourselves.

"I was a red-hot actress in my twenties," Jessica recalls. "My thirties were a lot cooler, and I used to be furious whenever a part I coveted went to someone else. 'Why not me?' I would fume—as if I expected God to come down into my dressing room and explain himself. Do I need to tell you, God never did. I worked consistently during my forties, my fifties, and my sixties. I am now in my seventies and still working. A lot of the actresses who were hot when I was not, burned out much earlier than I did. I have been blessed by a long and distinguished career. God's will for me, which I couldn't see, was that I would be a success in the long haul. I was simply far too impatient and shortsighted to see it. It is only in retrospect that I can believe that God was bringing me along like a fighter. I was always given just enough to be ready for the next thing and then just enough to be ready for the thing after that."

A divine plan for our life is continually unfolding. Our good is assured by divine planning for it. When we seek to align ourselves with God's will for us, we are aligning ourselves with this master plan. For every challenge, there is a resolution. There is no situation too challenging for God's aid. For every question, there is an answer. There is no question too troublesome for God's problem-solving nature. For every circumstance, there is an outworking that is in our best interest. Let us affirm, "God is quietly and constantly acting on my behalf."

As a child of God, I am worthy of a good life. I am worthy of fulfilling relationships, good health, peace of mind, and financial security. If I will cooperate with their unfolding, God is able to bring these blessings to my life. God has given me a world that is rich with opportunities and blessings. To receive the bounty that is mine, I need only cooperate, affirming by my actions and my prayers that I am God's child and worthy of all good that comes to me. I deserve good. This is God's will for me. There is no lack in God's kingdom. I do not need to compete with others to attract my good. I give thanks for what I have. I have faith in what is to come. God is generous to me. I have faith in God's generosity.

Because there is no competition for God's good, I can afford to be generous myself. I can pray for all people, asking in faith that all of them be blessed as I am blessed. I am what I was created to be: an expression of God's love. God has given me a heart filled with divine love and I draw on that love to extend myself to others. I am not threatened or jealous. Rather, I accept myself and others as unique creations. I choose not to be judgmental or critical. I raise my thoughts above such negativity. Love brings out the best in me and encourages me to see the best in others. With God's help, I am patient and understanding. I accept the highest good that God has to offer me, and I support the highest good that God has to offer to others. I believe that we are each uniquely endowed by a divine inheritance. What God gives to me does not deprive others. What God gives to others does not deprive me. There is sufficient good for all to enjoy God's bounty. I am blessed beyond measure, as are my brothers and sisters.

Wherever I am, I am always at home. Wherever I am, the presence of God surrounds and enfolds me. I allow my soul to be warmed and nurtured by God's love. I relax into the Divine Presence. I recognize that God intends to support and sustain me through any challenges I may experience. I experience a profound peace that enters my heart and assures me that I am not alone. All is well. I need only affirm that fact to feel that it is so.

Faith is a choice. Seeking to know and to do God's will, we are able to choose to extend ourselves in faith. Seeking to believe, we are able to choose to believe. We are able to proclaim spiritual truths by which we are able to live. We are told in Romans 15:13, "May the God of hope fill you with all joy and peace in believing." If we are to experience joy and peace, we must believe. If we doubt, we can always pray, "Lord, I believe, help my disbelief."

"My disbelief" is always a precise measure of what separates me from God. Faith is openended. We can always believe more than we do believe. With every additional jot of belief comes an additional jot of comfort. The outer world offers me many comforts, but none can compare to the joy of immersing myself in God's presence. The more I connect with God as the true source of joy, the more joy I am able to bring to my experience of life. "You may abound in hope by the power of the Holy Spirit," we are told in Romans 15:13.

When we are living in faith, we are also, always, living in hope. We trust and accept the blessings of each day as they come to us directly from God. We affirm we are exactly where we are intended to be. In good faith, we open our hearts to the abundance that God unfolds for us at each moment. Even as we do this, we look forward hopefully to further blessings coming to us from God's hand. God intends us nothing but further good. We affirm this fact and look toward the future with this in mind. As a result, we experience delight in living. We are able to live in hope. As we do so, joy, perhaps unexpectedly, courses through our veins. Joy ripples outward from our God-filled heart to all those whom we encounter. Our faith is contagious. We become a power of example. God is the source of our unlimited strength. As John 5:30 tells us, "I can do nothing on my own." On the other hand, "I seek to do not my own will but the will of him who sent me."

Margaret tries to lead a faith-centered life. As a writer, she has worked at her craft for more than thirty years, and during that time she has written many things "on spec" with no guarantee that there will be a buyer for her work. She is often asked, "How can you just go ahead and write something? What if you do all that work for nothing?"

"I write what seems to want to be written," Margaret says. "I know that what I do doesn't always seem sensible, but it is what I am called to do and so I just try to answer that calling. I am fortunate. I have a publisher who is responsive to what other people might think of as my 'whims.' He listens to what it is I think I should be writing, and he always urges me to just go ahead and try it—and so I do."

Following her callings, Margaret has written some twenty books in the past two decades. Her books have sold well—some best sellers, many with steady and substantial but nonspectacular sales. Her life looks stable and steady from the outside. She has an established reputation. She writes and writes consistently. There is no wobble in her trajectory. She always is at work on some stage of a project, and that project is always one that has come to her through her inner guidance.

"Sometimes I will get a book idea that just seems crazy," Margaret says. "I will have a plan to write book A when all of a sudden book B will come forward and insist on being written. I have learned to go along with the book that seems to have spiritual priority. This means I have to operate on faith. I have to believe there will be an audience for what I write, that I am not just writing into a vacuum, and yet many times I do feel as if I am writing into the void. I am certainly writing without a contract, without a guaranteed sale for the finished product. Often I feel a little bit like Beethoven did at the end of his career. After a red-hot youthful career, his reputation was somewhat diminished. His work was no longer being well received publically—it was too avant-garde—and after a period in which he experienced a near suicidal depression, he finally resolved to simply write music for himself and God. Well, I write books for myself and God. God willing, there is also an audience for them. I hope so, but I have to trust enough to write anyway."

"I have to trust enough" is a pivotal phrase. How much is "enough"? Usually it is just enough to take the indicated action, not so much that there is any deep comfort level.

When we trust God enough, we move out on faith. When we move out on faith, we often still have the heebie-jeebies. We still think, "I better be right about this." We are trying to act as if we have a sense of ease that we may not yet have. We are living the dictum, "Faith without works is dead."

"It's like this," explains Margaret. "I am always hoping that God is going to show up with some warm and wonderful guarantee, an L.L.Bean blanket to wrap my doubts in. I am always yearning for there to be a sense of real safety. You would think that my many years of striving for obedience would make it all a little more comfortable, but I still seem to always get asked to stretch beyond my comfort zone. God wants one more book from me just when I think I may not have another book to offer. 'Safety' comes to me through obedience, and obedience comes to me through willingness. I strive to be always willing. What I find is that when I take the action that I believe God is indicating for me, then I feel safe 'enough.'"

As Margaret makes clear, she still feels she is taking a risk when she tries to listen for and accomplish God's will. Her long years of listening to God have not made it any less necessary to listen. They have not made it any less necessary to risk.

"God seems to live squarely in the present," Margaret theorizes. "My past of being a faithful servant doesn't seem to cut me much slack. What God is interested in is what is my commitment today. I find that when I am willing to make a daily commitment, to be what I think God wants of me right now, then I am rewarded with a sense of conscious contact. I feel myself to be with God whenever I choose to be with God, but make no mistake, that choice is active and daily or it isn't worth much."

To hear Margaret tell it, there is no resting on our spiritual laurels. There is no point at which we can say, "Well. That's it. I have made it." How can we have made it when God is always making something more of us? And God is always making something more of us.

"I find that God seems to be interested in what I am doing right now, in the precise present. I cannot say, 'You see, God, I am a writer.' God wants to know what I am writing right now. I am afraid that God is terribly interested in our actions and not so interested in our good intentions. I don't get any-where with God saying I am 'going' to write a book. God has the book ready and waiting. I am the one who is stalling. I am always trying to take a few extra minutes of dawdling time before I have to go into action and put myself on the line. God is always willing to be on the line. I have never shown up to take a risk that I didn't find God there already, just waiting for me. It's as though God knows we could lead two lives in the time it takes to lead one. God has always got a new thing for me to move on to. I can resent this restlessness, or I can see it as something that draws me to God. I have come to think that my edginess is something that God instilled in me because only God can seem to soothe it. It is only when I am being obedient to God that I am really comfortable. Since God seems to have made me a writer. That means I tend to do an awful lot of writing. People will say to me, 'Oh, you are so prolific.' They don't know that my productivity is God's idea more than my own."

Margaret works at her relationship with God. She keeps it central because that is where it seems to want to be anyhow. She has tried over the years to make God less important and to focus on her work instead, but God seems to be present in her work and she exorcizes God at her own peril.

"I tried to write a whole book once just concentrating on the book and not thinking about God and how God wanted me to write the book and was going to help me write the book, et cetera. I was tired of my God books, and I thought I would enjoy just being a novelist, just telling a story, not a particularly spiritual story at that. What I found was that God became a very steady suitor. He was always there waiting for me when I finished each day's writing. He was always asking me, 'Well? How did it go?' When I look back on that book, a novel, I do not remember the solitude of writing it. I remember the sense of companionship I experienced. That's when I realized that there were two of us in this relationship of God's and mine and that I wasn't the only one making decisions about how close we should be. Over the years I have come to realize that God is keeping a pretty close eye on me."

God is keeping a pretty close eye on all of us. If we doubt that, we need only try to evade God for a while. A loneliness sets in and a restlessness. We are cornered back into relating with God because without God the world rapidly becomes untenable. If we begin to judge the world simply by its surface appearances, we quickly become sad. "Where is justice?" we wonder. "Where is peace?" In order to experience the good qualities of the world, we must experience the long view, and the long view includes God. Without God, the world is too upsetting; too many things do not make sense. There is too much tragedy and not enough hope. Our psyches begin to tilt toward darkness. We begin to experience fear and alienation. A world without God, a God-less world, is a world that is very difficult to live in. We can tell ourselves that we are only being "realists" and only being "modern" when we try to live without God, but there is some seemingly central part of ourselves that is left saddened and disenchanted by living a God-less life. Depression sets in and then its more somber sister, despair. We find ourselves wandering from place to place, never contented, and we finally wonder bleakly, "Is this all there is?"

"Is this all there is?" is a hopeless question. It is also the question that is asked during the dark night of the soul. We intuitively sense there has to be more than "this," and our psyches do not find a sense of balance until we begin to posit a spiritual something that undergirds the world as we seem to know it.

Logic itself seems to demand that "something" made all this. We turn in our despair to the question "What sort of something?" We begin to explore the idea of God, even if we do not turn to any known religion. We try to find something in ourselves that can relate to something that has created everything. We find that there is a part of ourselves that is humbler than we had imagined. That humble part of ourselves looks at the world with wonder and says, "Let me talk to whoever created the lily or perhaps the frog."

For implicit in the idea of there being a creator is the fact that there is much humor in the world and that we can experience none of it successfully without God. Without God, what is there to laugh at? We seem to be in dire straits. With God, we are able to pray, "Look at the pickle we have got ourselves in now. Please help."

When we get to the prayer "Please help," then we are on the right path. We are relating to Somebody or Something that is larger than ourselves and is benevolent. It doesn't seem to matter much how we conceptualize this something. God concepts can follow from experience rather than lead it. All that seems to matter is that we have become openminded about "the God idea," and from that openmindedness many experiences and theorems can follow.

"My concept of God seems to change as I change," Margaret says. "I have gone through periods where I thought of God as an energy, a force. I have had periods where God was more anthropomorphic than that. I have needed a more human God in those times. Then, too, at other times I have thought of God as a form of spiritual electricity, and I have thought of God as a law. I think that I have come close to many of the God concepts put forward by the world's great religions, but I have come to those concepts experientially.

"I seem to learn more about God by trying to relate to God than I do by listening to God experts," Margaret continues, aware of the irony that she herself is sometimes considered a "God expert." "Experts are somehow so off-putting, and God seems so intimate and personal and private. My God and your God may be two different things. By tomorrow, my God may be a different thing yet again. I never find that I can language God successfully. There always is something more left unsaid, something that is a matter of experience. I have written a great deal about God, and yet I find that I am just at the beginning. There are so many things one could say and they are all true. And yet they all seem like partial truths, like God is much bigger than anything we could say about God. Speaking for myself, I have always come back to the idea that God is real and somehow both within me and outside of me. And that is just the beginning."

A beginning seems to be all that is necessary in relating to God. God does not ask us for any dignified conclusions. God does not cause us to audition our knowledge before we can relate. With God, it seems to be possible to start anyplace at all. In AA, newcomers are told they must find for themselves their own concept of a "power greater than themselves." This power greater than themselves is necessary to maintaining sobriety, but it may be something as amorphous as the AA rooms themselves.

One newcomer thought of this power as the force that held the planets to their course. Another, half in jest, thought of God as Mick Jagger. Another chose sunspots as something wondrous that she could relate to. All of these newcomers stayed sober. All of them went on to forge other and even more personal versions of God, or a higher power. It did not seem to matter where a newcomer began or with what. God evidently had no aversion to being thought of as a Rolling Stone. Anyplace seemed to be a good enough place for a new-comer to start.

An AA newcomer is typically desperate, and such desperation breeds openmindedness on spiritual matters. When the choice is to believe in something or die, the newcomer is apt to find a something that can be believed in. I myself am a sober alcoholic, and I started out my idea of a higher power with a line from Dylan Thomas, "The force that through the green fuse drives the flower." That was a God of creativity and one that I could believe in. That I still believe in, although over the years of my sobriety, my God concept has shifted to keep pace with what I seemed to need for each era. I have not found that God makes hard terms with me. Rather, it has seemed to be enough that I am willing to believe in *something*.

The *something* that makes a higher power is entirely personal. I did not start with Mick Jagger, but I had sympathy for the newcomer who did. She was a rock-and-roll record producer, and she desperately needed a God who was hip. The woman who chose sunspots was a New York atheist, and she didn't want any anthropomorphic God that smacked of the kind of fairy-tale Santa Claus God she had been brought up to disdain. Desperate to gain sobriety, an AA newcomer might choose to believe in almost anything. It would matter less what he believed in than that he believed in something. The nature of that something would be an entirely personal and idiosyncratic choice.

Most spiritual seekers are not as desperate as AA

newcomers—at least not as overtly desperate. They may experience a haunting and urgent inner emptiness, but they do not have the gunpoint of a fatal disease urging them to choose a higher power—or else! Of their own free will, they are electing to get to know God, but except for their inner imperative, it is not critical that they do so. They may feel driven to know God, but they are driven by an inner impulse that may feel only to them unrelenting. All who seek God do so out of a self-acknowledged inner hunger. There is a spiritual thirst that can be sated only by spiritual means. "Ask and ye shall receive," we are told in John 16:24. Nowhere is this promise more beautifully kept than when a neophyte comes to God asking to be answered in faith.

"Whereas I was blind, now I see," John 9:25 tells us, and every newcomer who has discovered a fledgling faith feels this wondrous sense of spiritual awakening. Faith moves mountains, and many of the mountains that are moved are the inner mountains of cynicism and despair. Through an awareness of Spirit, we suddenly learn to look quietly and calmly upon every negative situation. With the eyes of newfound faith, we see through it to the other side, where the Great Creator is molding circumstances and conditions into a more nearly perfect whole. Faith is rejuvenating. It is tonic. As we drop confusion and entertain peace, we transcend doubt and fear. We are lifted to the hilltop of the Inner Life. Through faith, our consciousness rises to the realization of that Divine Presence that is always delivering itself to us. As we now are ready to accept, we receive.

Awakened in faith, we receive freedom from problems, whatever they may be. We are suddenly conscious of an infinite wisdom directing us. Whatever we ought to know, we do know, and whatever we ought to do, we do do. Our every thought and every decision is molded by our newly discovered higher power. Our problems and difficulties melt away as Divine Intelligence makes all things right in our life. Freedom and joy express themselves in our experience. As we seek to align ourselves and our thinking with God, there is nothing in us to obstruct the flow of good things into our realm of activity. There is a power operating through us, a Presence that inspires us, an immutable law that sustains us. Upon this Power, this Presence, and this law, we can place total reliance. Its sole desire for us is that we be happy, joyous, and free. Depending on God, we are those things. No adversity undermines us. As Romans 8:31 exclaims, "If God be for us, who can be against us?"

The law of God is absolute. This law is both perfect and exact. Nothing is outside of its reach. We can place our complete trust in this power. It operates in and through us. As we align ourselves with it, everything that is good and everything that is right is brought to pass. This law knows how to bring about everything that is necessary to our good. We can, therefore, trust to it today and every day. We are one with the infinite spirit of Love. "I delight in the law of God," exclaims Romans 7:22. When we understand the law of God to be a law of limitless love, we can well rejoice. We may begin with a God concept as hazy as sunspots, but sooner or later we will have the moment of awakening that tells us that

God is in us as us. We will discover that the highest God and innermost God is one God, not two. All of creation is God made manifest. God is what we are, although we are at the same time subject to God's law. We have greater abilities and resources than we have yet realized. With God, all things are possible.

Believing that there is an infinite Power in the universe, a power greater than ourselves, we can now accept that Power as acting in our life. Romans 13:1 tells us "There is no power but of God." Christ taught us "Not I but the Father doeth the works."

The secret of faith then lies in the realization that there is a Power of Good in the universe that is greater than we are and that we can use it. We are one with the Infinite Spirit. As we turn our will and our life over to the care of God, we are invoking this Greater Power. Accordingly, we must learn to accept and expect this Power to flow through everything that we do. Although our low self-worth might tell us otherwise, as we align ourselves with this power, we are the very embodiment of it—its energy and its action. We can strive to recognize ourselves as creations of God. We can strive to find delight in exploring the law of God. In other words, we can come to faith with some eagerness and not be merely cornered into it by our need.

In faith, we ask God to make of us what he will. This means that we ask to be as individual as a snowflake, unique in all creation. We ask to become fully and wholly ourselves. This means that we ask Spirit to make of us something new.

We ask to be original, a new creation. We are all just a little bit original. Each of us wears a different face, but God is behind us all. One life flows through all creation. This life is never monotonous. It is always making something new through each of us. We can affirm this newness of life. We can embrace with enthusiasm the changes that Spirit is bringing to pass in our lives. This means that we can experience a new zest for living. Divine Mind pours through each of us in an individual way. We can accept that grounded in God we are grounded in genius. New ideas and insights flow to us daily. We can continually invite right action, insight, and illumination.

John 3:7 tells us, "Ye must be born again." We *are* born again as we recognize our divine heritage. Everything draws its power, its strength, and its life from one divine source. As conscious beings, we have the gift of conscious faith. We can use our free will to align ourselves with the Divine Mind unfolding in our experience. We can affirm the action of God in our life. We can affirm the reality of good constantly manifesting. As we seek to live one day at a time, one minute at a time, in the conscious presence of God, there is nothing from the past that can hamper us and nothing from the future that can stand in our way. Knowing that God is all and we are a part of that all, we experience a new freedom and a new joy in living.

God is over all, in all, and through all. Affirmation can establish an inward recognition of this fact. As we affirm our faith, we strengthen it. We can lay aside every doubt and fear and enter into a newness of life, born again in faith. "Believe that you receive," we are told in Mark 11:24. This is an explicit instruction for effective prayer. We are told to believe that our prayers are answered even as we say them. This is God doing for me what I cannot do for myself.

Just as God can restore the shattered lives of newly sober alcoholics, God can restore all of us to sanity: the recognition that we are one with the Divine Presence and can consciously enter into communion with it. The Divine Presence is not only close to us, it is also within us.

Realizing that there is a law of Good active in my experi-ence, I now release every thought of limitation, doubt, and fear that my heart still harbors. I consciously accept the good that my heart desires. I accept my good here and now, in the present. The law works through me. I intuitively know what to do and how to do it. Furthermore, the law of God contains within it all the details of its creation. I do not need to outline and strain for my good to come into being. I need only accept that what law does for me, it does through me. There is a Power greater than myself on which I now rely. Nothing can oppose its right action in my life.

"The Lord is my shepherd. . . . He restoreth my soul," we are told in Psalms 23:1,3. When we reach to God in faith, we *do* experience a restoration. It is with great relief that we lay aside our every doubt and fear. Reaching both out and in to Divine Presence, we sense that we are one with the Divine and we consciously affirm our communion with it. We reach an inner Sanctuary, a place where the still, small voice speaks to us with clarity and authority. In that place, we know that God can both sustain us and restore us. We sense the strength of God and the gentleness of God. As the psalmist says, we experience God as the loving shepherd.

"I never put very much store by meditation," volunteers Albert, a self-made millionaire. "I was a very driven and motivated kind of guy. I had better things to do than sit around trying to contact God. It all seemed pretty airy-fairy to me, like trying to make contact with a UFO. I just didn't see how it could be practical. I wasn't an atheist. I was probably an agnostic. I couldn't be bothered to do the research. Then I hit my skid. I don't know whether to tell you it was a midlife crisis or a dark night of the soul. Whatever it was, it was pretty terrible.

"No matter how busy and how productive I tried to be there was an underlying depression that I just couldn't shake. I kept coming back to that old Peggy Lee song, 'Is That All There Is?' Nothing was really wrong, but nothing felt really right to me either. A friend suggested I try meditation, and one Saturday afternoon, I gave it a flier. I figured, 'What the hell. I've tried everything else. The next step is antidepressants and I don't want to do that.' Imagine my surprise when I consciously tried to quiet down and something or someone actually seemed to speak with me. I had an overwhelming impression that all was all right. It was the first time in a year when things seemed to be in place. Frankly, I was shocked. Now I know that what I had experienced was my first moment of 'conscious contact.' One little taste and I wanted more of it. I became a regular meditator, a frequent flier as I liked to joke."

"Commit thy way unto the Lord . . ." we are told in Psalms

37:5. Albert commited to God because he sensed instantly that God was willing to commit back. A practical man, Albert believed in results, and his first attempt at meditation brought him instant, although subtle, results. In order to know God, all that he needed to do—and this seemed huge to him for many years—was to shut everything else out and quietly affirm that God was at the center of his experience. He needed only to believe that there was Something and that that Something was capable of guiding him.

"I had always been active, perhaps hyperactive," Albert recalls. "Meditation was my first attempt at being receptive, of allowing something to happen to me instead of doing something myself. I said to myself, 'I believe God already knows the answer to this particular problem.' Then I let myself sense the Presence of God guiding and directing me. To my surprise, I could feel the answer forming where before there had been the problem. All I had to do was be willing to be openminded. I opened myself to receive new ideas and I did."

Albert is now a confirmed meditator. He sets aside daily quiet time and uses it to "check in" and see if he is on track. "There is a shift that occurred to me not too long after I began meditating," he relates. "When I started, I wanted meditation to be useful to me. I think I was really pretty self-centered. Gradually, as I practiced meditation, there was a shift. I found myself wanting to be useful to God. This was really novel for me. I started out taking quiet time to let God know what I needed. I ended up taking quiet time so that I could see if there was anything that God needed."

The shift that Albert describes is a shift between self-centeredness and God-centeredness. It is a shift that is well known to those familiar with AA. Induced through prayer and meditation, it is a spiritual awakening of what William James calls "the educational variety."

In order for Albert to undergo his spiritual transformation, he needed to be openminded. Pain made him openminded. Meditation first of all relieved his suffering; next it began giving him a shift to a life that would prove far less painful. As Albert sought to quit playing God and to instead see what role God would have him play, he began to experience a lightness of heart that came with trying to be right–size.

"Uphold me with thy free spirit," we are taught in Psalms 51:12. And we do experience a new freedom of spirit as we recognize that Divine Intelligence manifests everything, nurtures everything, and sustains everything. What a relief it is to know there is nothing outside the realm of Divine Presence. It is the source of all. It is fully capable of running our life if we are capable of relinquishing control and allowing it to do so. When Albert loosed the reins of his life, he found himself able to function better as a businessman than he ever had. Without the strain of feeling that he had to control and manipulate his world, he was free to act in it with a renewed vigor. As the Bible teaches us, there is "One God and Father of all, who is above all and through all, and in you all."

When we open ourselves up to the possibility that there is a higher power, we begin to sense a mystical presence that pervades the universe. We feel this Presence welling up in our consciousness. We experience its activity in our outer affairs. As we work to remain spiritually open, as we take time to meditate and to listen to what we experience, we begin to recognize that God is the source of all. We begin to recognize the Divine in everything and to see it everywhere. Rooted in God, we begin to experience our thoughts and ideas as free from limitation. The Indwelling Presence that we now acknowledge has an unlimited supply of fresh ideas and insights. Buoyed by this knowledge, we now can affirm, "My spirit is free of all limitations." We can accept the boundless constructive good that God intends for us. We can affirm, "I accept the actuality of God's good in my life."

"Decree a thing and it shall be established unto thee. . . ." So we are taught in Job 22:28. As we affirm that God is our source, we affirm that nothing can separate us from the Father within. We can affirm, "All that I am and all that I do is the Father within me expressing as me." As the great spiritual teacher Ernest Holmes declares, "The thoughts that I think and the words that I speak are brought to pass because it is God speaking them through me."

We are one with God. Nothing can separate us from the Father within. Committed to our belief that God is both everywhere and in everything, we affirm that all that we are and all that we do is the action of the One Power expressing itself through us. "Ye are God's building," 1 Corinthians 3:9 tells us. Our thoughts and words are the building blocks with which God can establish his kingdom. When we are negative, we are closed to God's action in our lives. When we are positive, we throw the switch that allows Divine Energy to act on our behalf. When I speak the word of joy, the Father Within frees me from sadness and loneliness.

"I did not realize the degree of loneliness I suffered every day," Albert muses. "When I began to meditate—which we must remember I did out of selfish motives, I was simply unhappy—I was almost instantly gifted with a sense of companionship. In God I found a partner. I no longer needed to have faith in myself as an isolated human being. Rather, I could have faith in myself because I was a part of the larger law of life."

The "larger law of life" is what we are reaching toward when we strive to have faith. Psalms 145:16 teaches God's nature. The psalmist praises God, "Thou . . . satisfieth the desire of every living thing." The Psalms are not theory. They are written out of spiritual experience. We can rely upon their information. What they say is true: God satisfies our desires, either by fulfilling them as we ask or by tutoring us until we desire what God desires for us to have. Like Albert, we may approach God with a selfish motivation only to find that as we get to know God, we genuinely desire to do God's will.

When we feel consciously that we are union with a divine source, then we have a feeling of abundance in everything that we do. As Ernest Holmes remarks, "It would be unthinkable to believe that the creative Intelligence of the universe could lack anything, or that it could plan for its creation to lack that which expresses its own being." We believe that our source contains all things, whether we think of them as large or as small. We expect good to manifest in our experience. As Holmes explains, "The Divine could only intend good and abundance for its creation and we need to know that its nature is forever flowing into everything that we do."

Attuned to God as source, we automatically find a betterment in our lives; we find new experiences and new opportunities for self-expression. As we commit to living by spiritual law, joy, peace, and serenity become our immediate companions. Optimism returns. Why should we go through life as if we must endure it? Spiritual law teaches differently. We are intended to live more abundantly. As God finds a fuller outlet through us, we find a fuller outlet through God. The Divine Influx fills our cup to overflowing. Our perception shifts; now our cup is half full instead of half empty. We expect good, and good is what we increasingly experience. The Divine Source pours its bounty upon us. Scripture prepares us for this happening. "Every good gift . . . cometh down from the Father . . ." states James 1:17.

The law of faith does not promise something for nothing. It does promise us, however, that as we consciously realize the presence of a power greater than ourselves active in our affairs, a betterment of conditions will occur. "I delight in the law of God," exclaims Romans 7:22.

As we affirm that we are creations of God, we can find this promised delight. We can learn to accept and to expect this Power to flow through everything that we do. The law of good is absolute and complete. It operates in and through us. It brings about everything that is good and right. The law knows how to bring about everything needed for our good. We can place our whole trust in law. We can accept the perfect action of law as governing our world. We are the very embodiment of this Power. Setting aside our human frailty, we sense strength and vitality coming to us and through us. Grounded in faith, we have greater abilities and resources than we have yet realized.

Caroline turned to God in the wake of a devastating divorce. "My life was in ashes," she now recalls. "Life as I knew it was over for me. I was still in love with my husband. Despite his infidelity, I couldn't imagine a life without him. In fact, I couldn't imagine any life at all—I didn't want one—and this is why I turned to prayer. I had a year-old daughter to raise, and I was frankly suicidal. I knew there had to be some spiritual way out of my difficulties because I had exhausted all the worldly ways I could think of. I asked God to please, please help me—and God did.

"I prayed for guidance and I got the urge to walk. This, I think, was spiritual guidance, certainly not my temperament, which was frankly sedentary. Almost against my will, I began going for daily walks, a first for me. I would leave the house, turn left and left again, and hike up the log hill just behind our house. I would stretch my legs, and I would seem to stretch my thoughts as well. It's hard to admire the jacaranda trees and think of suicide at the same time.

"At first, I thought my feelings would kill me," she remembers. "I missed my husband so much. But before too long, I began to notice my surroundings—the cat on the wall, the salmon-colored rose behind a garden fence. I began to get ideas of things that I could try for myself and for the baby. I got clear guidance to call one place about a job, and when I called them, there was a job for me there—amazing, I thought. Despite my desperation, I was still quite skeptical. Every time God came through for me, I acted like it was some kind of a fluke, a once-in-a-lifetime coincidence."

To hear her tell it, Caroline had placed her dependency on a higher power, but she wasn't ready to admit it. "I did pray, but I didn't trust prayer," she confirms. "I prayed on my walks, but I didn't call it praying. I called it mulling. God heard my mulling loud and clear, luckily for me."

Caroline's first job led to a second job, another "God shot," another case of her being in the right place at the right time. "God was doing for me what I was unable to do for myself," she says now. "I was being led in very concrete and specific ways, but I was blind to the leading and so ungrateful. I still whined all the time about my husband who had left me. It didn't matter that he was a louse and God was coming through for me. I still wanted the louse."

Caroline continued to walk and continued to mull. She asked for guidance about how to get her husband back and was instead guided to a divorce lawyer that she could afford. "My lawyer broke it to me gently that my husband was already living with somebody else and didn't seem to be thinking much about me or the baby. I didn't want to hear it, but I did. About the same time I got a promotion and my mother started dying from cancer. It was as if the universe simply had 'real life' for me to deal with and not the fantasy of some fantastic, miraculous reconciliation.

"I think it was watching my mother die that finally led me over the bridge to faith," says Caroline. "A friend of mine gave me a copy of Raymond Moody's book *Life After Life*. Desperately sad about my mother, I began to explore the possibility that there was more to life than daily living. Moody was sure that there was more and that he had actually encountered it. According to him, there was a spiritual dimension where I believed my mother was going and from where we could be guided and helped. I asked God to help my mother with her transition, and her death was a peaceful one. In my gratitude for this, I found myself talking to God daily, and I finally had to admit that I did pray. In fact, I prayed a lot."

Prayer got Caroline through her mother's death and through her divorce. Prayer got her through difficult situations at work. Prayer helped her know in what ways she could be a better parent to her young daughter. There seemed to be no arena of her life that prayer didn't encapsulate—if she was only willing to pray about it.

"At first when I met Michael, I was terrified. We worked together and I thought, 'The last thing I need is a complication in the work area.' Michael was friendly to me, too friendly, and I tried to ignore him. I thought I could just freeze him out, that my life was full enough without a man, and certainly I did not want a man like Michael. I knew from our conversations at the water cooler that he was not your ordinary kettle of fish. I knew from office scuttlebutt that he was divorced and had custody of his son."

Determined to play it cool, Caroline feigned lack of interest when Michael asked her for drinks after dinner on a night when they had both worked overtime to finish a project.

"Oh, c'mon," Michael said. "What are the odds of our both ever getting babysitters on the same night again?" His humor won Caroline over, and she agreed to go for drinks—except that Michael didn't drink. "I'll just tell you this up front and get it over with," he said. "I am a sober alcoholic. I haven't had a drink in five years, and I hope, a day at a time, to never have another drink again. I'll have a Coke, but I don't mind if you have a white wine or something."

Caroline had a white wine—and a very good conversation. She learned that Michael's ex-wife was a cocaine addict who was still using the drug and that Michael had taken custody of their son out of concern. He simply didn't feel the child was safe with his ex-wife, and if that really put the pressure on him to stay sober, well, so be it.

"I thought he was awfully nice but awfully intense," Caroline recalls. "And I wasn't used to candor from a man. I found it disarming. So disarming I agreed to see him again."

Michael was persuasive. Caroline was charmed and then overwhelmed. The first time they went to bed together, he was so tender that she started crying.

"'I can't do this,' I thought to myself," she recalls. "But by then my habit of walking and praying was ingrained. I would start each walk determined to end things with Michael, and then I would pray and listen, and by the time I walked back home, Michael seemed like a good idea again. But staying with him was honestly a one-day-at-a-time only-through-the-power-of-prayer proposition."

It is now fifteen years since Caroline accepted Michael's offer of an after-work drink. They have been married thirteen years now and Caroline cannot imagine what life would be like for her without Michael and his son, Nick.

"God had to tame me," Caroline explains. "I was just so crazy when I started praying. I was wild with pain and filled with mistrust. I was so used to bad things and bad people that anything good felt wrong to me. God had to gentle me into accepting things—I am so glad that he did."

"Commit thy way unto the Lord," we are told in Psalms 37:5. Caroline committed her way unto the Lord, and he straightened out the tangled mess of her affairs. He gave her help with parenting, help with money, help with a difficult divorce. He gave her help with her mother's prolonged and difficult cancer death, help with her new courtship, help with her subsequent marriage and newly acquired stepson. God helps her still.

"God helped me in all the ways I could imagine and in a lot of ways I couldn't," Caroline now concludes. She still feels she was "cornered" into faith, but she now thanks God for the circumstances that did the cornering. "Michael tells me that he believes in G.O.D.—Good Orderly Direction. That is what God has given me."

"I and the Father are one," Jesus announced. He was proclaiming the unity of all life. There is one God, and out of this unity flows every thing that is. When we reach to God in faith, we affirm this unity. Mankind is one with God and cannot be separated from God. Our word has power because it embodies the action of God within us. When we pray, we activate all the power that there is. Our guidance is the action of an all-knowing God working for us and through us. The power of God exists and is real. We do not need to invent or create it. No matter what our problem, God contains the answer—and God is at the center of our being. Directly from that center we receive inspiration. I can ask in faith for God to govern my every act and every thought. My guidance is certain, as I can now accept the all-knowing creative action of God through what I am. This is the meaning of faith.

When we ask in faith for God's guidance, we accept that the Mind of God is guiding and directing our thoughts and acts. When we bring to God a specific problem, we believe that God already knows the answer to this particular problem and we therefore are able to lose our anxiety and concern. We let go of the problem and we listen for the answer. The answer already exists in the Mind of God, and it is revealed to my mind now. Something is leading and directing me. Something in me knows what to do and how to do it. I accept this guidance.

Turning to God in faith, I am open to new ideas. That which recently seemed a problem is now a problem no longer. The Mind of God, which knows the answer, communes directly with my individual mind. I affirm the Divine Guidance and feel a sense of calm replacing my anxiety. There is an Intelligence that knows how to bring to pass the right things for us. God has dominion over all things. As I affirm this and I affirm my unity with God, my difficulties melt away, replaced by serenity and the conviction that God is working through me, as me. I affirm the Divine Presence and actually believe that it is guiding me. From the Giver of all life, I accept the answer to my dilemma. "To be spiritually minded is life and peace," Romans 8:6 tells us. Grounded in faith, we find this to be true.

Faith engenders receptivity. We no longer try to force our will upon life. Instead, we ask to receive God's will into our experience. Jesus taught that it is our Father's good pleasure to give us the kingdom. It is our job, therefore, to be ready to receive it. We need to bear in mind always that we are the recipients of Life's bounty. We did not invent the acorn, and yet we can witness the mighty oak. Each prayer we take to God is a kernel from which great goodness can flow. Our job is to stand ready to receive this goodness.

James was an author who had fallen upon hard times. He had a shy but fiery temperament and a distaste for dishonesty in all forms. He suffered a falling out with his literary agent because he felt the man was one step shy of a con artist, promising miracles that James was not sure he could deliver.

"You can't sell me like snake oil," James had lashed out at his agent. "My new book isn't going to fix all the wrongs of the world. I can't guarantee you it will be a best seller. Can't we try to sell it on its own merits? Do we have to promise publishing houses that they are going to make their fortune off this work?"

James's agent was angered by being questioned and called him to task. "You do the writing. I do the selling," he told James. "How I sell you is really none of your business, *that* I sell you is what you need to be concerned with." James begged to differ, and he and his agent came to a bitter parting of the ways. A shy man, James retreated to his own company. He did not know how to seek another agent for his work. He told himself that another agent would have to find him—not a circumstance that many would consider very likely.

"I know I should be a better businessman, but I really am not. I am comfortable with the writing part of a writing career, not the career part. I am perfectly good at sitting alone in a room putting words on the page. I am less good at selling myself. I believe that my ideas can speak for themselves—of course, they need a chance to do that, and left to my own devices, I don't give them many."

With his money dwindling and his once "hot" career growing colder by the moment, James knew that he had to do something, but he wasn't sure what. He was awkward on the telephone and couldn't picture himself calling other literary agents cold and trying to schmooze his way into their good graces. Knowing he should be doing something more practical, he did what seemed serviceable to him. He went on a spiritual retreat.

"Away from the distractions of my life, I was free to see exactly what rotten shape my career was really in." James laughs. "I went on a retreat to get away from it all, but I found I brought it all with me. My big spiritual awakening was the realization that I really needed a new literary agent, that I was exactly not the kind of personality who could get along without one.

"OK, God, you are going to have to help me on this one," James prayed. "You know all about literary agents, and I am fresh out of ideas. Help me please."

Having said his prayers, James went back to writing. This was what he knew how to do. He also had an idea for a new book, and this was what he wanted to get onto the page while the idea was still crystalline for him.

"James, call me. I have some interesting news," he fielded a phone call from a former colleague. Early in their careers, they had been very close, even co-writing a book together. Years and distance had separated them, but James still instantly recognized his friend's voice and was only too glad to return his call.

"How's life as a successful author?" James began his call. He wanted to make a nod to his friend's many accomplishments since last they spoke.

"Life as a successful author is very nice, which is why I am calling you. For the past week, I have had it in my head to call you about my literary agent. He's a great guy, really grounded, and I think you would like him. You aren't shopping for a new agent, are you?"

"Actually I am," James answered. He tried not to sound too thunderstruck.

"Well, I'm glad to hear it. I thought the guy you were with was a bit of an ambulance chaser," his friend volunteered. "I wasn't really sure how well your styles would mesh. Did you burn out on him?"

"I think he may have burned out on me," James admitted. "I questioned him about a few things and he didn't like it."

"I'll bet he didn't. Look. I took the liberty of already talking to my agent about you. I told him you always had strong ideas but weren't too strong on the schmooze factor. He said that sounded refreshing and that he would love to talk to you or read anything you wanted him to read."

"It's really the damnedest thing, your calling me up out of the blue like this," James managed. "I am really grateful."

"Well, yeah. I was hoping you wouldn't think I was being too pushy, but I just kept getting this impulse and I couldn't get rid of it without acting on it. I am glad you're not pissed."

James was far from pissed. In fact, he was deeply grateful. First of all, to his generous friend, and secondly to God. He had no doubt that his friend was operating out of spiritual urgings. Telling himself to just be open, he placed the phone call to the agent. Stumbling and stuttering, he introduced himself and his work. The man was gracious, even laughing a little in a collegial way over James's shyness.

"Let me see whatever you've got," the agent concluded.

"You mean my ideas can speak for themselves?"

"That's always the best way, isn't it?" the agent asked.

James put a packet into the mail. The result was everything he hoped.

"The Father is in me, and I in him," we are told in John 10:38. This text affirms the unity of all life. James prayed and his prayer was answered. All of life is One Life. Every physical substance derives from One Energy. There is one Life Principle, which is God. As we turn to God in faith, we are also turning within, for it is there as well as without that God is found. If all of life is one life, our life not only derives from God, it *is* God. When we ask for faith in God, we are also asking for faith in ourselves. Jesus said, "Be ye therefore perfect, even as your Father which is in heaven [within you] is perfect."

Turning to God in faith, we can affirm that the life of God is our life now. In God we live and enjoy our being. We are called to realize this great fact: God lives in us and through us. We ask to identify ourselves with God's perfection. We ask to accept it as real to us. We ask, too, to so live as to express this perfection through our faithful actions. God acts through us, as us. We are creations and we are intended, in turn, to be creative ourselves. Our creativity is our gift back to our Creator. No matter how discordant something may appear to be on the surface, beneath appearances there is the action of God creating a more perfect whole. We affirm this fact as we turn to God in faith. We can affirm, "There is One Life. That Life is God. That life is our life now. God's will be done."

When we pray for God's will to be done, we are actually

praying for our own good to come to pass. As we ask God for us to live and move in God, we are asking that anything that separates us from God be removed from us. "As a deer longs for the running brooks: so longs my soul for you, O God," states Psalms 42:1. The psalmist continues, "My soul's thirsty for God, thirsty for the living God." We turn to God in faith because we are thirsty for God. We have exhausted our own human devices, and we have seen that we do not have the sufficient power to run our lives as we see fit. There has to be something better, and that something has to be God. "My tears have been my food day and night," the psalmist tells us in Psalms 42:3.

Most of us do not come to God out of sanctity. We come instead out of our very human need. Life without God doesn't work for us. Therefore, we come to God. "God is our refuge and strength: a very present help in trouble," Psalms 46:1 promises us. And so it is that most of us come to God, not because we are good but because we are troubled. We come to God because we need God. Without God, our life does not "work." With God, our life does work. When we see with the eyes of faith, all works toward the good.

Ernest Holmes teaches us, "A universal and infinite Intelligence governs everything, holds everything in its place, and directs the course of everything. The Intelligence that governs the planets in their courses is the same Intelligence that is manifesting in the mind of man. The personal use we make of it to direct and govern our activities depends upon our personal choice."

Free will makes us unique in creation. Unlike the trees and the flowers, we can choose whether or not we will cooperate with our growth. We have the freedom to turn toward God or away from God. Exhausted by self-will, most of us only turn to God feeling battered and worn down. We can say with Psalms 56:1, "Be merciful to me, O God, for men are treading me down: all day long my adversary presses upon me."

In turning to God, we dissolve our adversarial position with the world. We affirm that the Power of Good is with us. We affirm that the One Power is supreme over every antagonist. As Ernest Holmes tells us, "We should cherish no fear, for when we neither fear nor hate we come to understand the unity of life. The nature of God cannot be other than that of peace and love."

Turning to God in faith, we enter into God's peace and love and protection. Our hearts can be without fear. We can place confidence in God within us, guiding and directing us. We can affirm that God sustains and upholds us. We can affirm that the Power of Good is with us. We can enter into a conscious union with God, who makes plain the path before us. Every sense of fear or doubt is wiped away as we affirm, "Today is the day that God has made and I rejoice in it."

When we believe we are living in God's day, we can experience a sense of relief and humor. We can live this day with joy and look forward to tomorrow with courage and confidence. In short, we are at peace. As Ernest Holmes remarks,

"Without peace there is no happiness. Without happiness there can be no enthusiasm. Without enthusiasm there can be no joy in life."

At root, it is joy in life that we are seeking when we seek to turn to God in faith. We take to heart a message such as the one found in 2 Corinthians 9:8: "And God is able to provide you with every blessing in abundance; so that by always having enough of everything, you may share abundantly in every good work." It is this sense of "enough" that we are lacking when we are in despair. It is this sense of "enough" that makes faith such an emotional comfort.

"I trust in the steadfast love of God forever and ever," Psalms 52:8 tells us. It is this trust that we are seeking when we look for faith. As we trust in the goodness of God, we are able to make decisions that are not based on fear. Knowing that God is guiding us, we make choices that bring us the greatest joy and fulfillment.

"May the God of steadfastness and encouragement grant you to live with harmony with one another," we read in Romans 15:5. When we turn to God in faith, we turn toward others in harmony. We no longer seek to wrest our will from a hostile world. The world is no longer hostile. Connected to God, we are connected to all creation. There is a great unity flowing through all of life, and upon that unity we can depend. Affirming that Divine Order is what we desire, we can allow God to arrange the happenings in our life. We can believe there is a purpose to all that occurs to us. Nothing is placed in our life without cause and nothing is removed from our life without equal cause. God is working to bring to pass a greater and greater harmony. What we may at first perceive as chaos is actually the shifting of circumstances to create a new beginning. Turning to God in faith, we become flexible and teachable. We trust the greater good that God is accomplishing. We pray always to accept the highest good, to accept God's plan and purpose for our lives.

Listen to Psalms 16:11: "You show me the path of life. In your presence there is fullness of joy; in your right hand are pleasures forevermore." The psalmist is describing the joy of a life lived in faith. We do not face any challenge alone. An all-knowing, all-powerful, all-loving God faces our obstacles with us. There is no problem too difficult for the Creator. Trusting God, we can relax into the assurance that all is well.

Galatians 5:22 speaks to us of faith: "The fruit of the Spirit is love, joy, peace, patience, kindness, generosity, faithfulness." When we turn to God in faith, we release anxiety. We remind ourselves that God knows the desires of our hearts and knows, too, what is best for us. No prayer goes unanswered. No request goes unfulfilled—although the answer may not come in the form that we think we desire. God knows everything that we need upon our spiritual path. Knowing this, we do well not to let ourselves be too concerned by our prayers not being answered the way we think they should be. We should affirm that God is answering our prayers even when no answer is immediately apparent to us. God's timing and our timing may differ. We do well to defer to God who has in mind the harmony of the whole of which we are a part. There is no limit to the good that God can accomplish. As Romans 1:20 tells us, "Ever since the creation of the world his eternal power and divine nature, invisible though they are, have been understood and seen through the things he has made."

Our faith is the kernel from which great things come to pass for ourselves and others. With faith we recognize the blessings we currently receive and we anticipate with eagerness the future blessings that are coming to bear. Our eyes are opened to the reality of God all around us and within us. God can accomplish greater things through us than we can yet perceive. Proverbs 19:21 tells us, "The human mind may devise many plans, but it is the purpose of the Lord that will be established."

The purpose of the Lord is good beyond our imagining. We come to God with our troubles, and God renders back to us his gifts. No adversity is too great to be transformed. As the psalmist exclaims in Psalms 98:1: "O sing to the Lord a new song; for he has done marvelous things."

The marvelous things the Lord is able to do come to us as we come to him. Ernest Holmes explains it this way: "All things are possible to the Spirit, therefore everything is possible to you in such a degree as you can believe in and accept the operation of Spirit in your life."

Psalms 97:1 exclaims, "The Lord is King; let the earth rejoice." When we reach to God in faith, we, too, are able to rejoice. We can allow the Divine Energy to flow through us in ever-widening circles of activity. Our every sense of limitation can melt away. God, the Inner Source, is limitless. As partners of that God, so are we. Every good we have experienced can increase. Every joy can be multiplied. In full knowledge that life gives according to our faith, we now see clearly that our divine birthright is freedom and joy. No longer divided against ourselves by doubt and fear, we now accept as truth what Romans 8:31 affirms, "If God be for us, who can be against us?"

Discover Julia Cameron's Creative Kingdom

©Aloma

To order call 1-800-788-6262 or visit our website at www.penguin.com

BOOKS IN *THE ARTIST'S WAY* **SERIES**

The Artist's Way
- ISBN 978-1-58542-147-3 (hardcover)
- ISBN 978-1-58542-146-6 (trade paper)
- ISBN 978-0-14-305825-0 (audio, CDs)

Walking in This World
ISBN 978-1-58542-261-6 (trade paper)

Finding Water
- ISBN 978-1-58542-463-4 (hardcover)
- ISBN 978-1-58542-777-2 (trade paper)

The Artist's Way Workbook
ISBN 978-1-58542-533-4 (trade paper)

The Artist's Way Morning Pages Journal
ISBN 978-0-87477-886-1 (trade paper)

The Complete Artist's Way
ISBN 978-1-58542-630-0 (hardcover)

The Artist's Way Every Day
ISBN 978-1-58542-747-5 (trade paper)

The Artist's Date Book
ISBN 978-0-87477-653-9 (trade paper)

Inspirations: Meditations from
  The Artist's Way
ISBN 978-1-58542-102-2 (trade paper)

OTHER BOOKS ON CREATIVITY

The Right to Write
ISBN 978-1-58542-009-4 (trade paper)

The Sound of Paper
ISBN 978-1-58542-354-5 (trade paper)

The Writing Diet
ISBN 978-1-58542-698-0 (trade paper)

The Vein of Gold
ISBN 978-0-87477-879-3 (trade paper)

How to Avoid Making Art (or Anything
  Else You Enjoy)
ISBN 978-1-58542-438-2 (trade paper)

The Writer's Life: Insights from The Right to
  Write
ISBN 978-1-58542-103-9 (trade paper)

Supplies: A Troubleshooting Guide for
  Creative Difficulties
ISBN 978-1-58542-212-8

About the Author

Julia Cameron has been an active artist for more than thirty years. She is the author of more than thirty books, fiction and nonfiction, including her bestselling works on the creative process *The Artist's Way, Walking in This World, Finding Water, The Writing Diet, The Right to Write*, and *The Sound of Paper*. A novelist, playwright, songwriter, and poet, Cameron has multiple credits in theater, film, and television.